THE Foundation

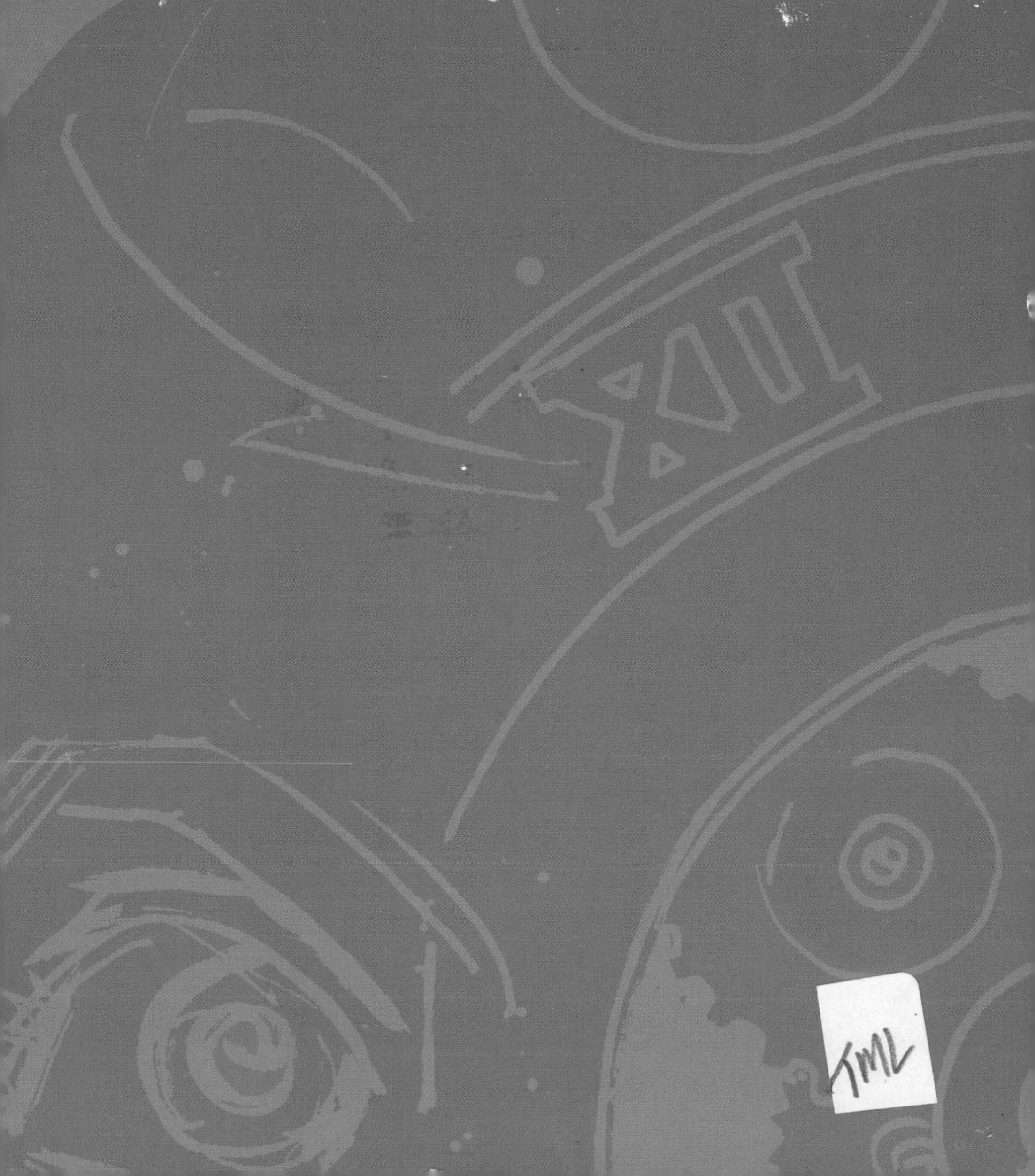

THE Foundation

THE FOUNDATION created by Kody Chamberlain

COVER ART __Paul Azaceta__

CHAPTER ART __Paul Azaceta__ {Chapter 1}
__& Chee__ {Chapters 2-5}

WRITER **John Rozum**

ART **Chee**

COLORIST **Pablo Quiligotti**

LETTERERS **Marshall Dillon & Terri Delgado**

MANAGING EDITOR **Marshall Dillon**

ANDREW COSBY
ROSS RICHIE
founders

MARK WAID
editor-in-chief

ADAM FORTIER
vice president,
new business

CHIP MOSHER
marketing &
sales director

MATT GAGNON
managing editor

ED DUKESHIRE
designer

Office of publication: 6310 San Vicente Blvd, Ste 404, Los Angeles, CA 90048-5457.

First Edition: July 2008
10 9 8 7 6 5 4 3 2 1
PRINTED IN KOREA

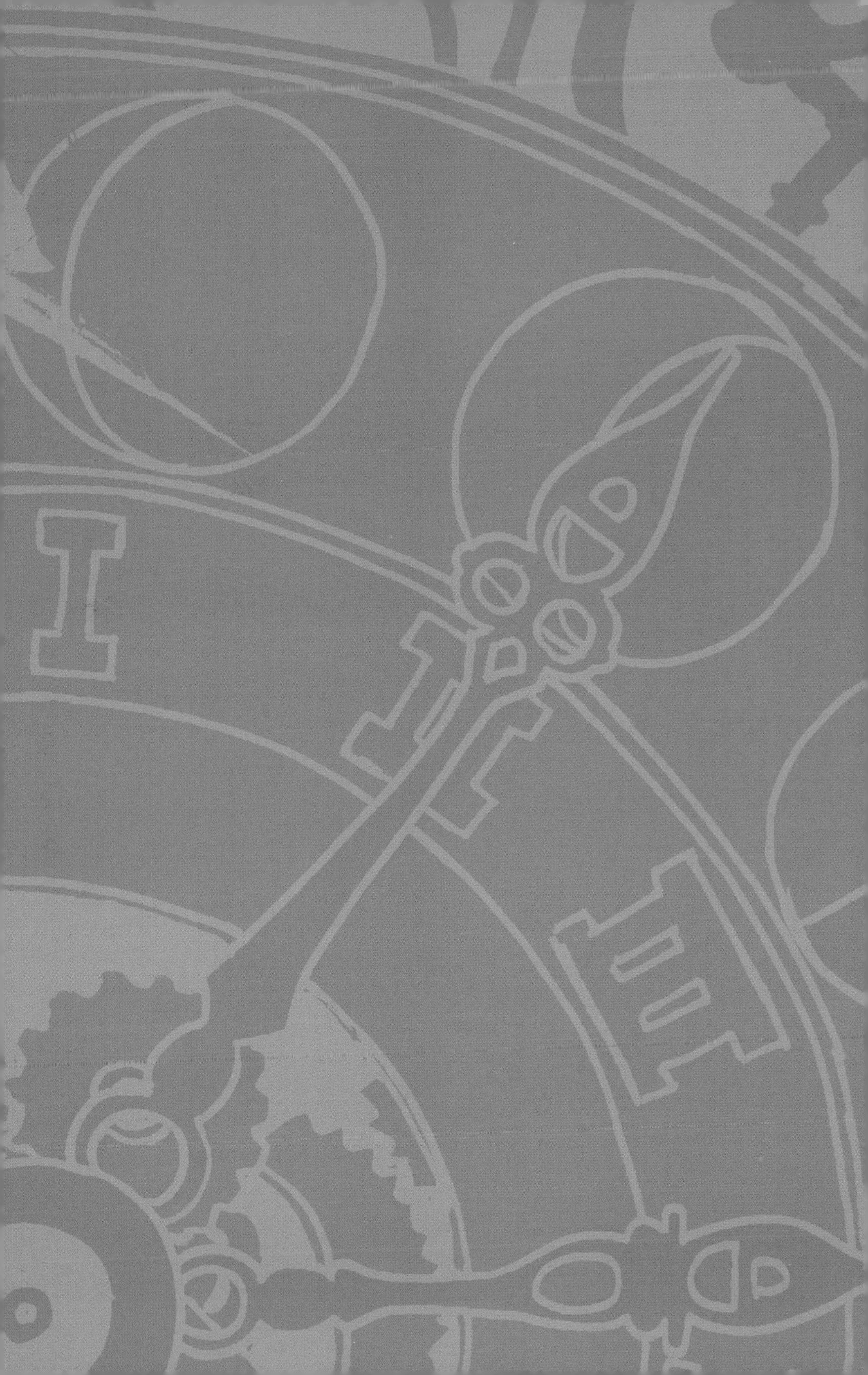

Chapter One

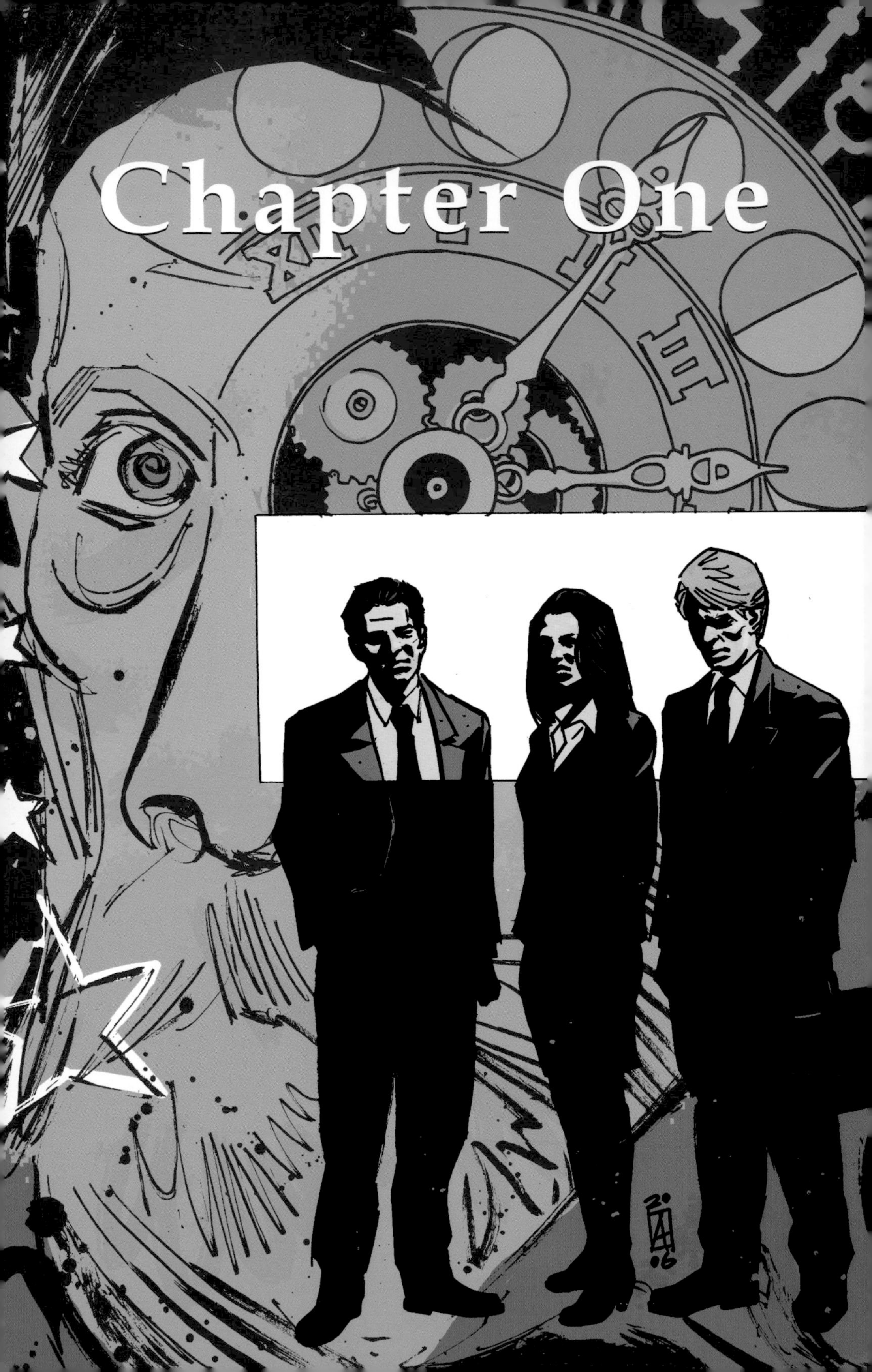

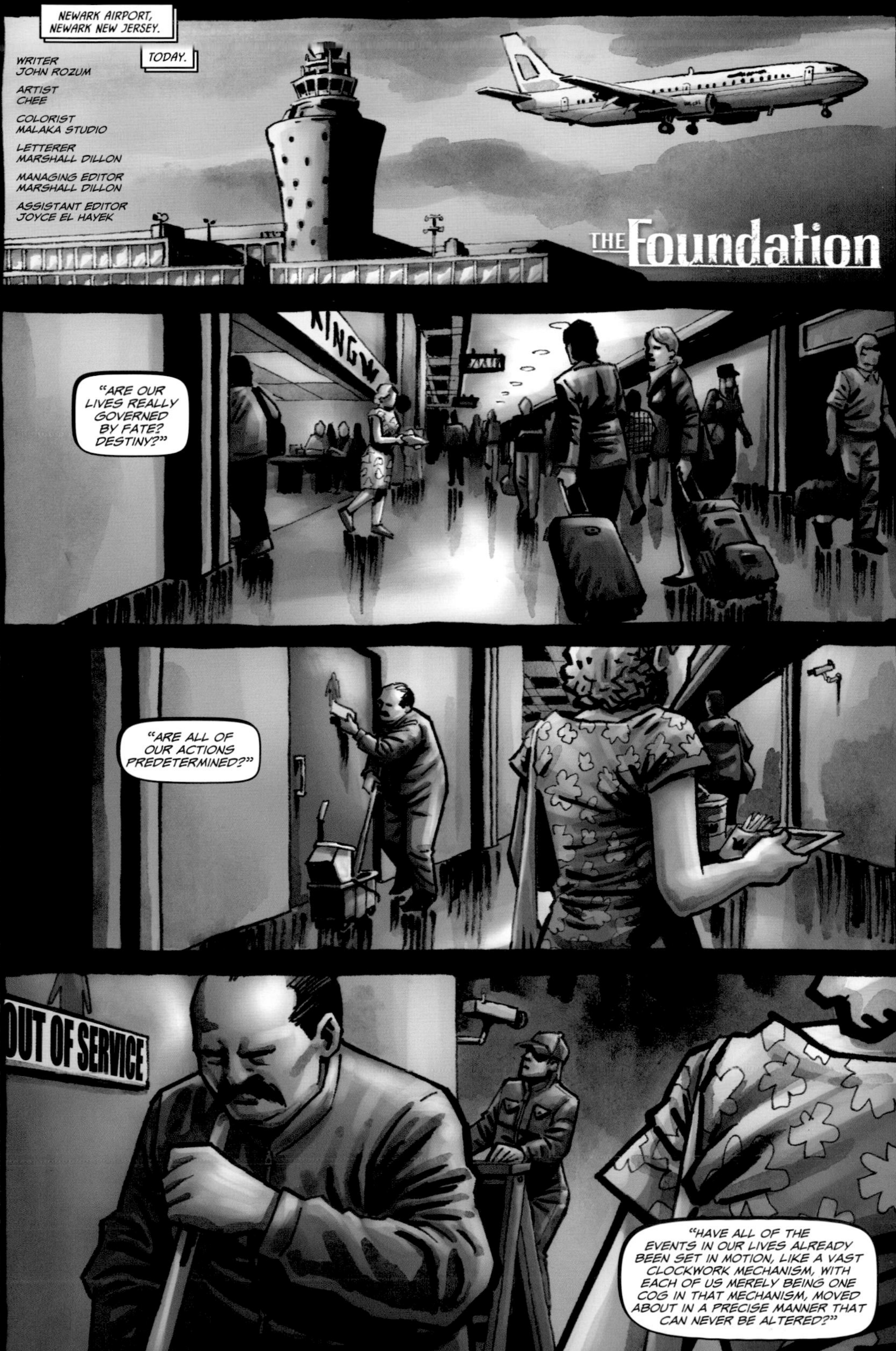

NEWARK AIRPORT, NEWARK NEW JERSEY.
TODAY.
WRITER JOHN ROZUM
ARTIST CHEE
COLORIST MALAKA STUDIO
LETTERER MARSHALL DILLON
MANAGING EDITOR MARSHALL DILLON
ASSISTANT EDITOR JOYCE EL HAYEK
THE Foundation
"ARE OUR LIVES REALLY GOVERNED BY FATE? DESTINY?"
"ARE ALL OF OUR ACTIONS PREDETERMINED?"
OUT OF SERVICE
"HAVE ALL OF THE EVENTS IN OUR LIVES ALREADY BEEN SET IN MOTION, LIKE A VAST CLOCKWORK MECHANISM, WITH EACH OF US MERELY BEING ONE COG IN THAT MECHANISM, MOVED ABOUT IN A PRECISE MANNER THAT CAN NEVER BE ALTERED?"

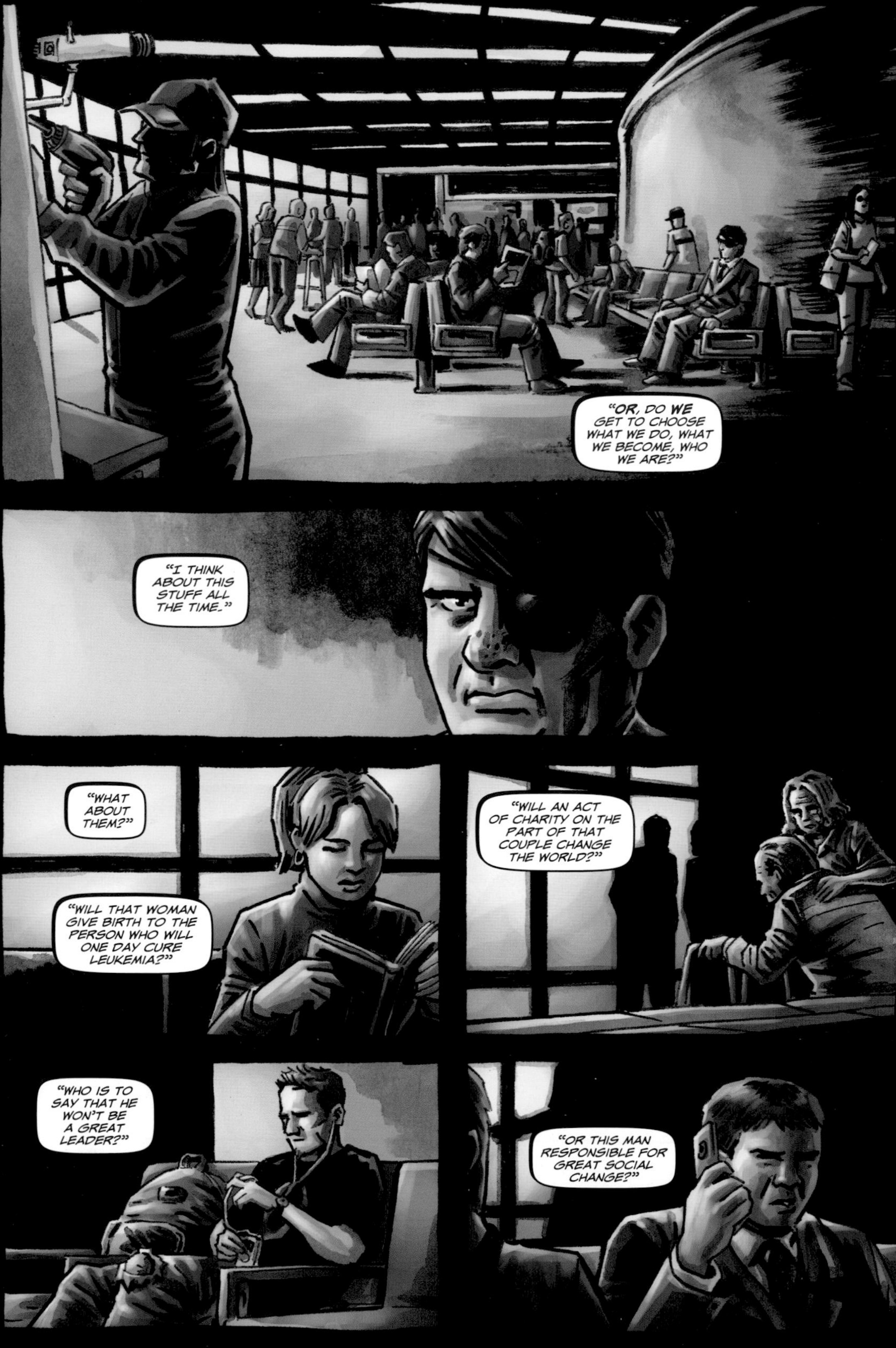
"OR, DO WE GET TO CHOOSE WHAT WE DO, WHAT WE BECOME, WHO WE ARE?"
"I THINK ABOUT THIS STUFF ALL THE TIME."
"WHAT ABOUT THEM?"
"WILL THAT WOMAN GIVE BIRTH TO THE PERSON WHO WILL ONE DAY CURE LEUKEMIA?"
"WILL AN ACT OF CHARITY ON THE PART OF THAT COUPLE CHANGE THE WORLD?"
"WHO IS TO SAY THAT HE WON'T BE A GREAT LEADER?"
"OR THIS MAN RESPONSIBLE FOR GREAT SOCIAL CHANGE?"

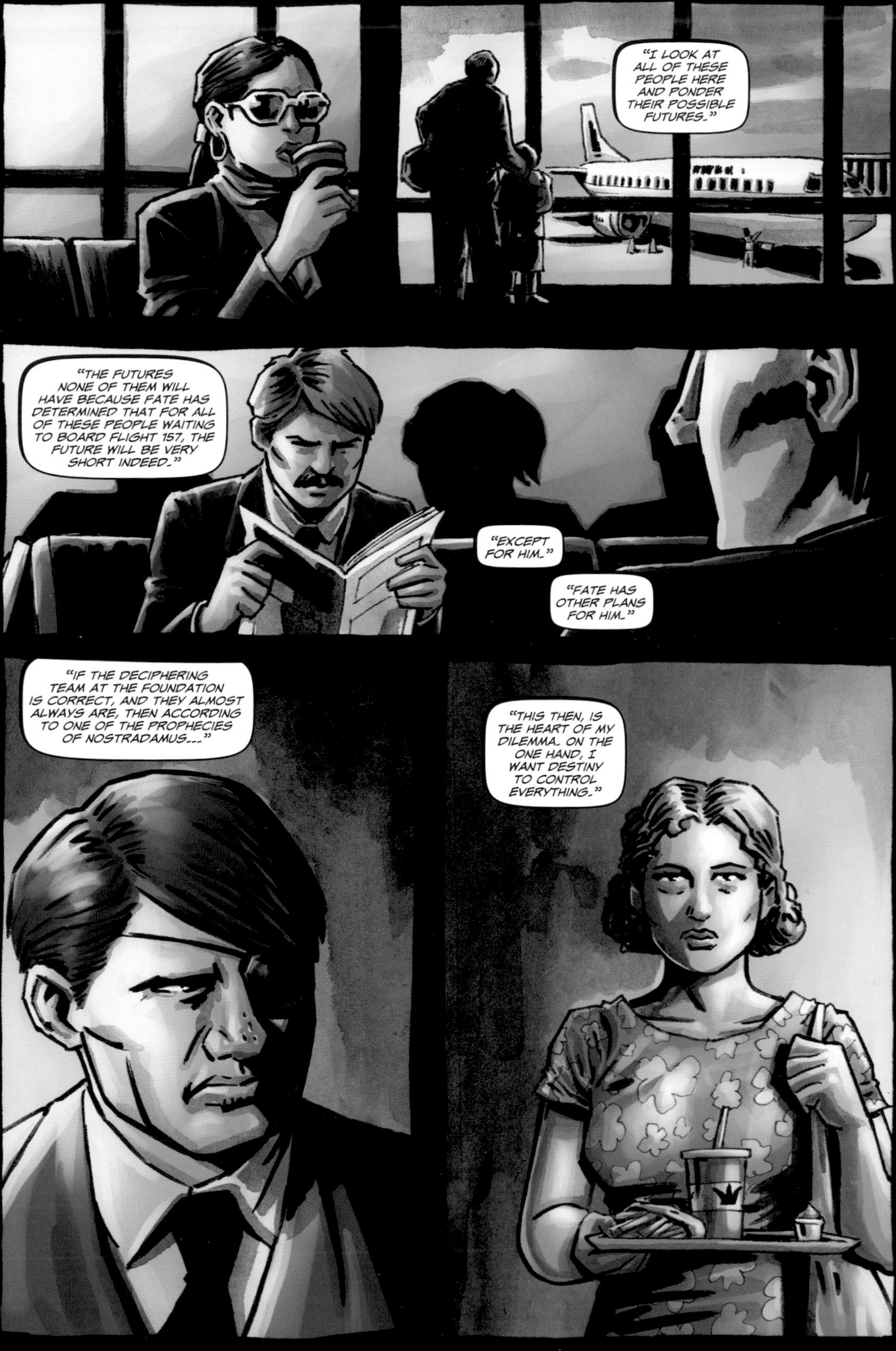
"I LOOK AT ALL OF THESE PEOPLE HERE AND PONDER THEIR POSSIBLE FUTURES."
"THE FUTURES NONE OF THEM WILL HAVE BECAUSE FATE HAS DETERMINED THAT FOR ALL OF THESE PEOPLE WAITING TO BOARD FLIGHT 157, THE FUTURE WILL BE VERY SHORT INDEED."
"EXCEPT FOR HIM."
"FATE HAS OTHER PLANS FOR HIM."
"IF THE DECIPHERING TEAM AT THE FOUNDATION IS CORRECT, AND THEY ALMOST ALWAYS ARE, THEN ACCORDING TO ONE OF THE PROPHECIES OF NOSTRADAMUS..."
"THIS THEN, IS THE HEART OF MY DILEMMA. ON THE ONE HAND, I WANT DESTINY TO CONTROL EVERYTHING."

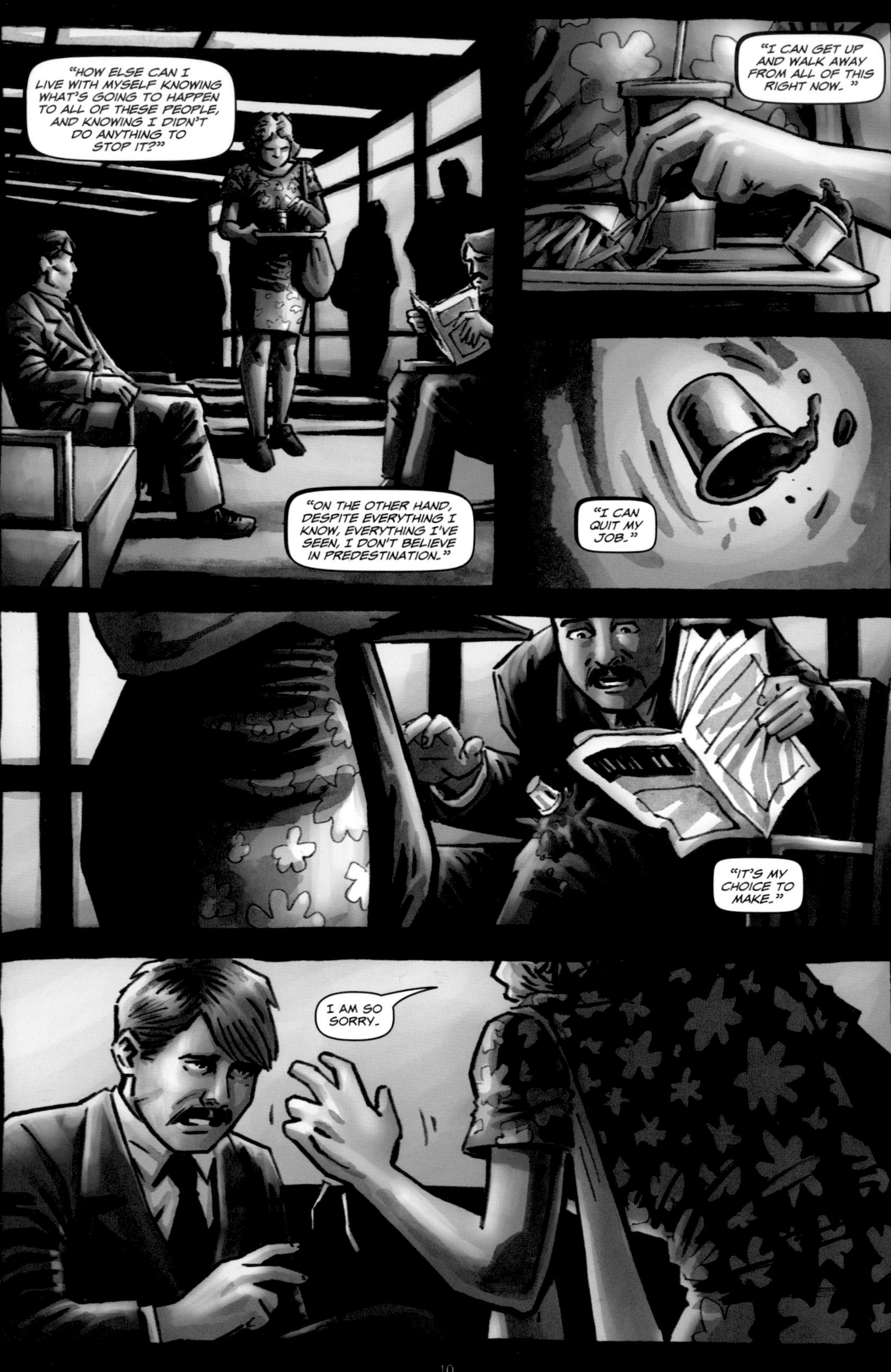
"HOW ELSE CAN I LIVE WITH MYSELF KNOWING WHAT'S GOING TO HAPPEN TO ALL OF THESE PEOPLE, AND KNOWING I DIDN'T DO ANYTHING TO STOP IT?"
"ON THE OTHER HAND, DESPITE EVERYTHING I KNOW, EVERYTHING I'VE SEEN, I DON'T BELIEVE IN PREDESTINATION."
"I CAN GET UP AND WALK AWAY FROM ALL OF THIS RIGHT NOW."
"I CAN QUIT MY JOB."
"IT'S MY CHOICE TO MAKE."
I AM SO SORRY.

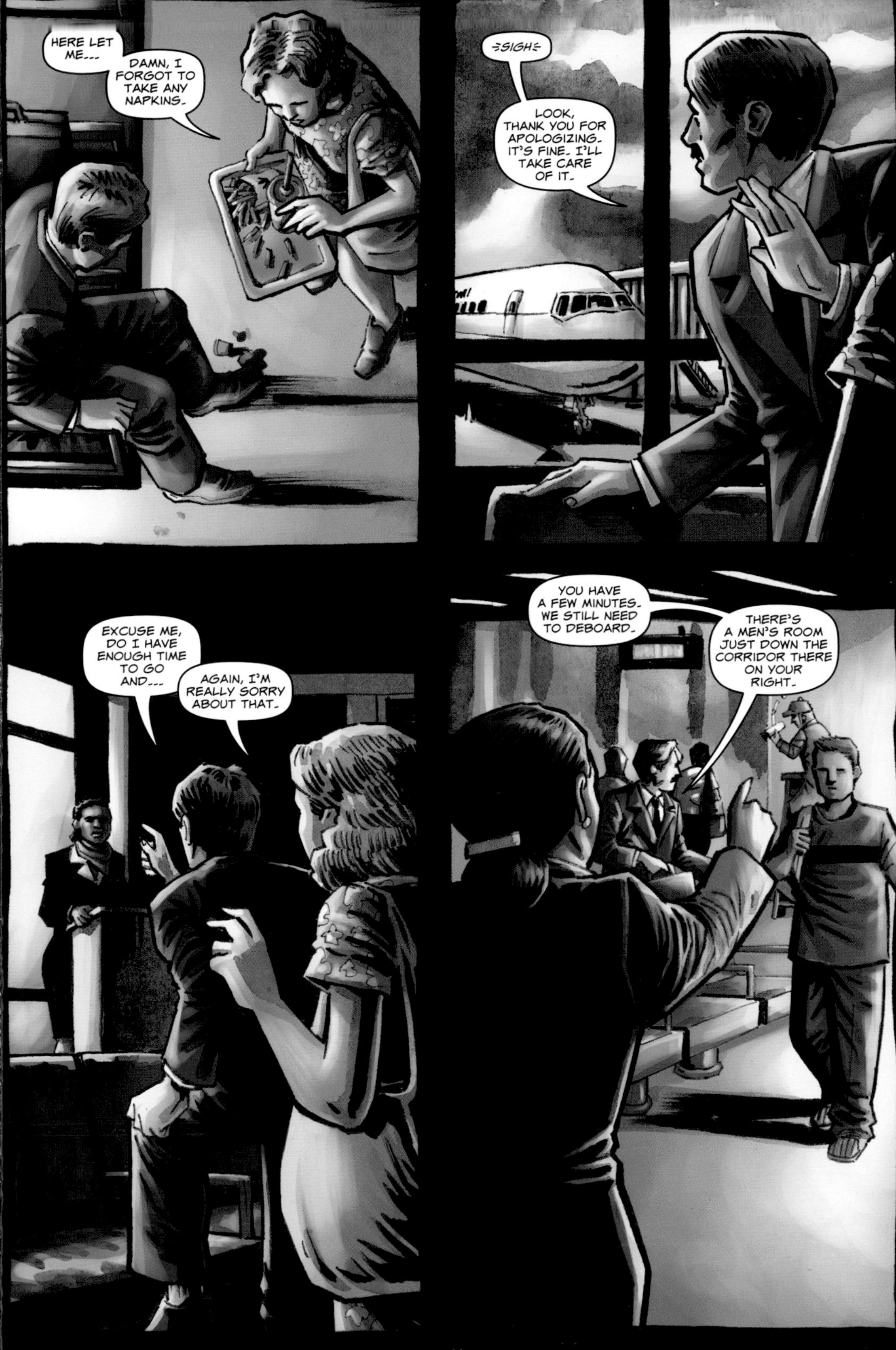
HERE LET ME...
DAMN, I FORGOT TO TAKE ANY NAPKINS.
≠SIGH≠
LOOK, THANK YOU FOR APOLOGIZING. IT'S FINE. I'LL TAKE CARE OF IT.
EXCUSE ME, DO I HAVE ENOUGH TIME TO GO AND...
AGAIN, I'M REALLY SORRY ABOUT THAT.
YOU HAVE A FEW MINUTES. WE STILL NEED TO DEBOARD.
THERE'S A MEN'S ROOM JUST DOWN THE CORRIDOR THERE ON YOUR RIGHT.

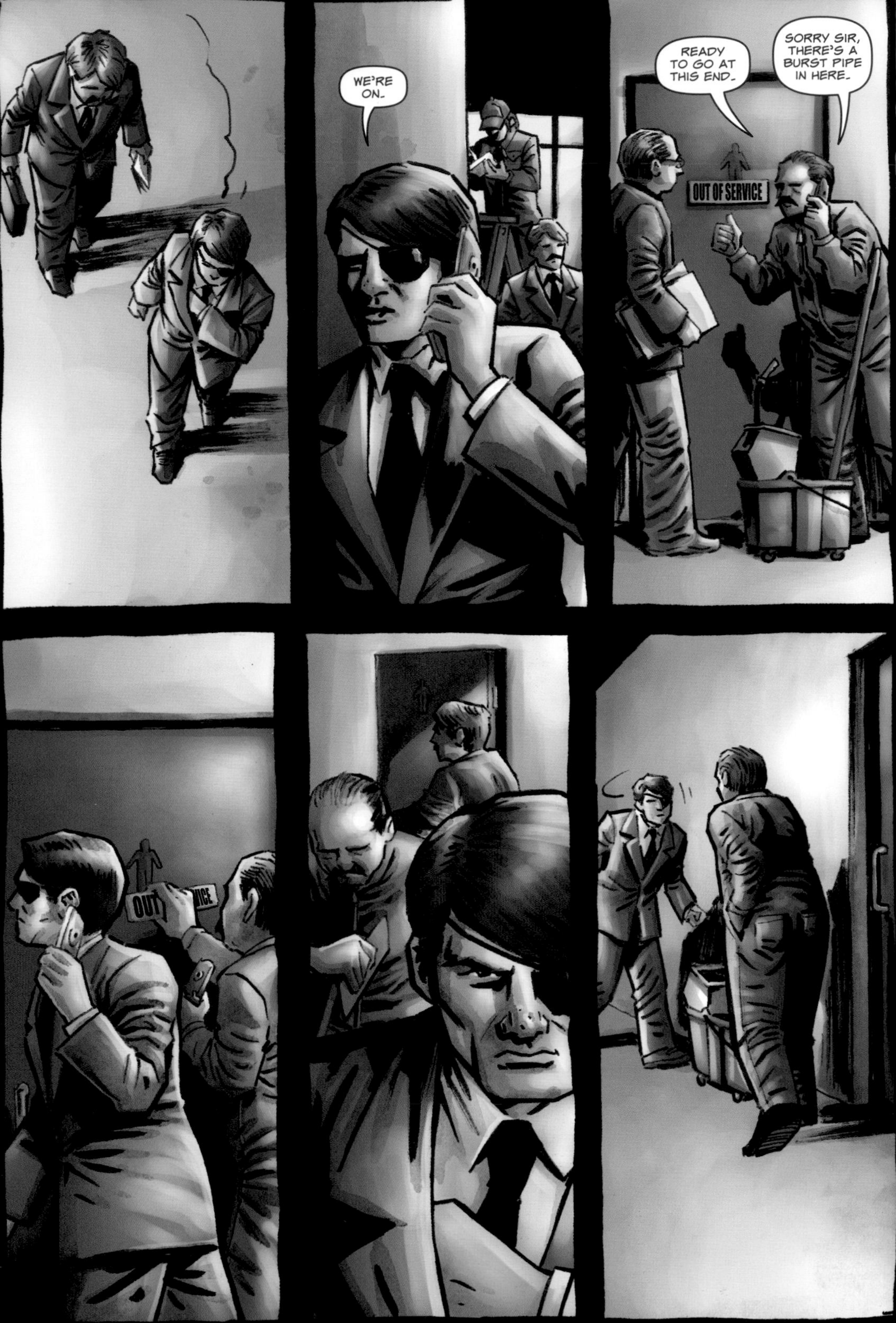
WE'RE ON.
READY TO GO AT THIS END.
SORRY SIR, THERE'S A BURST PIPE IN HERE.
OUT OF SERVICE

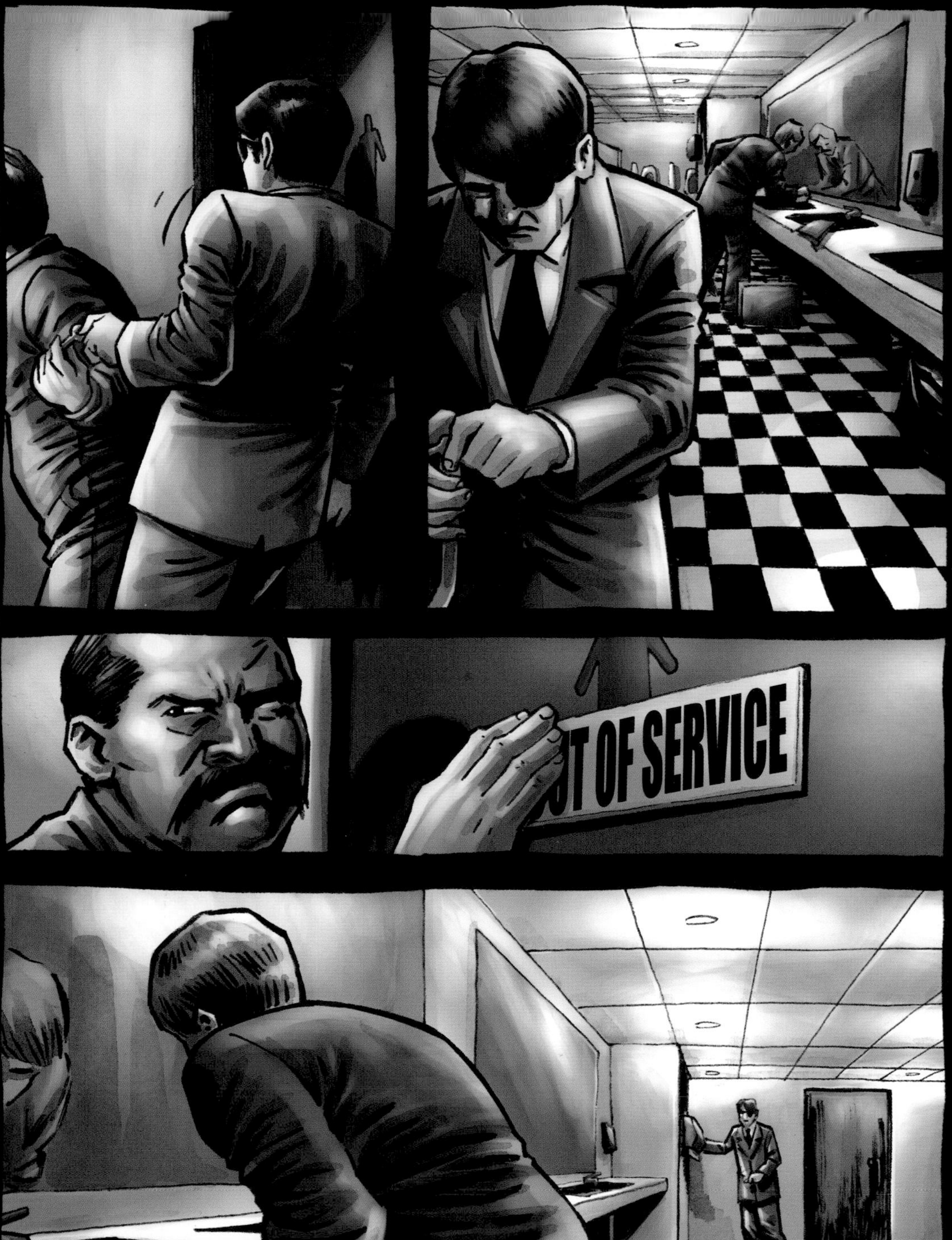
UT OF SERVICE

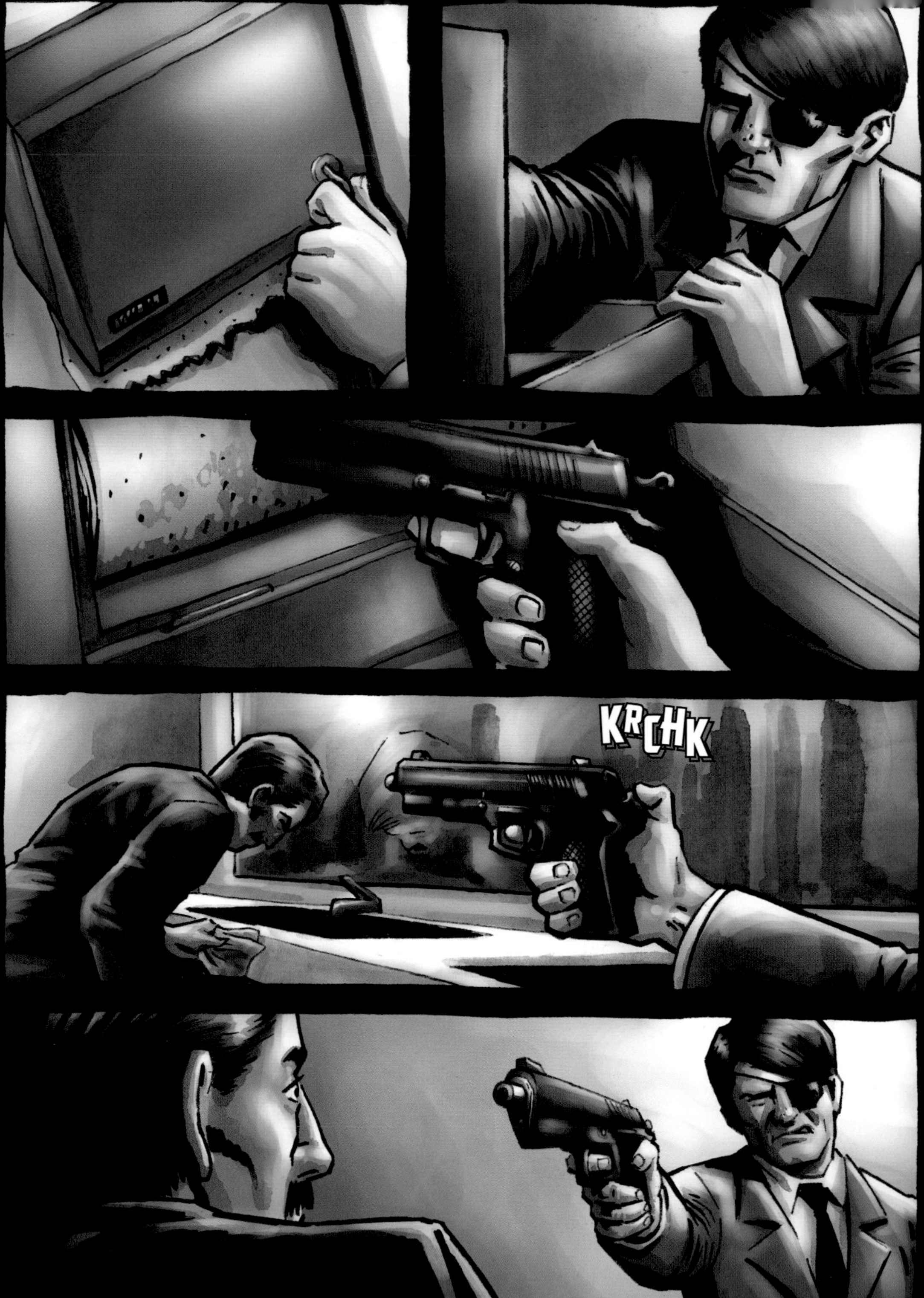
KRCHK

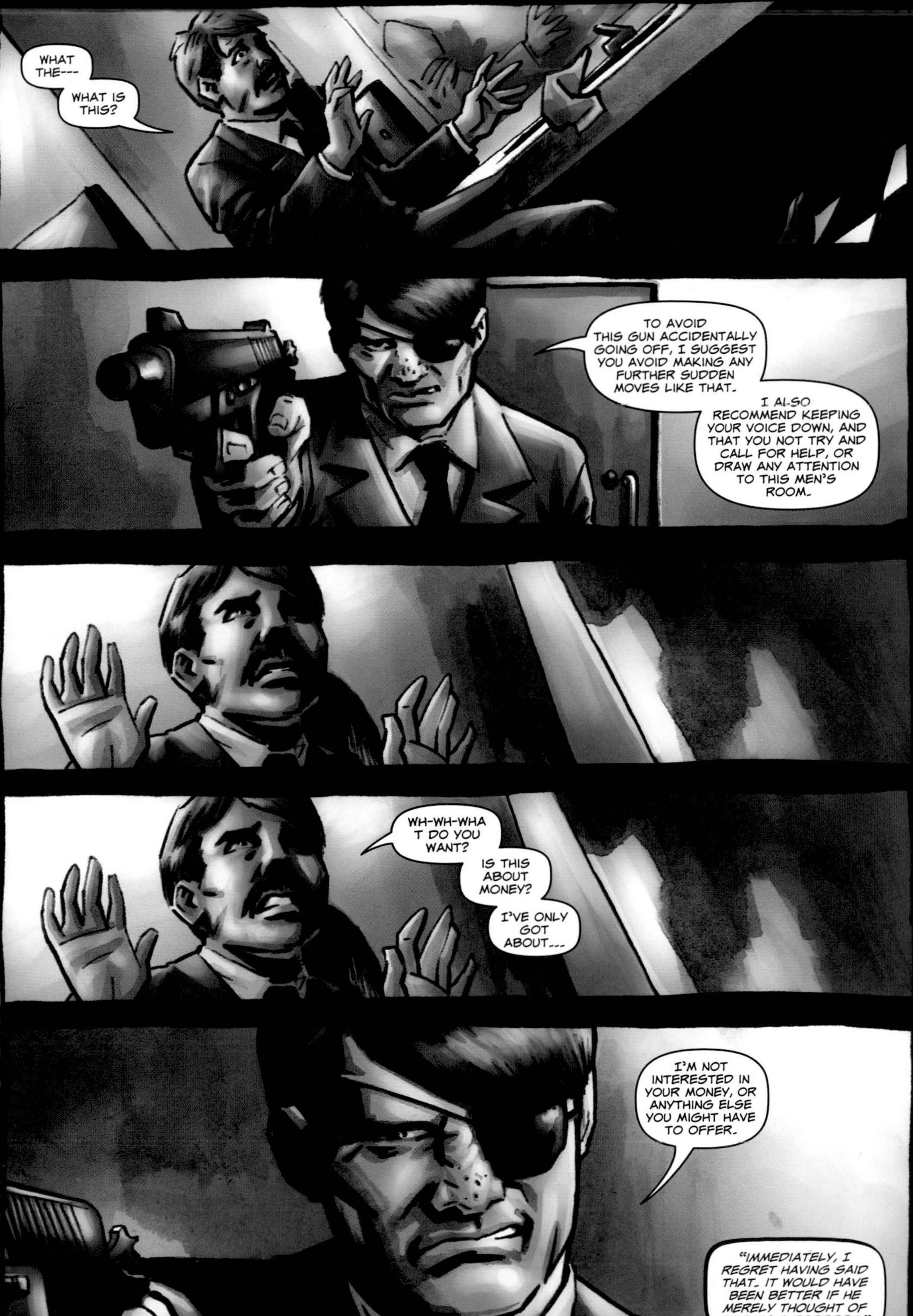
WHAT THE---
WHAT IS THIS?
TO AVOID THIS GUN ACCIDENTALLY GOING OFF, I SUGGEST YOU AVOID MAKING ANY FURTHER SUDDEN MOVES LIKE THAT.
I ALSO RECOMMEND KEEPING YOUR VOICE DOWN, AND THAT YOU NOT TRY AND CALL FOR HELP, OR DRAW ANY ATTENTION TO THIS MEN'S ROOM.
WH-WH-WHA T DO YOU WANT?
IS THIS ABOUT MONEY?
I'VE ONLY GOT ABOUT---
I'M NOT INTERESTED IN YOUR MONEY, OR ANYTHING ELSE YOU MIGHT HAVE TO OFFER.
"IMMEDIATELY, I REGRET HAVING SAID THAT. IT WOULD HAVE BEEN BETTER IF HE MERELY THOUGHT OF THIS AS A ROBBERY."

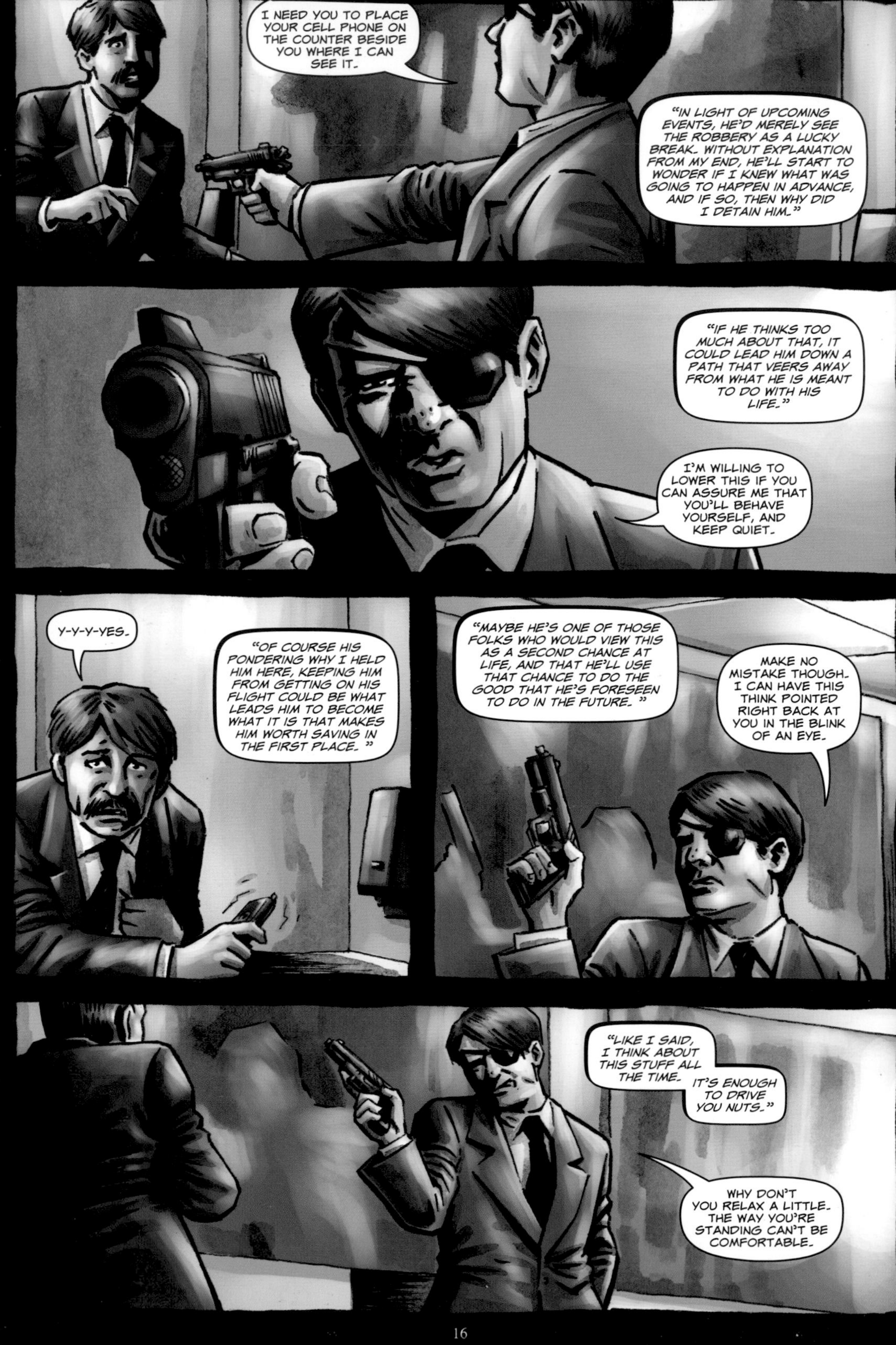
I NEED YOU TO PLACE YOUR CELL PHONE ON THE COUNTER BESIDE YOU WHERE I CAN SEE IT.
"IN LIGHT OF UPCOMING EVENTS, HE'D MERELY SEE THE ROBBERY AS A LUCKY BREAK. WITHOUT EXPLANATION FROM MY END, HE'LL START TO WONDER IF I KNEW WHAT WAS GOING TO HAPPEN IN ADVANCE, AND IF SO, THEN WHY DID I DETAIN HIM."
"IF HE THINKS TOO MUCH ABOUT THAT, IT COULD LEAD HIM DOWN A PATH THAT VEERS AWAY FROM WHAT HE IS MEANT TO DO WITH HIS LIFE."
I'M WILLING TO LOWER THIS IF YOU CAN ASSURE ME THAT YOU'LL BEHAVE YOURSELF, AND KEEP QUIET.
Y-Y-Y-YES.
"OF COURSE HIS PONDERING WHY I HELD HIM HERE, KEEPING HIM FROM GETTING ON HIS FLIGHT COULD BE WHAT LEADS HIM TO BECOME WHAT IT IS THAT MAKES HIM WORTH SAVING IN THE FIRST PLACE."
"MAYBE HE'S ONE OF THOSE FOLKS WHO WOULD VIEW THIS AS A SECOND CHANCE AT LIFE, AND THAT HE'LL USE THAT CHANCE TO DO THE GOOD THAT HE'S FORESEEN TO DO IN THE FUTURE."
MAKE NO MISTAKE THOUGH. I CAN HAVE THIS THINK POINTED RIGHT BACK AT YOU IN THE BLINK OF AN EYE.
"LIKE I SAID, I THINK ABOUT THIS STUFF ALL THE TIME.
IT'S ENOUGH TO DRIVE YOU NUTS."
WHY DON'T YOU RELAX A LITTLE. THE WAY YOU'RE STANDING CAN'T BE COMFORTABLE.

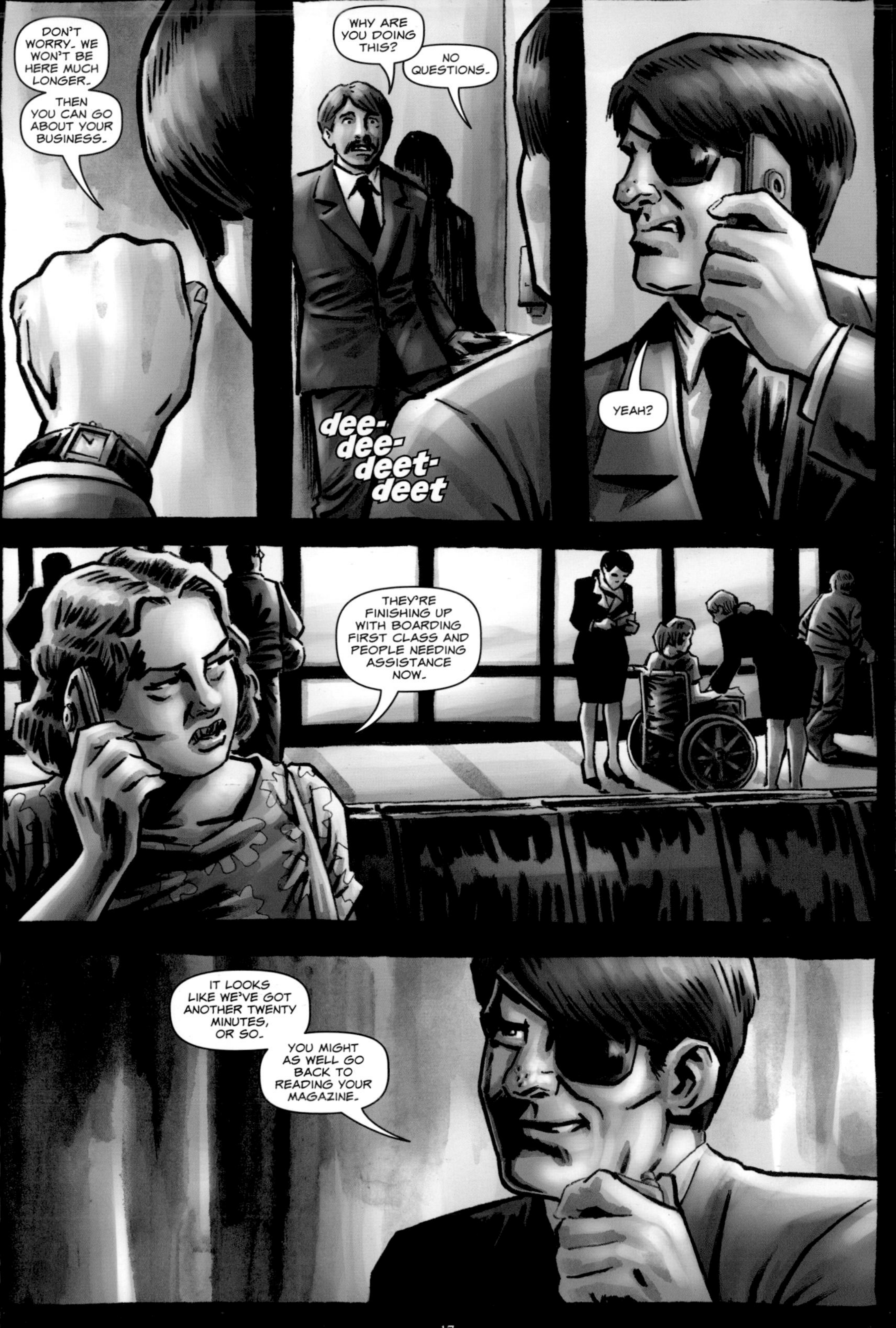
DON'T WORRY. WE WON'T BE HERE MUCH LONGER.
THEN YOU CAN GO ABOUT YOUR BUSINESS.
WHY ARE YOU DOING THIS?
NO QUESTIONS.
dee-dee-deet-deet
YEAH?
THEY'RE FINISHING UP WITH BOARDING FIRST CLASS AND PEOPLE NEEDING ASSISTANCE NOW.
IT LOOKS LIKE WE'VE GOT ANOTHER TWENTY MINUTES, OR SO.
YOU MIGHT AS WELL GO BACK TO READING YOUR MAGAZINE.

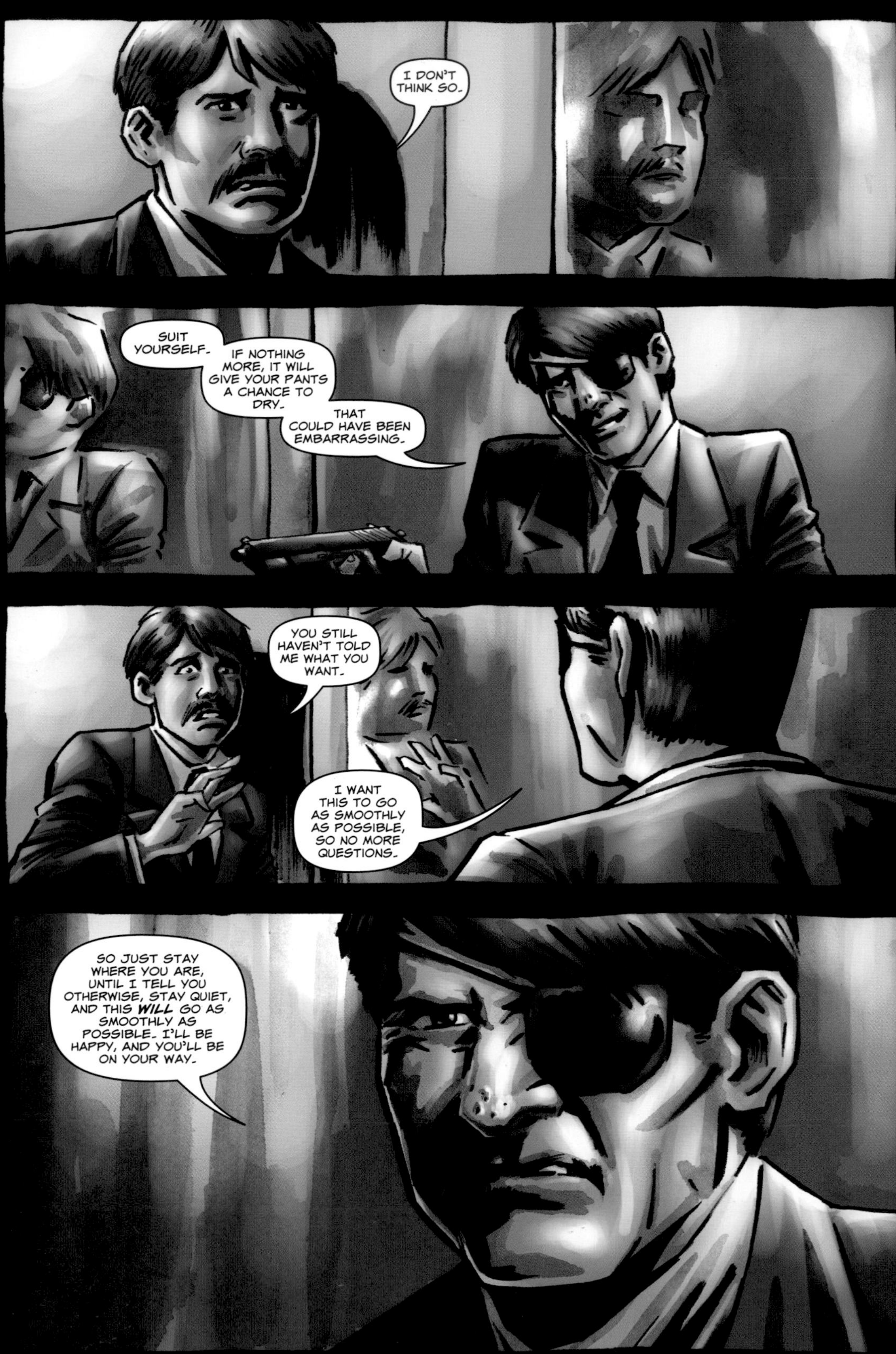
I DON'T THINK SO.
SUIT YOURSELF.
IF NOTHING MORE, IT WILL GIVE YOUR PANTS A CHANCE TO DRY.
THAT COULD HAVE BEEN EMBARRASSING.
YOU STILL HAVEN'T TOLD ME WHAT YOU WANT.
I WANT THIS TO GO AS SMOOTHLY AS POSSIBLE, SO NO MORE QUESTIONS.
SO JUST STAY WHERE YOU ARE, UNTIL I TELL YOU OTHERWISE, STAY QUIET, AND THIS WILL GO AS SMOOTHLY AS POSSIBLE. I'LL BE HAPPY, AND YOU'LL BE ON YOUR WAY.

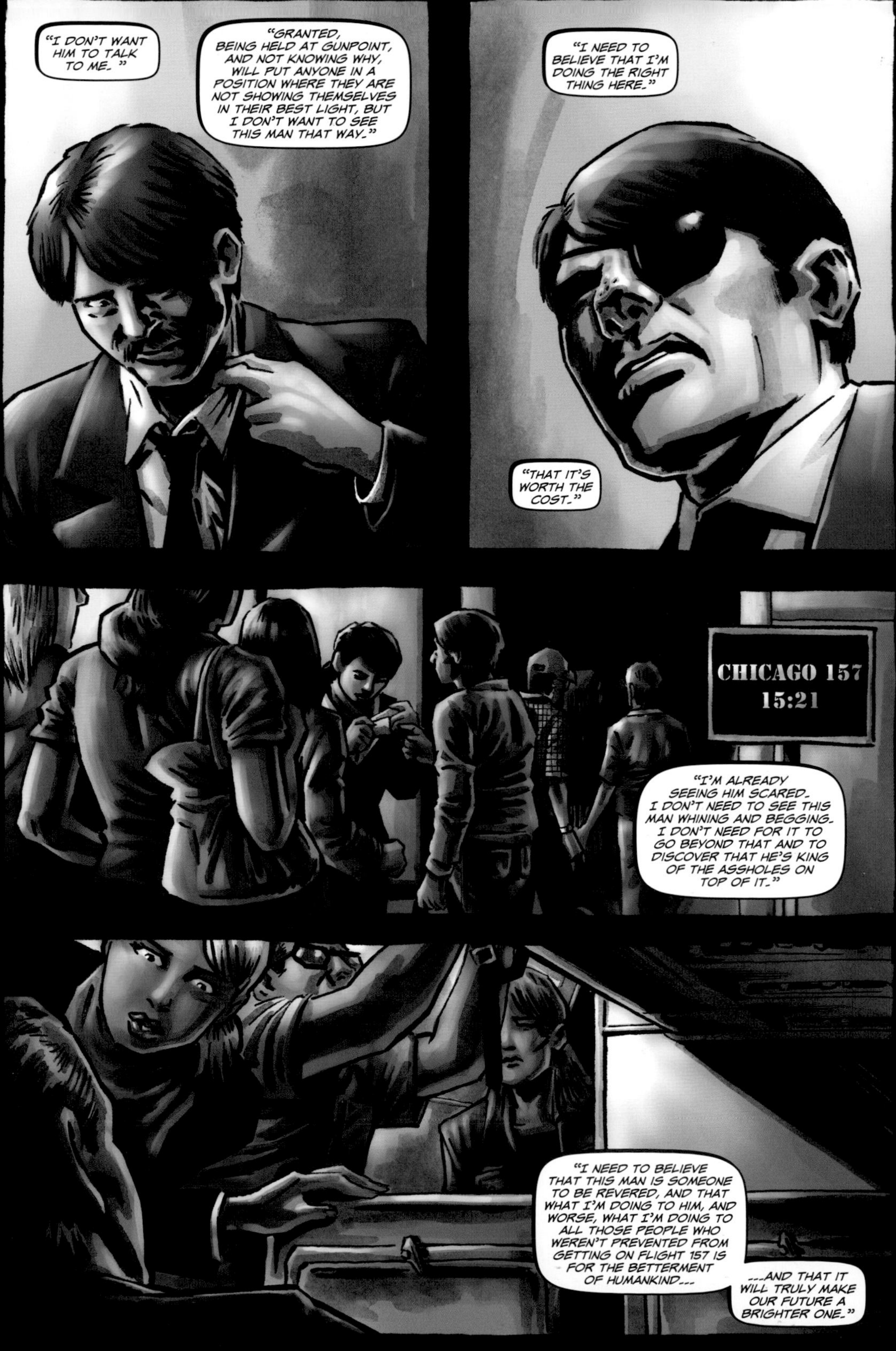
"I DON'T WANT HIM TO TALK TO ME."
"GRANTED, BEING HELD AT GUNPOINT, AND NOT KNOWING WHY, WILL PUT ANYONE IN A POSITION WHERE THEY ARE NOT SHOWING THEMSELVES IN THEIR BEST LIGHT, BUT I DON'T WANT TO SEE THIS MAN THAT WAY."
"I NEED TO BELIEVE THAT I'M DOING THE RIGHT THING HERE."
"THAT IT'S WORTH THE COST."
CHICAGO 157
15:21
"I'M ALREADY SEEING HIM SCARED. I DON'T NEED TO SEE THIS MAN WHINING AND BEGGING. I DON'T NEED FOR IT TO GO BEYOND THAT AND TO DISCOVER THAT HE'S KING OF THE ASSHOLES ON TOP OF IT."
"I NEED TO BELIEVE THAT THIS MAN IS SOMEONE TO BE REVERED, AND THAT WHAT I'M DOING TO HIM, AND WORSE, WHAT I'M DOING TO ALL THOSE PEOPLE WHO WEREN'T PREVENTED FROM GETTING ON FLIGHT 157 IS FOR THE BETTERMENT OF HUMANKIND...
...AND THAT IT WILL TRULY MAKE OUR FUTURE A BRIGHTER ONE."

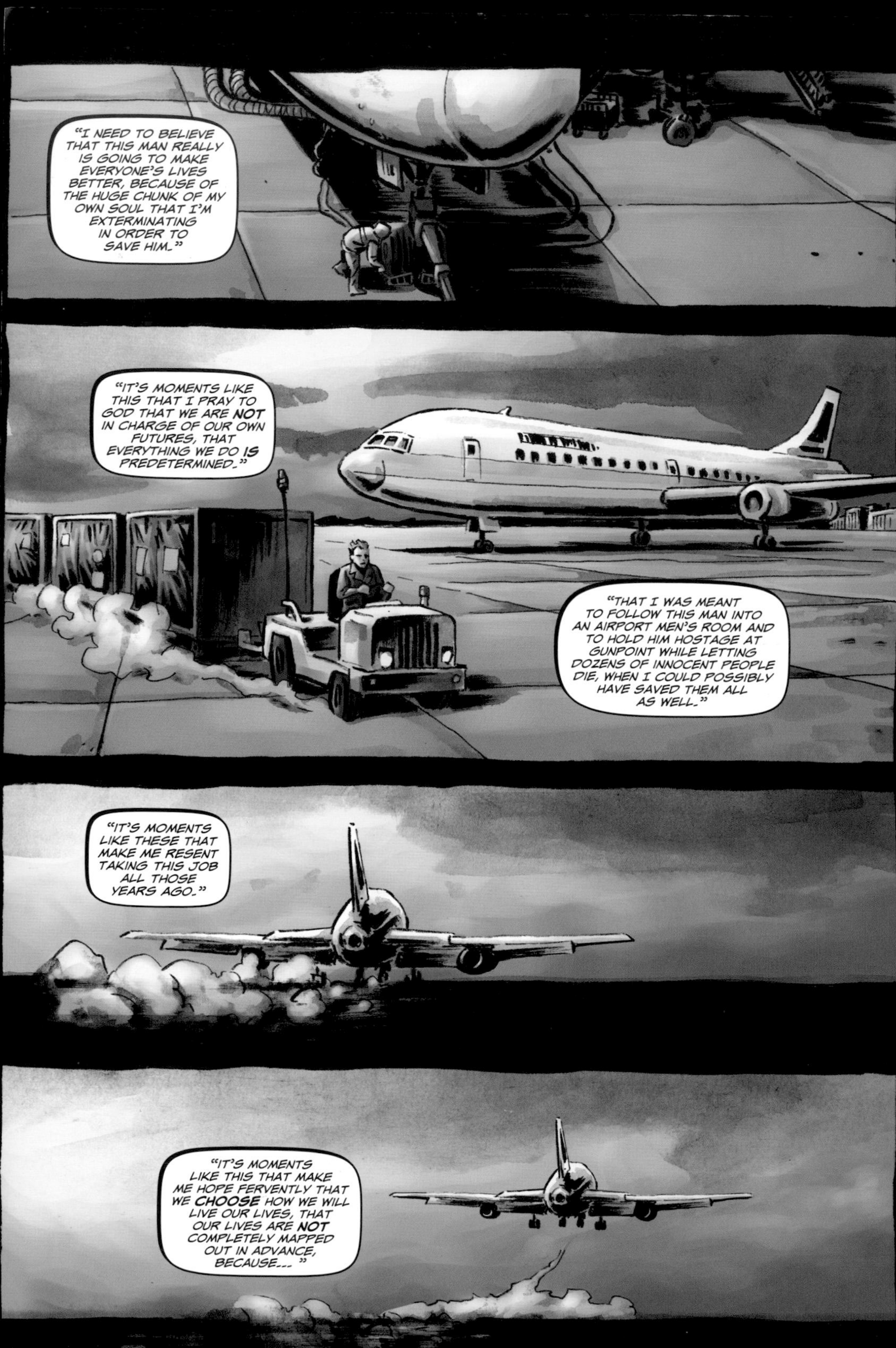
"I NEED TO BELIEVE THAT THIS MAN REALLY IS GOING TO MAKE EVERYONE'S LIVES BETTER, BECAUSE OF THE HUGE CHUNK OF MY OWN SOUL THAT I'M EXTERMINATING IN ORDER TO SAVE HIM."
"IT'S MOMENTS LIKE THIS THAT I PRAY TO GOD THAT WE ARE **NOT** IN CHARGE OF OUR OWN FUTURES, THAT EVERYTHING WE DO **IS** PREDETERMINED."
"THAT I WAS MEANT TO FOLLOW THIS MAN INTO AN AIRPORT MEN'S ROOM AND TO HOLD HIM HOSTAGE AT GUNPOINT WHILE LETTING DOZENS OF INNOCENT PEOPLE DIE, WHEN I COULD POSSIBLY HAVE SAVED THEM ALL AS WELL."
"IT'S MOMENTS LIKE THESE THAT MAKE ME RESENT TAKING THIS JOB ALL THOSE YEARS AGO."
"IT'S MOMENTS LIKE THIS THAT MAKE ME HOPE FERVENTLY THAT WE **CHOOSE** HOW WE WILL LIVE OUR LIVES, THAT OUR LIVES ARE **NOT** COMPLETELY MAPPED OUT IN ADVANCE, BECAUSE..."

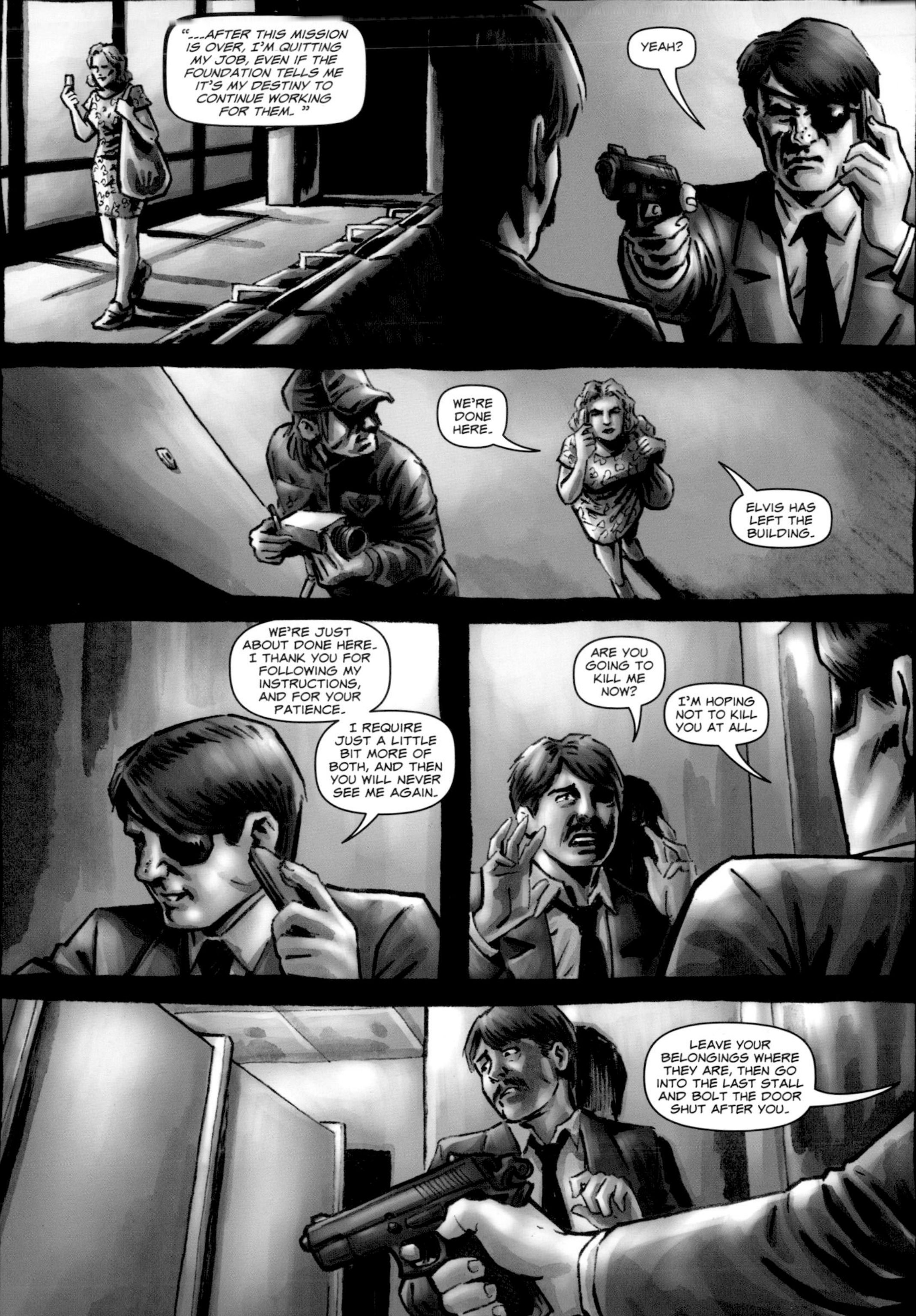
"...AFTER THIS MISSION IS OVER, I'M QUITTING MY JOB, EVEN IF THE FOUNDATION TELLS ME IT'S MY DESTINY TO CONTINUE WORKING FOR THEM."
YEAH?
WE'RE DONE HERE.
ELVIS HAS LEFT THE BUILDING.
WE'RE JUST ABOUT DONE HERE. I THANK YOU FOR FOLLOWING MY INSTRUCTIONS, AND FOR YOUR PATIENCE.
I REQUIRE JUST A LITTLE BIT MORE OF BOTH, AND THEN YOU WILL NEVER SEE ME AGAIN.
ARE YOU GOING TO KILL ME NOW?
I'M HOPING NOT TO KILL YOU AT ALL.
LEAVE YOUR BELONGINGS WHERE THEY ARE, THEN GO INTO THE LAST STALL AND BOLT THE DOOR SHUT AFTER YOU.

"DON'T COME OUT OF THERE, NO MATTER WHAT YOU HEAR, OR..."

...DON'T HEAR. IN A FEW MINUTES, YOU'LL BE GIVEN A SIGNAL TELLING YOU IT'S OKAY TO COME OUT. WHAT YOU DO AFTER THAT IS ENTIRELY UP TO YOU.

"AS I SAID..."

YOU WILL NEVER SEE ME AGAIN.

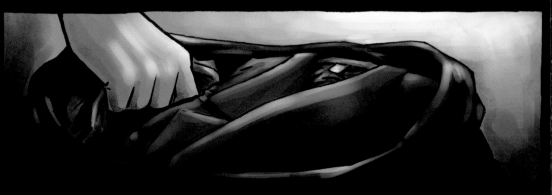

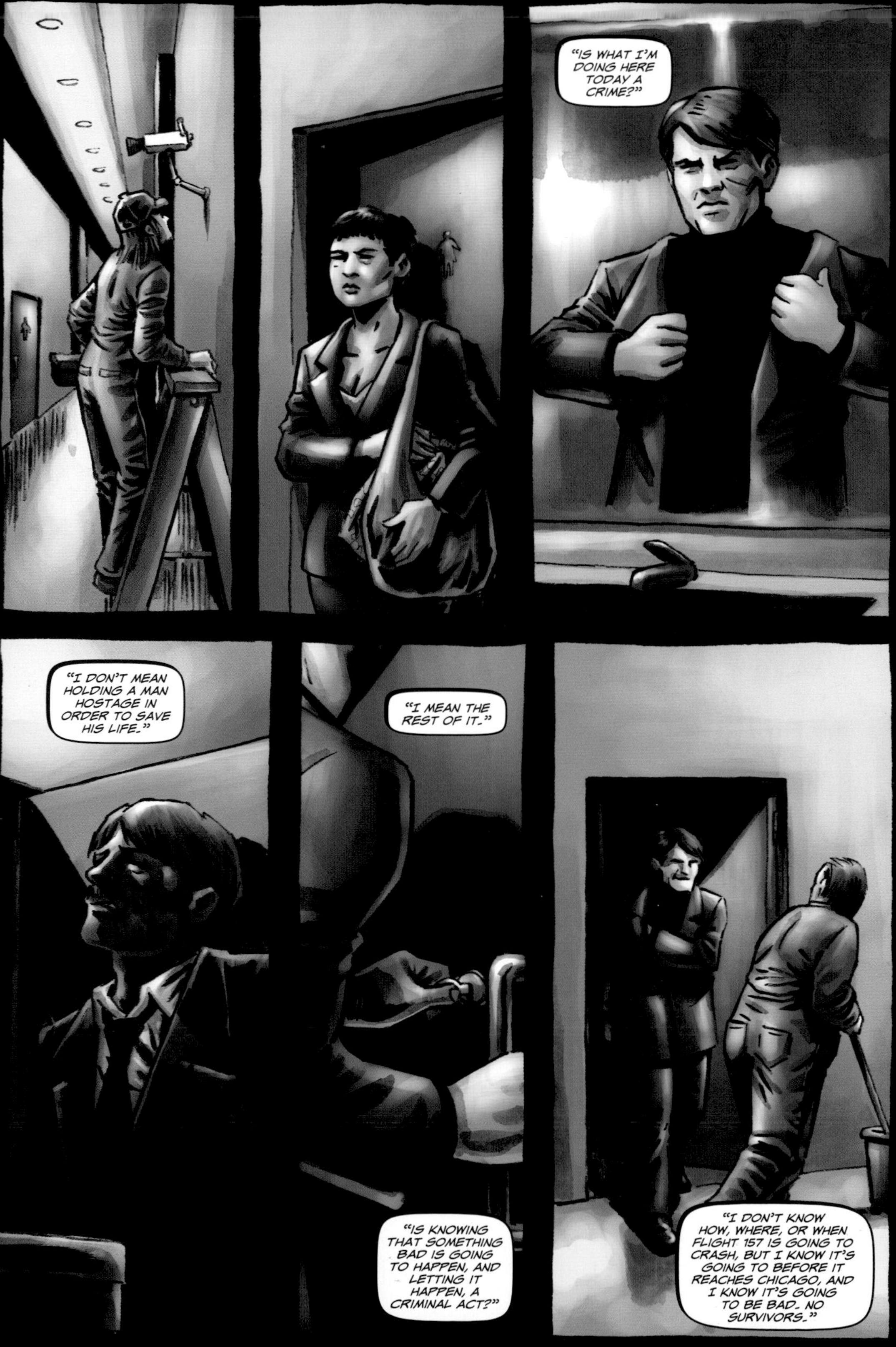
"IS WHAT I'M DOING HERE TODAY A CRIME?"
"I DON'T MEAN HOLDING A MAN HOSTAGE IN ORDER TO SAVE HIS LIFE."
"I MEAN THE REST OF IT."
"IS KNOWING THAT SOMETHING BAD IS GOING TO HAPPEN, AND LETTING IT HAPPEN, A CRIMINAL ACT?"
"I DON'T KNOW HOW, WHERE, OR WHEN FLIGHT 157 IS GOING TO CRASH, BUT I KNOW IT'S GOING TO BEFORE IT REACHES CHICAGO, AND I KNOW IT'S GOING TO BE BAD. NO SURVIVORS."

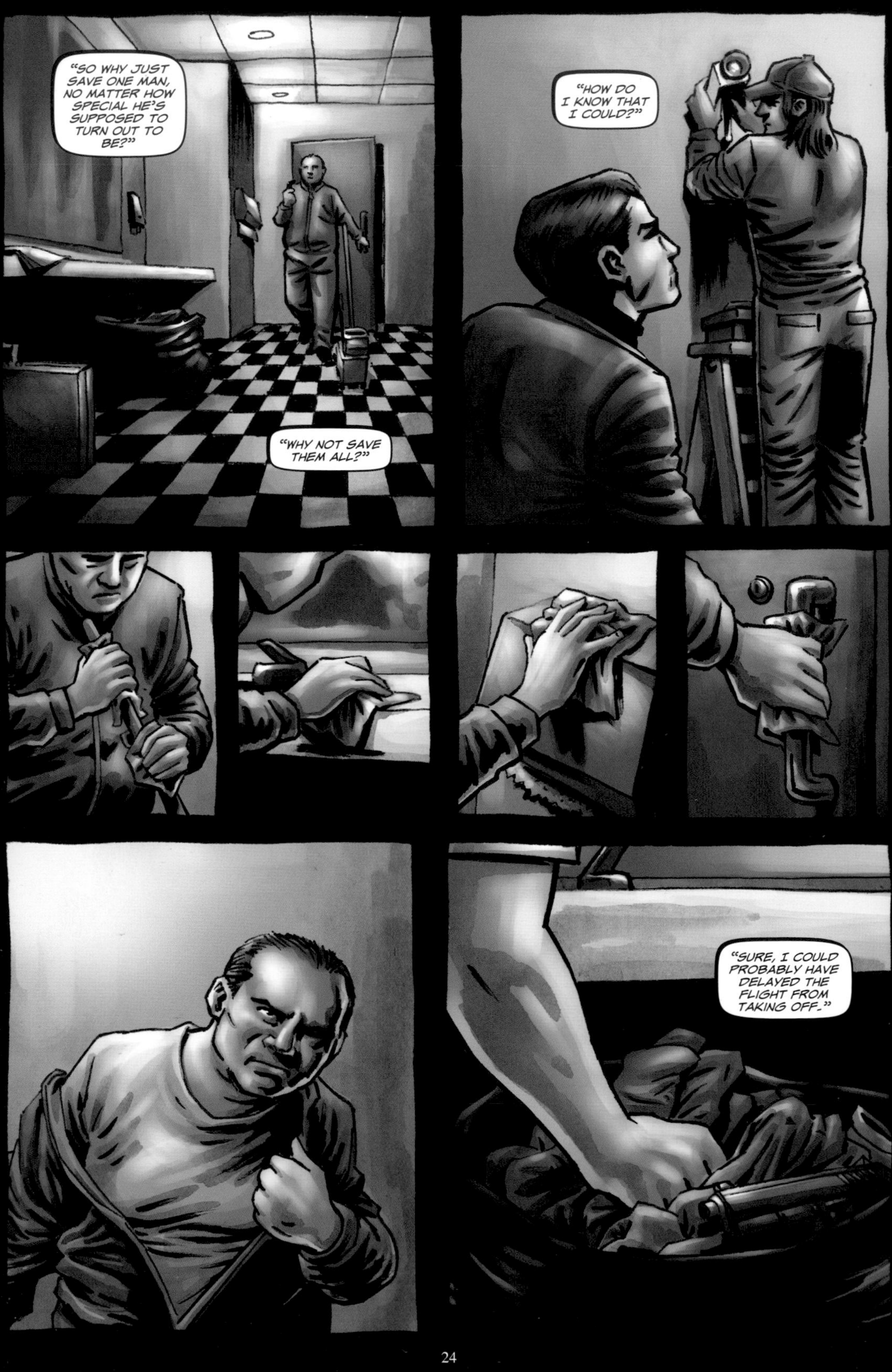
"SO WHY JUST SAVE ONE MAN, NO MATTER HOW SPECIAL HE'S SUPPOSED TO TURN OUT TO BE?"
"WHY NOT SAVE THEM ALL?"
"HOW DO I KNOW THAT I COULD?"
"SURE, I COULD PROBABLY HAVE DELAYED THE FLIGHT FROM TAKING OFF-"

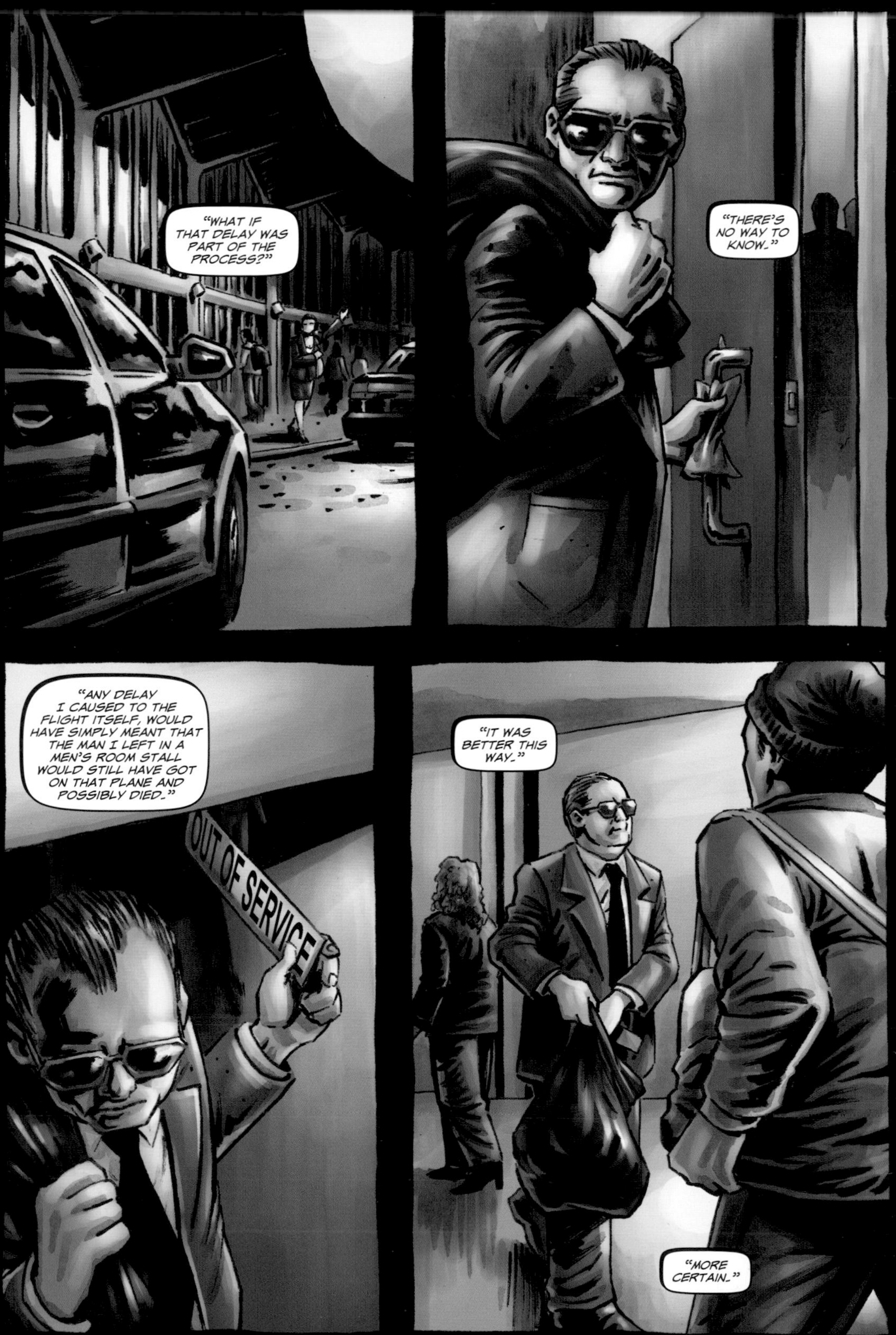
"WHAT IF THAT DELAY WAS PART OF THE PROCESS?"
"THERE'S NO WAY TO KNOW."
"ANY DELAY I CAUSED TO THE FLIGHT ITSELF, WOULD HAVE SIMPLY MEANT THAT THE MAN I LEFT IN A MEN'S ROOM STALL WOULD STILL HAVE GOT ON THAT PLANE AND POSSIBLY DIED."
OUT OF SERVICE
"IT WAS BETTER THIS WAY."
"MORE CERTAIN."

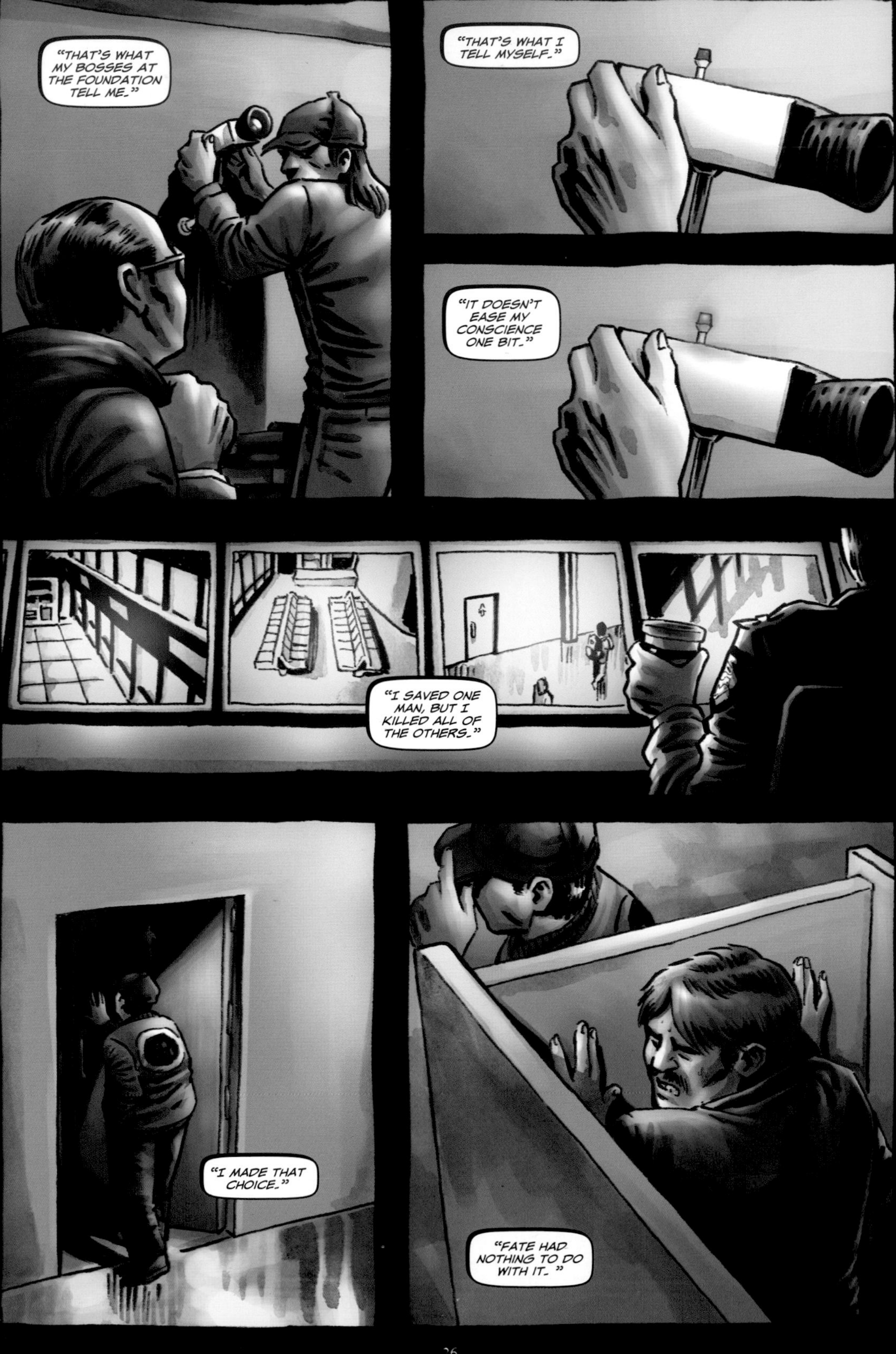
"THAT'S WHAT MY BOSSES AT THE FOUNDATION TELL ME."
"THAT'S WHAT I TELL MYSELF."
"IT DOESN'T EASE MY CONSCIENCE ONE BIT."
"I SAVED ONE MAN, BUT I KILLED ALL OF THE OTHERS."
"I MADE THAT CHOICE."
"FATE HAD NOTHING TO DO WITH IT."

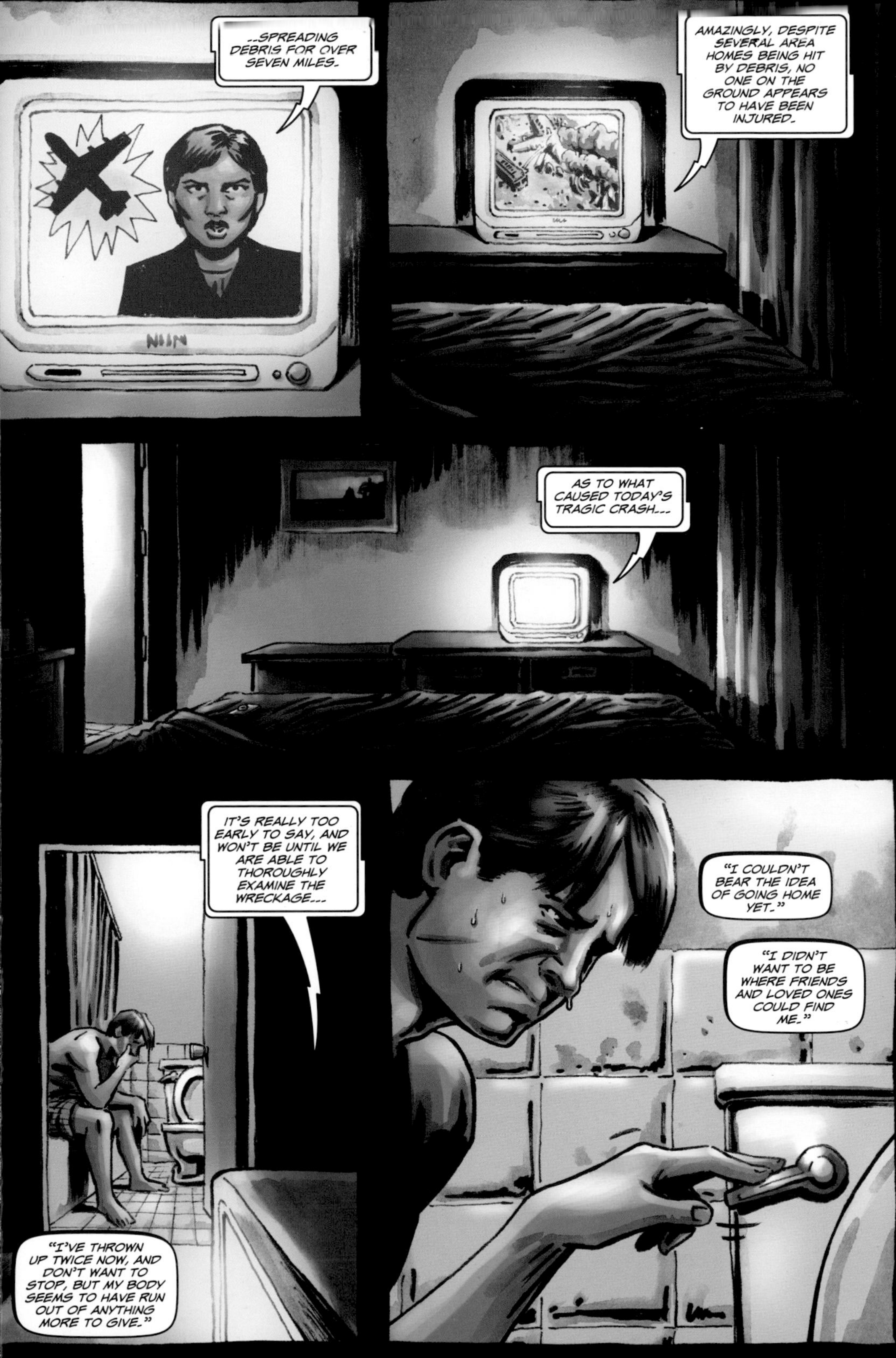
--SPREADING DEBRIS FOR OVER SEVEN MILES.
AMAZINGLY, DESPITE SEVERAL AREA HOMES BEING HIT BY DEBRIS, NO ONE ON THE GROUND APPEARS TO HAVE BEEN INJURED.
AS TO WHAT CAUSED TODAY'S TRAGIC CRASH...
IT'S REALLY TOO EARLY TO SAY, AND WON'T BE UNTIL WE ARE ABLE TO THOROUGHLY EXAMINE THE WRECKAGE...
"I'VE THROWN UP TWICE NOW, AND DON'T WANT TO STOP, BUT MY BODY SEEMS TO HAVE RUN OUT OF ANYTHING MORE TO GIVE."
"I COULDN'T BEAR THE IDEA OF GOING HOME YET."
"I DIDN'T WANT TO BE WHERE FRIENDS AND LOVED ONES COULD FIND ME."

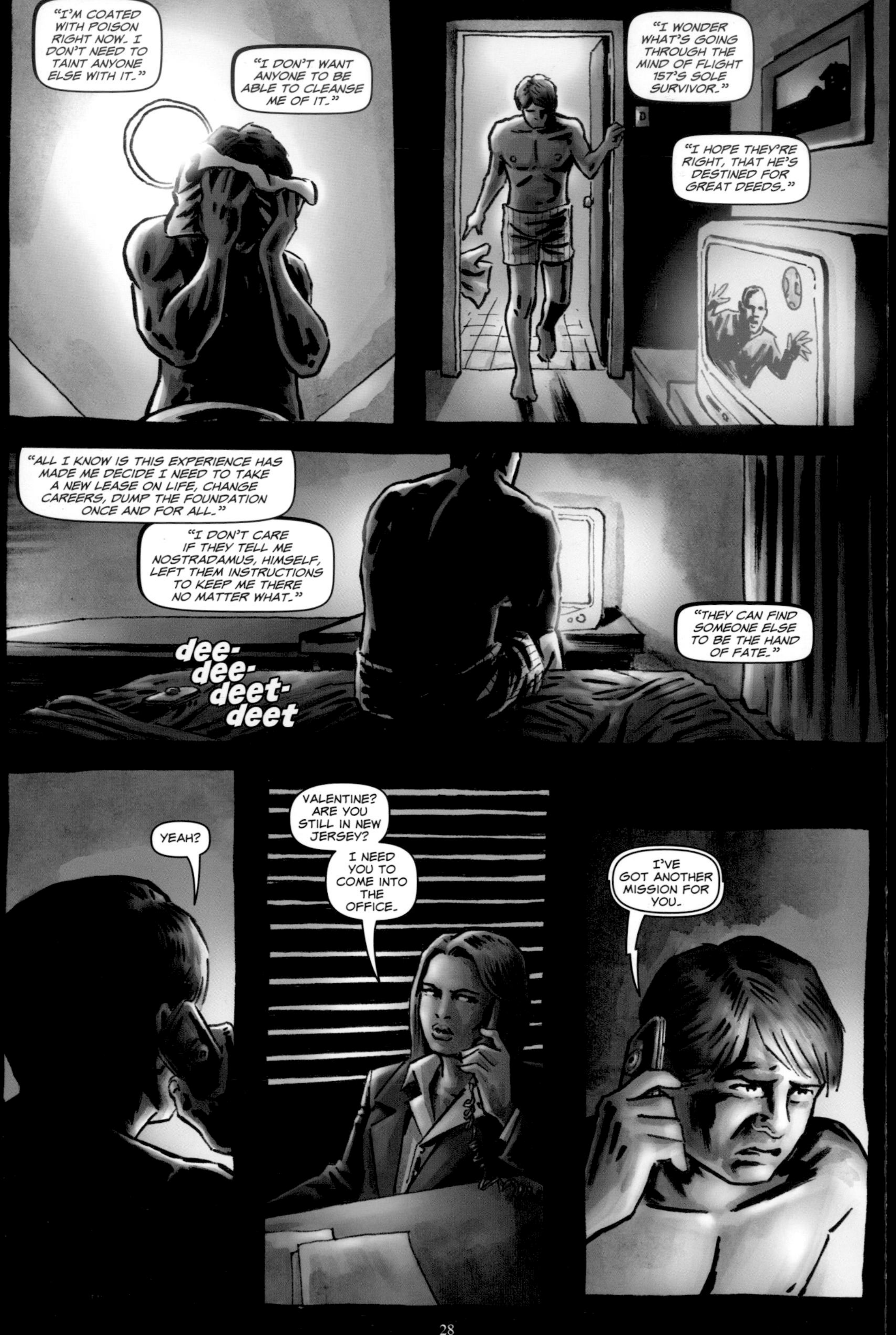
"I'M COATED WITH POISON RIGHT NOW. I DON'T NEED TO TAINT ANYONE ELSE WITH IT."
"I DON'T WANT ANYONE TO BE ABLE TO CLEANSE ME OF IT."
"I WONDER WHAT'S GOING THROUGH THE MIND OF FLIGHT 157'S SOLE SURVIVOR."
"I HOPE THEY'RE RIGHT, THAT HE'S DESTINED FOR GREAT DEEDS."
"ALL I KNOW IS THIS EXPERIENCE HAS MADE ME DECIDE I NEED TO TAKE A NEW LEASE ON LIFE, CHANGE CAREERS, DUMP THE FOUNDATION ONCE AND FOR ALL."
"I DON'T CARE IF THEY TELL ME NOSTRADAMUS, HIMSELF, LEFT THEM INSTRUCTIONS TO KEEP ME THERE NO MATTER WHAT."
"THEY CAN FIND SOMEONE ELSE TO BE THE HAND OF FATE."
dee-dee-deet-deet
YEAH?
VALENTINE? ARE YOU STILL IN NEW JERSEY?
I NEED YOU TO COME INTO THE OFFICE.
I'VE GOT ANOTHER MISSION FOR YOU.

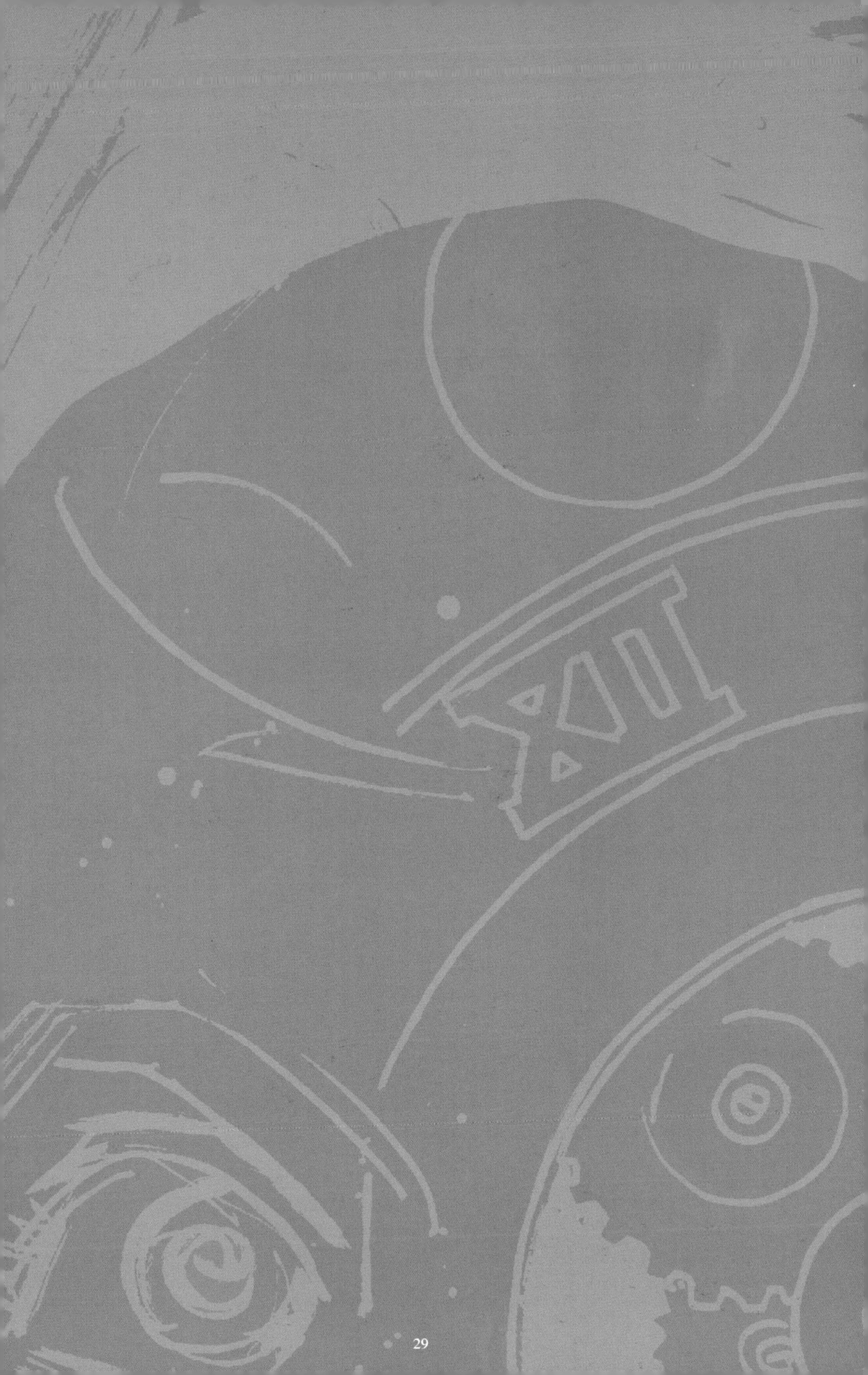
XII

Chapter Two

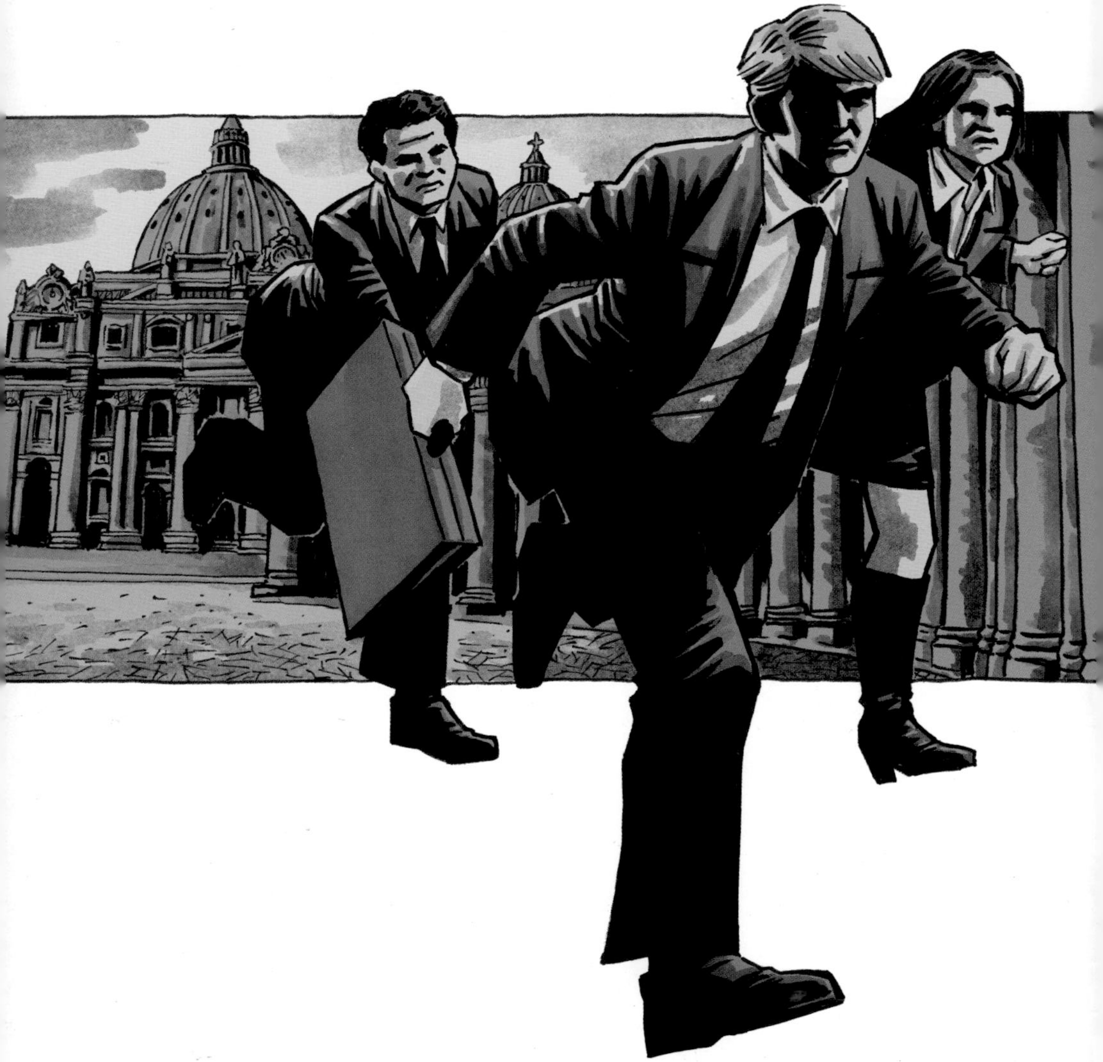

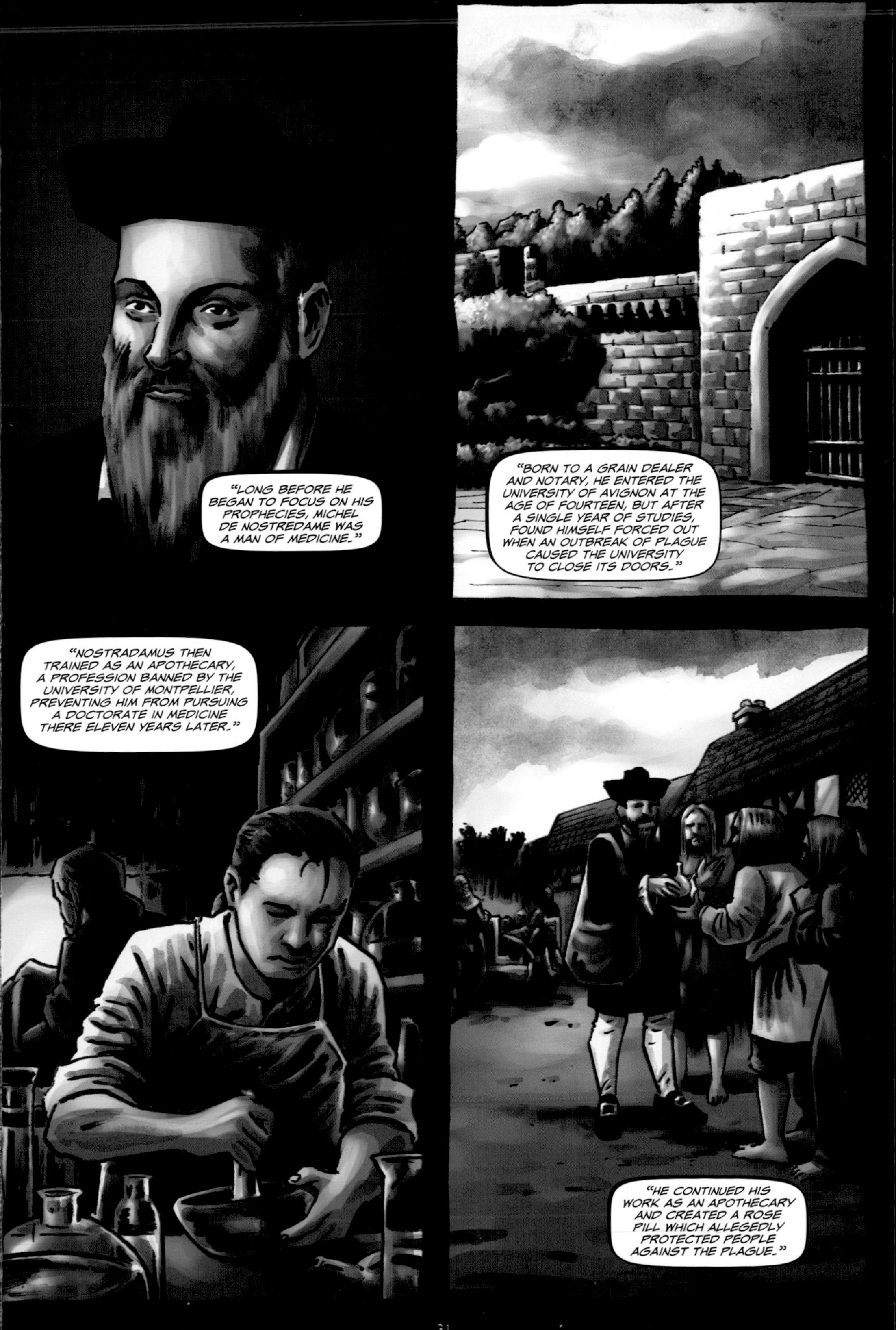
"LONG BEFORE HE BEGAN TO FOCUS ON HIS PROPHECIES, MICHEL DE NOSTREDAME WAS A MAN OF MEDICINE..."
"BORN TO A GRAIN DEALER AND NOTARY, HE ENTERED THE UNIVERSITY OF AVIGNON AT THE AGE OF FOURTEEN, BUT AFTER A SINGLE YEAR OF STUDIES, FOUND HIMSELF FORCED OUT WHEN AN OUTBREAK OF PLAGUE CAUSED THE UNIVERSITY TO CLOSE ITS DOORS..."
"NOSTRADAMUS THEN TRAINED AS AN APOTHECARY, A PROFESSION BANNED BY THE UNIVERSITY OF MONTPELLIER, PREVENTING HIM FROM PURSUING A DOCTORATE IN MEDICINE THERE ELEVEN YEARS LATER..."
"HE CONTINUED HIS WORK AS AN APOTHECARY AND CREATED A ROSE PILL WHICH ALLEGEDLY PROTECTED PEOPLE AGAINST THE PLAGUE..."

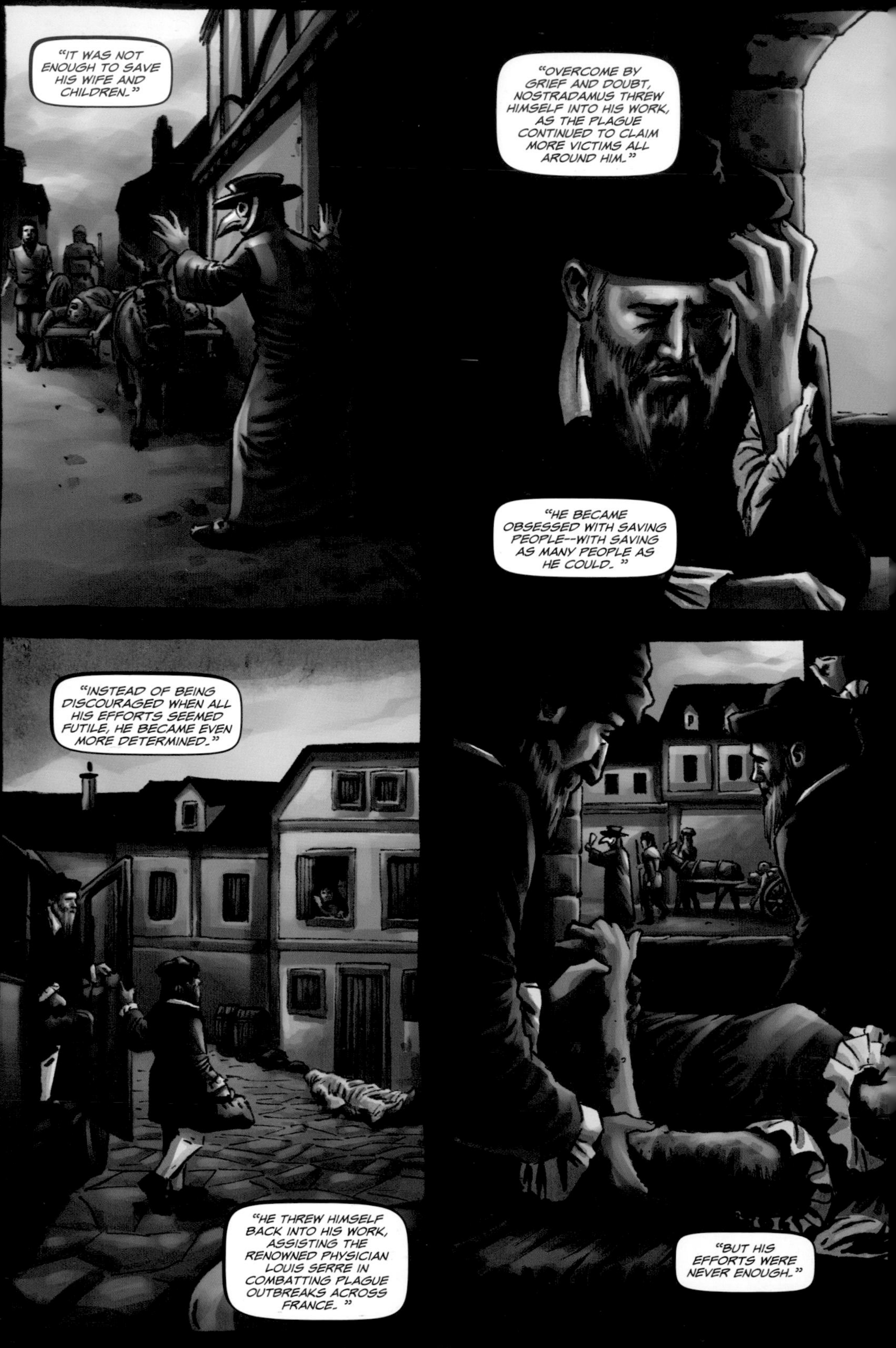
"IT WAS NOT ENOUGH TO SAVE HIS WIFE AND CHILDREN."
"OVERCOME BY GRIEF AND DOUBT, NOSTRADAMUS THREW HIMSELF INTO HIS WORK, AS THE PLAGUE CONTINUED TO CLAIM MORE VICTIMS ALL AROUND HIM."
"HE BECAME OBSESSED WITH SAVING PEOPLE--WITH SAVING AS MANY PEOPLE AS HE COULD."
"INSTEAD OF BEING DISCOURAGED WHEN ALL HIS EFFORTS SEEMED FUTILE, HE BECAME EVEN MORE DETERMINED."
"HE THREW HIMSELF BACK INTO HIS WORK, ASSISTING THE RENOWNED PHYSICIAN LOUIS SERRE IN COMBATTING PLAGUE OUTBREAKS ACROSS FRANCE."
"BUT HIS EFFORTS WERE NEVER ENOUGH."

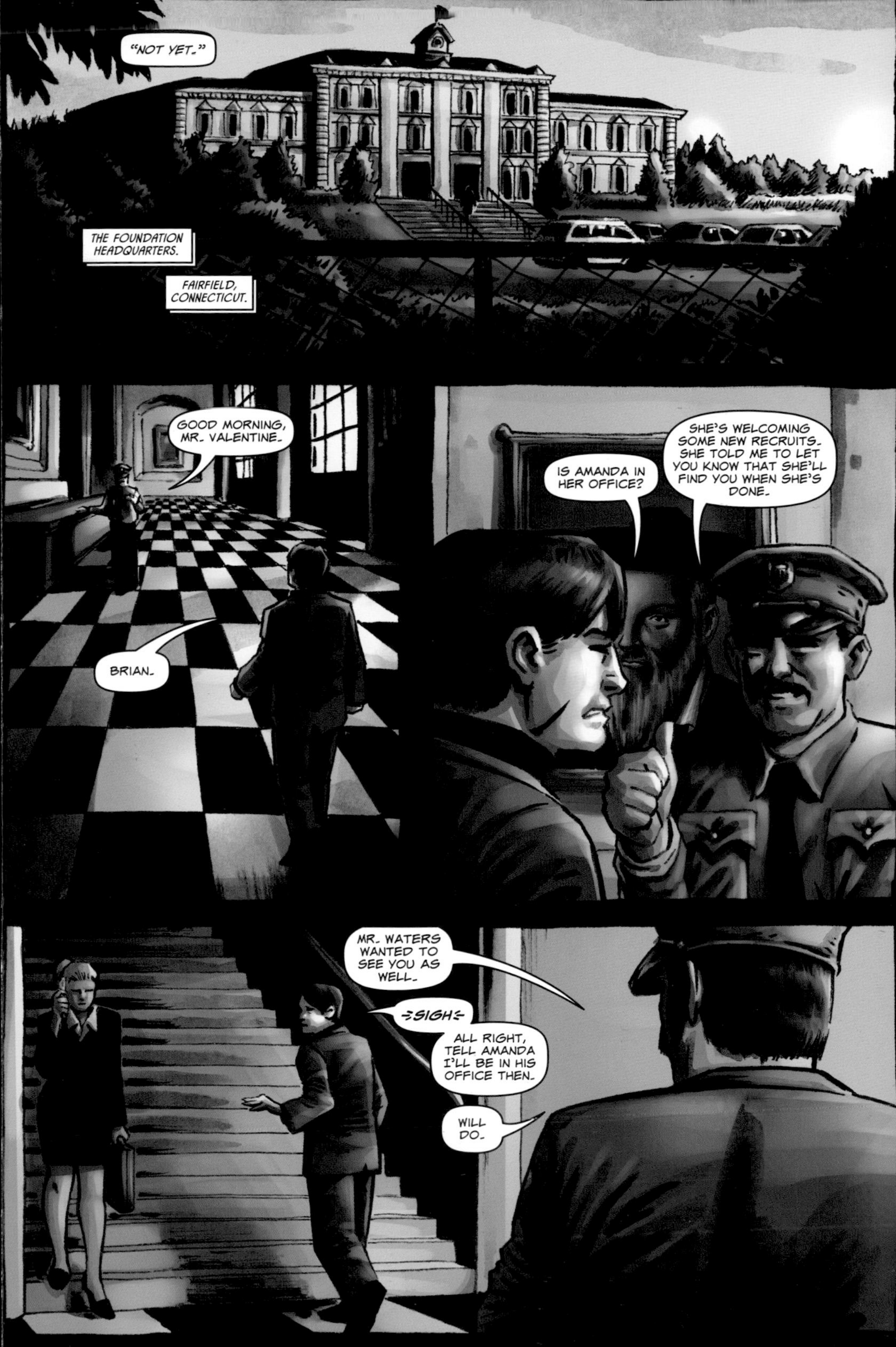
"NOT YET."
THE FOUNDATION HEADQUARTERS.
FAIRFIELD, CONNECTICUT.
GOOD MORNING, MR. VALENTINE.
BRIAN.
IS AMANDA IN HER OFFICE?
SHE'S WELCOMING SOME NEW RECRUITS. SHE TOLD ME TO LET YOU KNOW THAT SHE'LL FIND YOU WHEN SHE'S DONE.
MR. WATERS WANTED TO SEE YOU AS WELL.
=SIGH=
ALL RIGHT, TELL AMANDA I'LL BE IN HIS OFFICE THEN.
WILL DO.

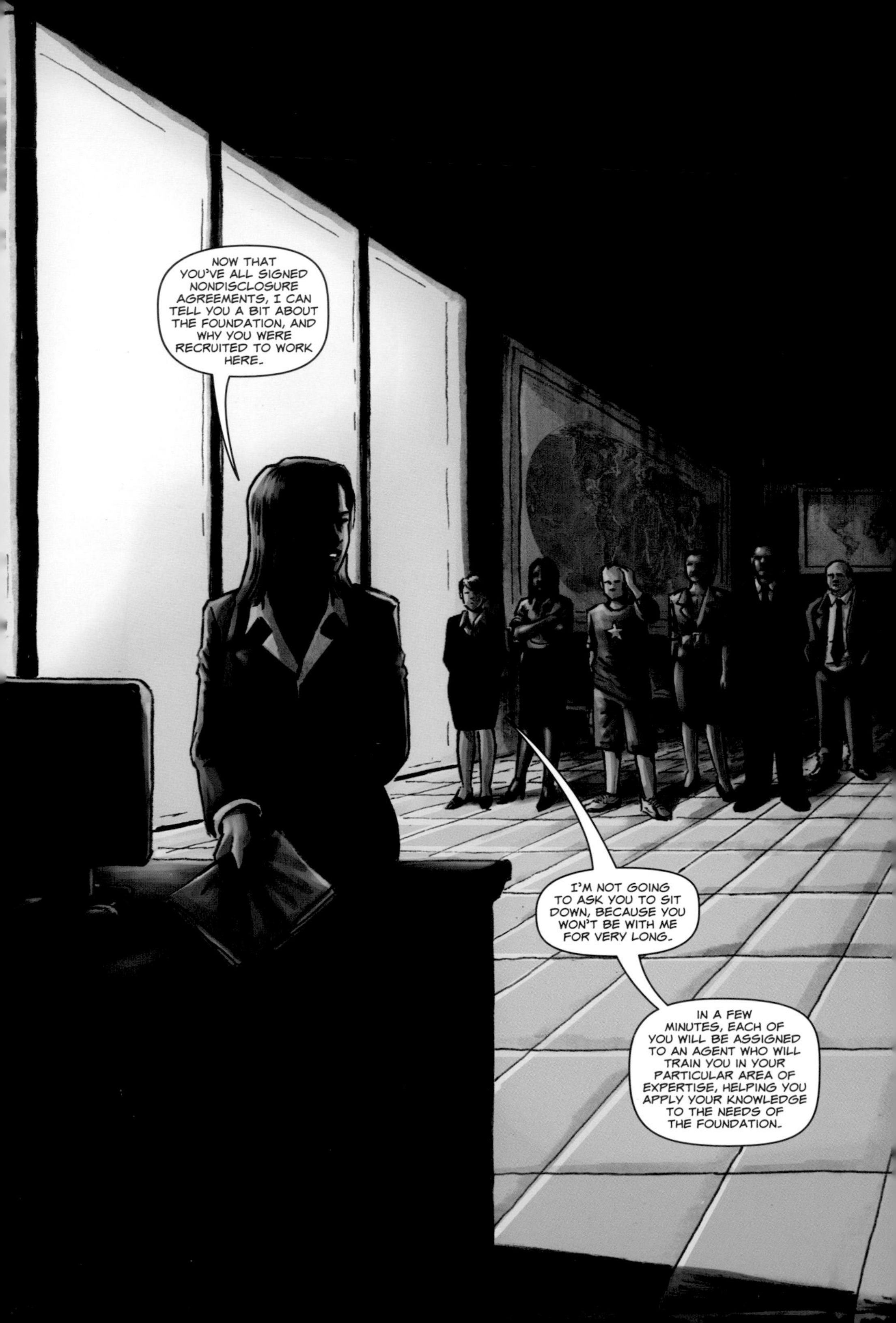
NOW THAT YOU'VE ALL SIGNED NONDISCLOSURE AGREEMENTS, I CAN TELL YOU A BIT ABOUT THE FOUNDATION, AND WHY YOU WERE RECRUITED TO WORK HERE.
I'M NOT GOING TO ASK YOU TO SIT DOWN, BECAUSE YOU WON'T BE WITH ME FOR VERY LONG.
IN A FEW MINUTES, EACH OF YOU WILL BE ASSIGNED TO AN AGENT WHO WILL TRAIN YOU IN YOUR PARTICULAR AREA OF EXPERTISE, HELPING YOU APPLY YOUR KNOWLEDGE TO THE NEEDS OF THE FOUNDATION.

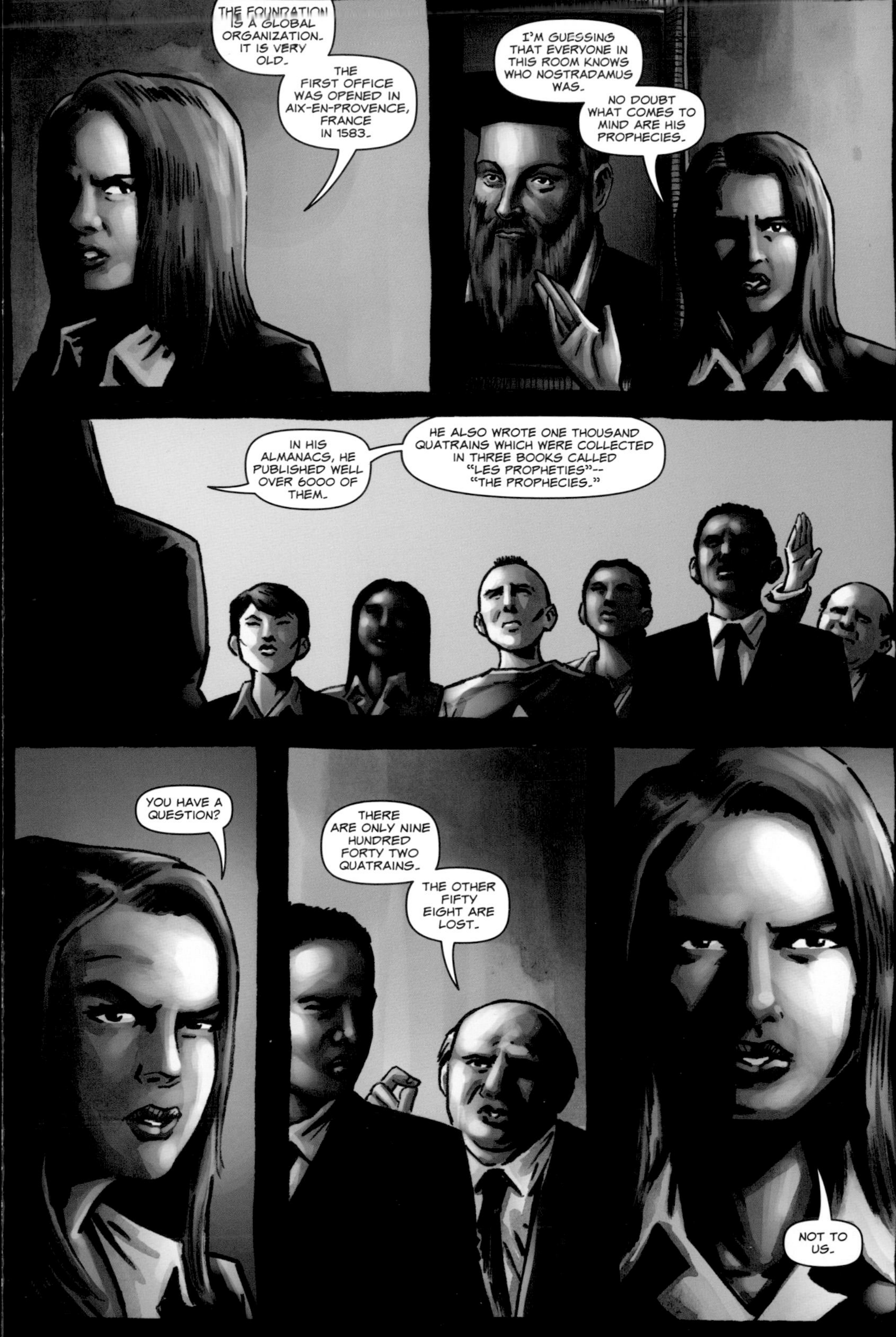
THE FOUNDATION IS A GLOBAL ORGANIZATION. IT IS VERY OLD.
THE FIRST OFFICE WAS OPENED IN AIX-EN-PROVENCE, FRANCE IN 1583.
I'M GUESSING THAT EVERYONE IN THIS ROOM KNOWS WHO NOSTRADAMUS WAS.
NO DOUBT WHAT COMES TO MIND ARE HIS PROPHECIES.
IN HIS ALMANACS, HE PUBLISHED WELL OVER 6000 OF THEM.
HE ALSO WROTE ONE THOUSAND QUATRAINS WHICH WERE COLLECTED IN THREE BOOKS CALLED "LES PROPHETIES"-- "THE PROPHECIES."
YOU HAVE A QUESTION?
THERE ARE ONLY NINE HUNDRED FORTY TWO QUATRAINS.
THE OTHER FIFTY EIGHT ARE LOST.
NOT TO US.

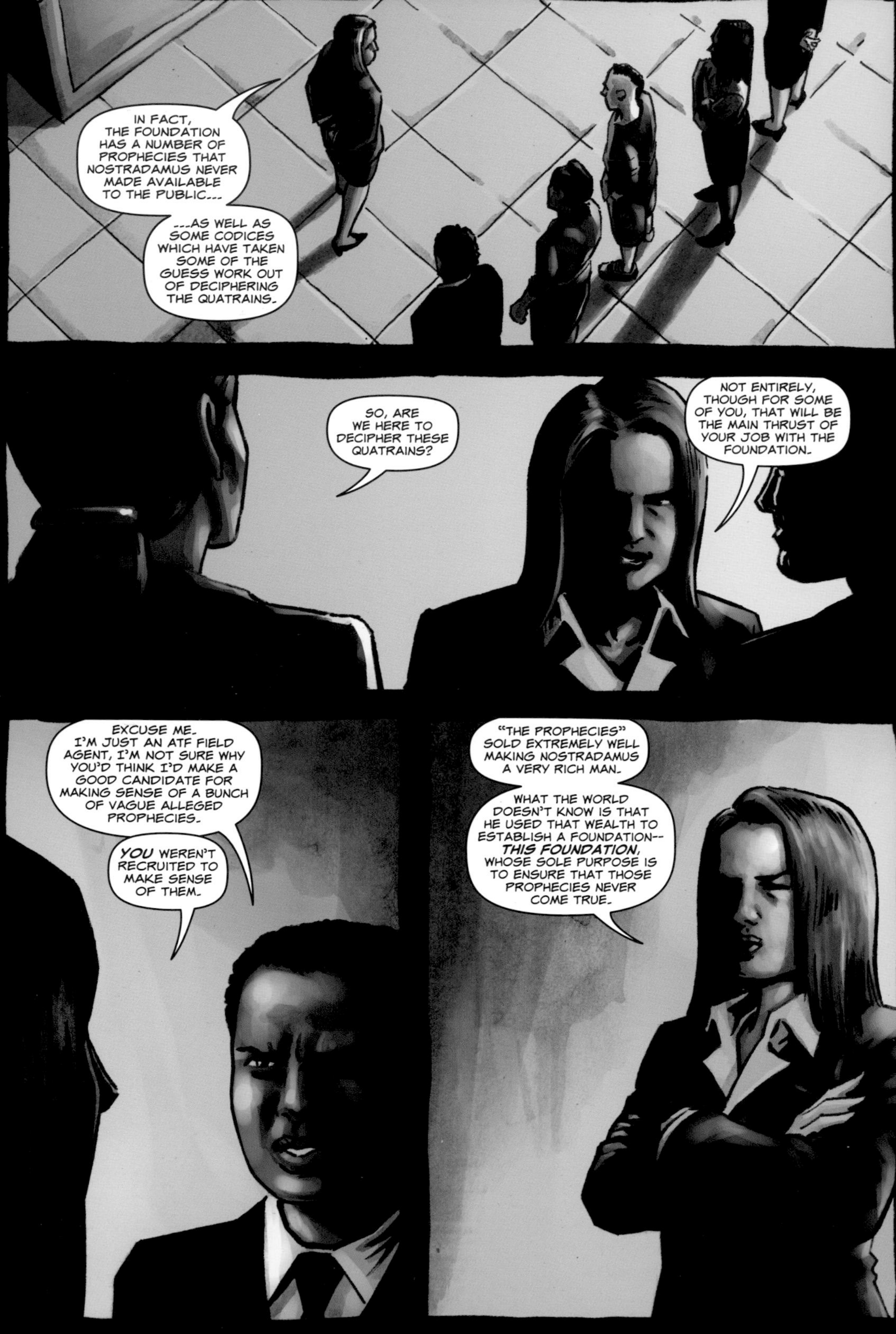
IN FACT, THE FOUNDATION HAS A NUMBER OF PROPHECIES THAT NOSTRADAMUS NEVER MADE AVAILABLE TO THE PUBLIC...
...AS WELL AS SOME CODICES WHICH HAVE TAKEN SOME OF THE GUESS WORK OUT OF DECIPHERING THE QUATRAINS.
SO, ARE WE HERE TO DECIPHER THESE QUATRAINS?
NOT ENTIRELY, THOUGH FOR SOME OF YOU, THAT WILL BE THE MAIN THRUST OF YOUR JOB WITH THE FOUNDATION.
EXCUSE ME. I'M JUST AN ATF FIELD AGENT, I'M NOT SURE WHY YOU'D THINK I'D MAKE A GOOD CANDIDATE FOR MAKING SENSE OF A BUNCH OF VAGUE ALLEGED PROPHECIES.
YOU WEREN'T RECRUITED TO MAKE SENSE OF THEM.
"THE PROPHECIES" SOLD EXTREMELY WELL MAKING NOSTRADAMUS A VERY RICH MAN.
WHAT THE WORLD DOESN'T KNOW IS THAT HE USED THAT WEALTH TO ESTABLISH A FOUNDATION-- THIS FOUNDATION, WHOSE SOLE PURPOSE IS TO ENSURE THAT THOSE PROPHECIES NEVER COME TRUE.

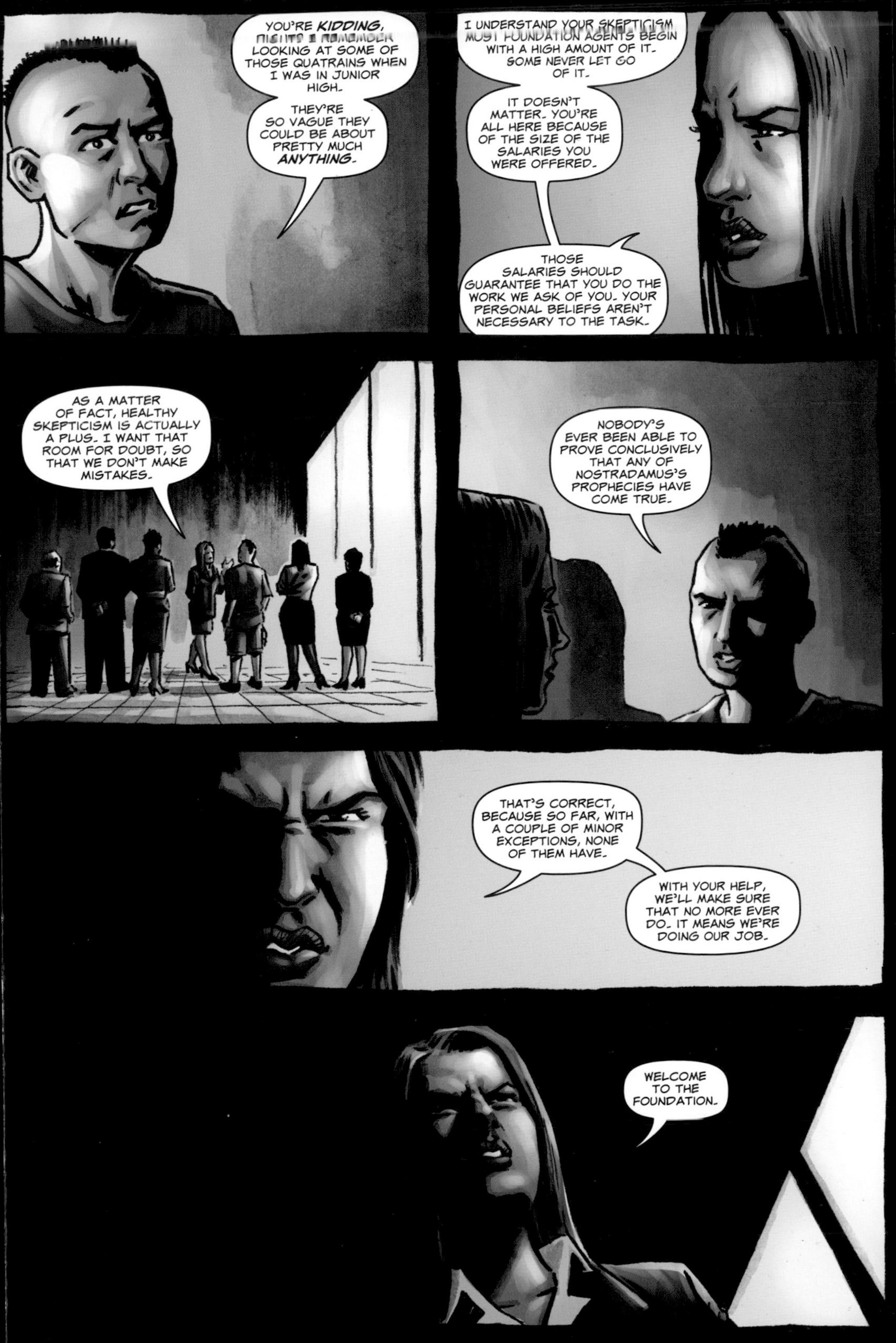

YOU'RE *KIDDING*,
LOOKING AT SOME OF THOSE QUATRAINS WHEN I WAS IN JUNIOR HIGH.
THEY'RE SO VAGUE THEY COULD BE ABOUT PRETTY MUCH *ANYTHING*.
I UNDERSTAND YOUR SKEPTICISM. MOST FOUNDATION AGENTS BEGIN WITH A HIGH AMOUNT OF IT. SOME NEVER LET GO OF IT.
IT DOESN'T MATTER. YOU'RE ALL HERE BECAUSE OF THE SIZE OF THE SALARIES YOU WERE OFFERED.
THOSE SALARIES SHOULD GUARANTEE THAT YOU DO THE WORK WE ASK OF YOU. YOUR PERSONAL BELIEFS AREN'T NECESSARY TO THE TASK.
AS A MATTER OF FACT, HEALTHY SKEPTICISM IS ACTUALLY A PLUS. I WANT THAT ROOM FOR DOUBT, SO THAT WE DON'T MAKE MISTAKES.
NOBODY'S EVER BEEN ABLE TO PROVE CONCLUSIVELY THAT ANY OF NOSTRADAMUS'S PROPHECIES HAVE COME TRUE.
THAT'S CORRECT, BECAUSE SO FAR, WITH A COUPLE OF MINOR EXCEPTIONS, NONE OF THEM HAVE.
WITH YOUR HELP, WE'LL MAKE SURE THAT NO MORE EVER DO. IT MEANS WE'RE DOING OUR JOB.
WELCOME TO THE FOUNDATION.

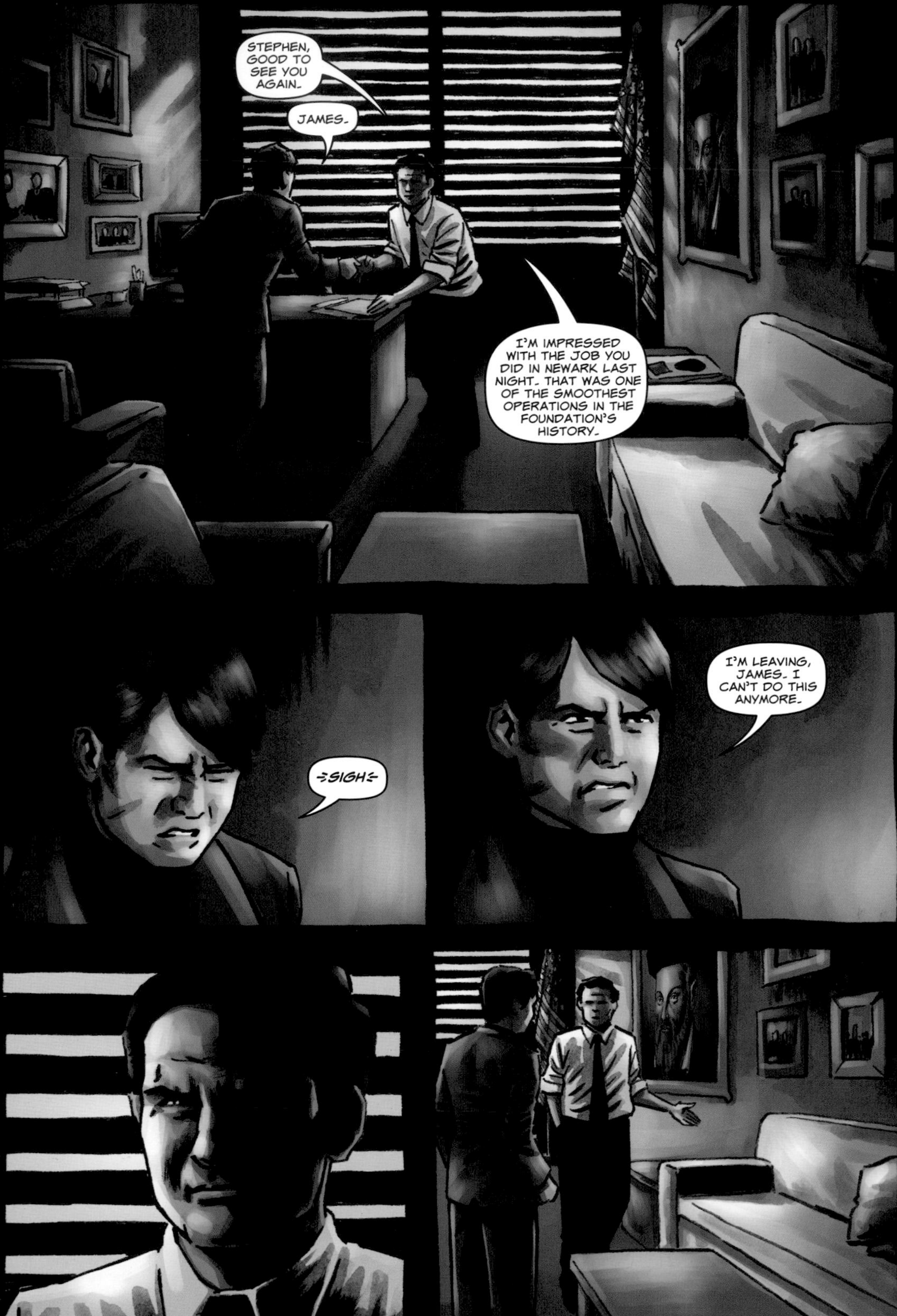
STEPHEN, GOOD TO SEE YOU AGAIN.
JAMES.
I'M IMPRESSED WITH THE JOB YOU DID IN NEWARK LAST NIGHT. THAT WAS ONE OF THE SMOOTHEST OPERATIONS IN THE FOUNDATION'S HISTORY.
=SIGH=
I'M LEAVING, JAMES. I CAN'T DO THIS ANYMORE.

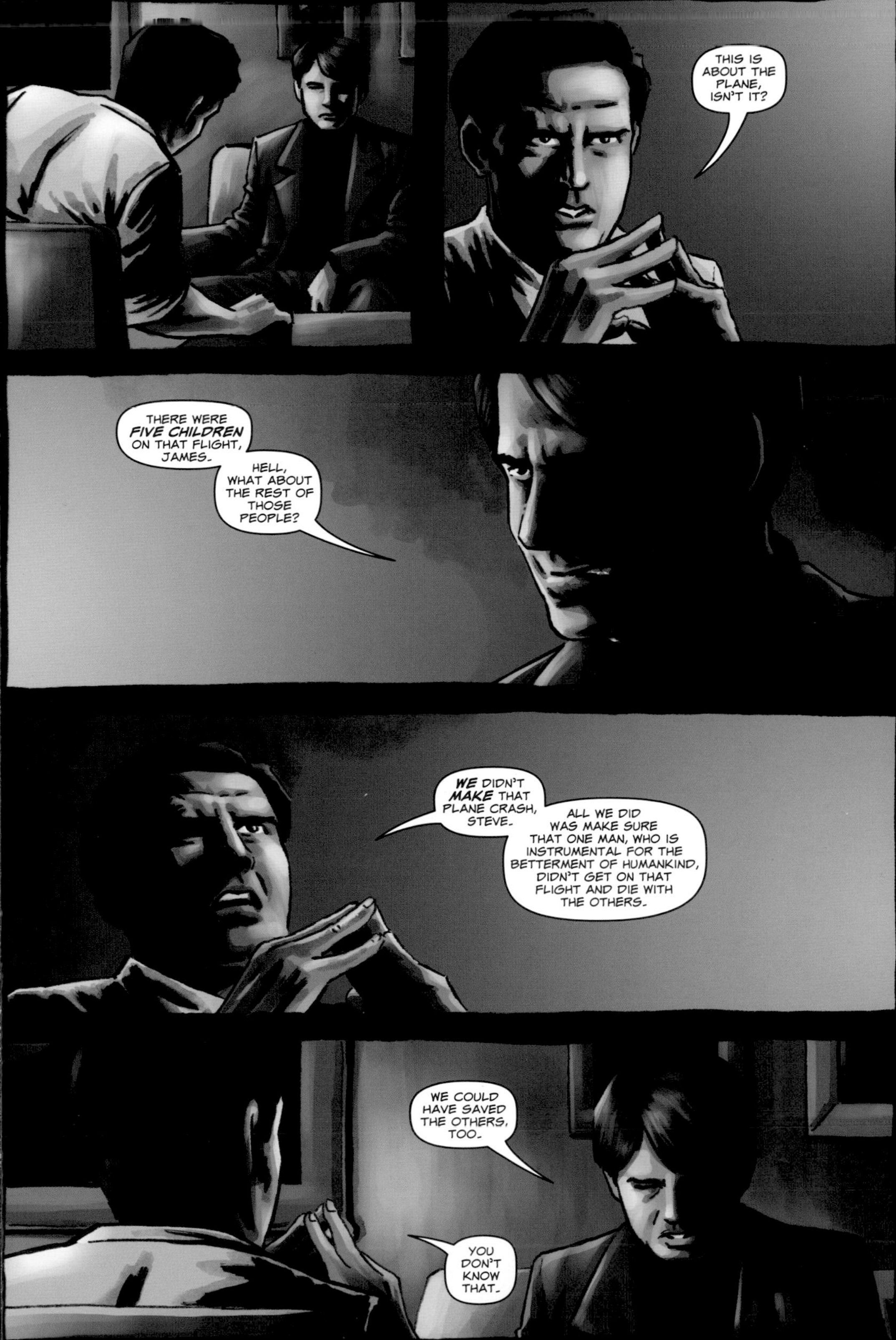
THIS IS ABOUT THE PLANE, ISN'T IT?
THERE WERE FIVE CHILDREN ON THAT FLIGHT, JAMES.
HELL, WHAT ABOUT THE REST OF THOSE PEOPLE?
WE DIDN'T MAKE THAT PLANE CRASH, STEVE.
ALL WE DID WAS MAKE SURE THAT ONE MAN, WHO IS INSTRUMENTAL FOR THE BETTERMENT OF HUMANKIND, DIDN'T GET ON THAT FLIGHT AND DIE WITH THE OTHERS.
WE COULD HAVE SAVED THE OTHERS, TOO.
YOU DON'T KNOW THAT.

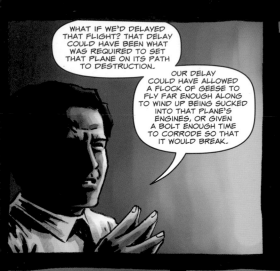

WHAT IF WE'D DELAYED THAT FLIGHT? THAT DELAY COULD HAVE BEEN WHAT WAS REQUIRED TO SET THAT PLANE ON ITS PATH TO DESTRUCTION.

OUR DELAY COULD HAVE ALLOWED A FLOCK OF GEESE TO FLY FAR ENOUGH ALONG TO WIND UP BEING SUCKED INTO THAT PLANE'S ENGINES, OR GIVEN A BOLT ENOUGH TIME TO CORRODE SO THAT IT WOULD BREAK.

ALL THAT, AND THE MAN WE *DID* SAVE, MOST LIKELY WOULD HAVE ENDED UP ON THE FLIGHT, AND NOW BE *DEAD* ALONG WITH ALL THE OTHERS.

I KNOW ALL THIS.

SO MUCH OF WHAT WE DO DEPENDS ON THE ASSUMPTION THAT FATE IS PREDETER-MINED.

OBVIOUSLY, IT'S NOT THOUGH. OUR WHOLE PURPOSE IS CHEATING FATE; CHANGING IT.

THAT MAN WE SAVED WAS SUPPOSED TO DIE WITH THE OTHERS. WE DECIDED HIS LIFE WAS MORE VALUABLE THAN EVERY OTHER ONE OF HIS FELLOW PASSENGERS.

WE SAVED HIM AT THE EXPENSE OF EVERYONE ELSE'S POSSIBLE FUTURES.

THAT MAKES US THE ONES WHO ARE PREDETERMINING THE FATE OF OTHERS.

I'M NO LONGER COMFORTABLE WITH THAT.

I'M ONLY COMFORTABLE WITH DETERMINING MY OWN FATE NOW.

THAT MEANS I'M FINISHED WORKING FOR THE FOUNDATION.

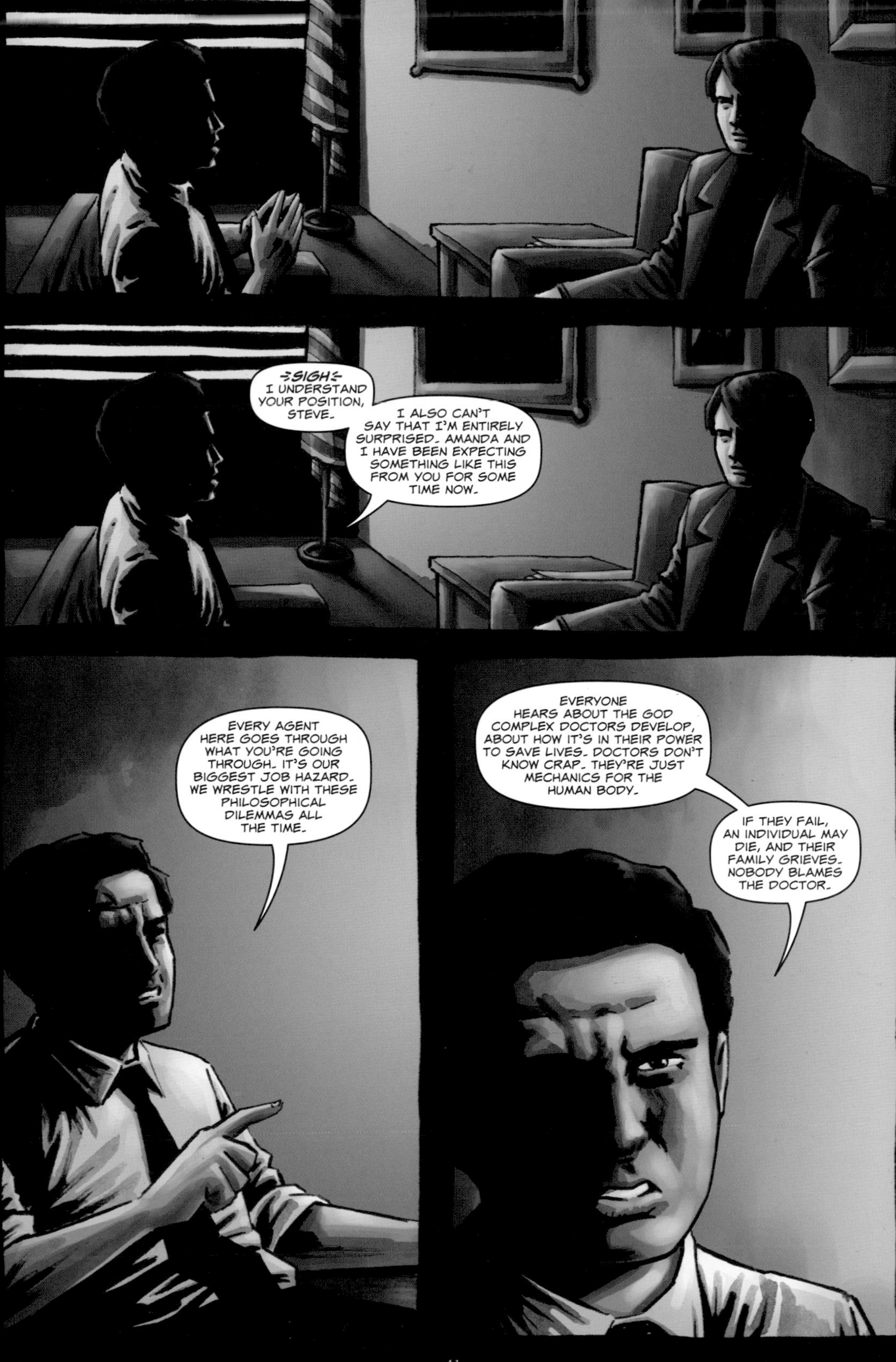

-SIGH- I UNDERSTAND YOUR POSITION, STEVE.
I ALSO CAN'T SAY THAT I'M ENTIRELY SURPRISED. AMANDA AND I HAVE BEEN EXPECTING SOMETHING LIKE THIS FROM YOU FOR SOME TIME NOW.
EVERY AGENT HERE GOES THROUGH WHAT YOU'RE GOING THROUGH. IT'S OUR BIGGEST JOB HAZARD. WE WRESTLE WITH THESE PHILOSOPHICAL DILEMMAS ALL THE TIME.
EVERYONE HEARS ABOUT THE GOD COMPLEX DOCTORS DEVELOP, ABOUT HOW IT'S IN THEIR POWER TO SAVE LIVES. DOCTORS DON'T KNOW CRAP. THEY'RE JUST MECHANICS FOR THE HUMAN BODY.
IF THEY FAIL, AN INDIVIDUAL MAY DIE, AND THEIR FAMILY GRIEVES. NOBODY BLAMES THE DOCTOR.

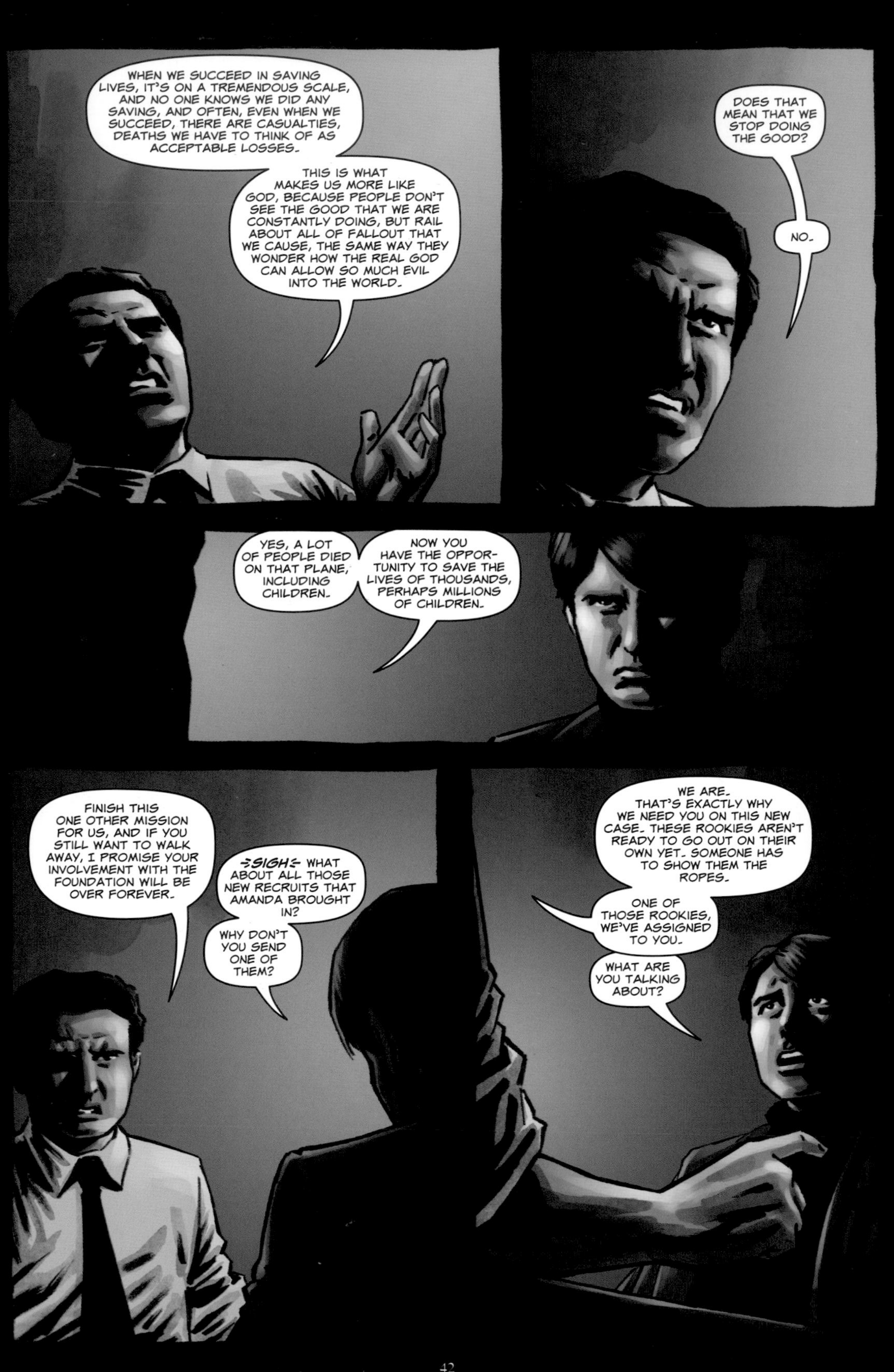
WHEN WE SUCCEED IN SAVING LIVES, IT'S ON A TREMENDOUS SCALE, AND NO ONE KNOWS WE DID ANY SAVING, AND OFTEN, EVEN WHEN WE SUCCEED, THERE ARE CASUALTIES, DEATHS WE HAVE TO THINK OF AS ACCEPTABLE LOSSES.
THIS IS WHAT MAKES US MORE LIKE GOD, BECAUSE PEOPLE DON'T SEE THE GOOD THAT WE ARE CONSTANTLY DOING, BUT RAIL ABOUT ALL OF FALLOUT THAT WE CAUSE, THE SAME WAY THEY WONDER HOW THE REAL GOD CAN ALLOW SO MUCH EVIL INTO THE WORLD.
DOES THAT MEAN THAT WE STOP DOING THE GOOD?
NO.
YES, A LOT OF PEOPLE DIED ON THAT PLANE, INCLUDING CHILDREN.
NOW YOU HAVE THE OPPORTUNITY TO SAVE THE LIVES OF THOUSANDS, PERHAPS MILLIONS OF CHILDREN.
FINISH THIS ONE OTHER MISSION FOR US, AND IF YOU STILL WANT TO WALK AWAY, I PROMISE YOUR INVOLVEMENT WITH THE FOUNDATION WILL BE OVER FOREVER.
SIGH WHAT ABOUT ALL THOSE NEW RECRUITS THAT AMANDA BROUGHT IN?
WHY DON'T YOU SEND ONE OF THEM?
WE ARE. THAT'S EXACTLY WHY WE NEED YOU ON THIS NEW CASE. THESE ROOKIES AREN'T READY TO GO OUT ON THEIR OWN YET. SOMEONE HAS TO SHOW THEM THE ROPES.
ONE OF THOSE ROOKIES, WE'VE ASSIGNED TO YOU.
WHAT ARE YOU TALKING ABOUT?

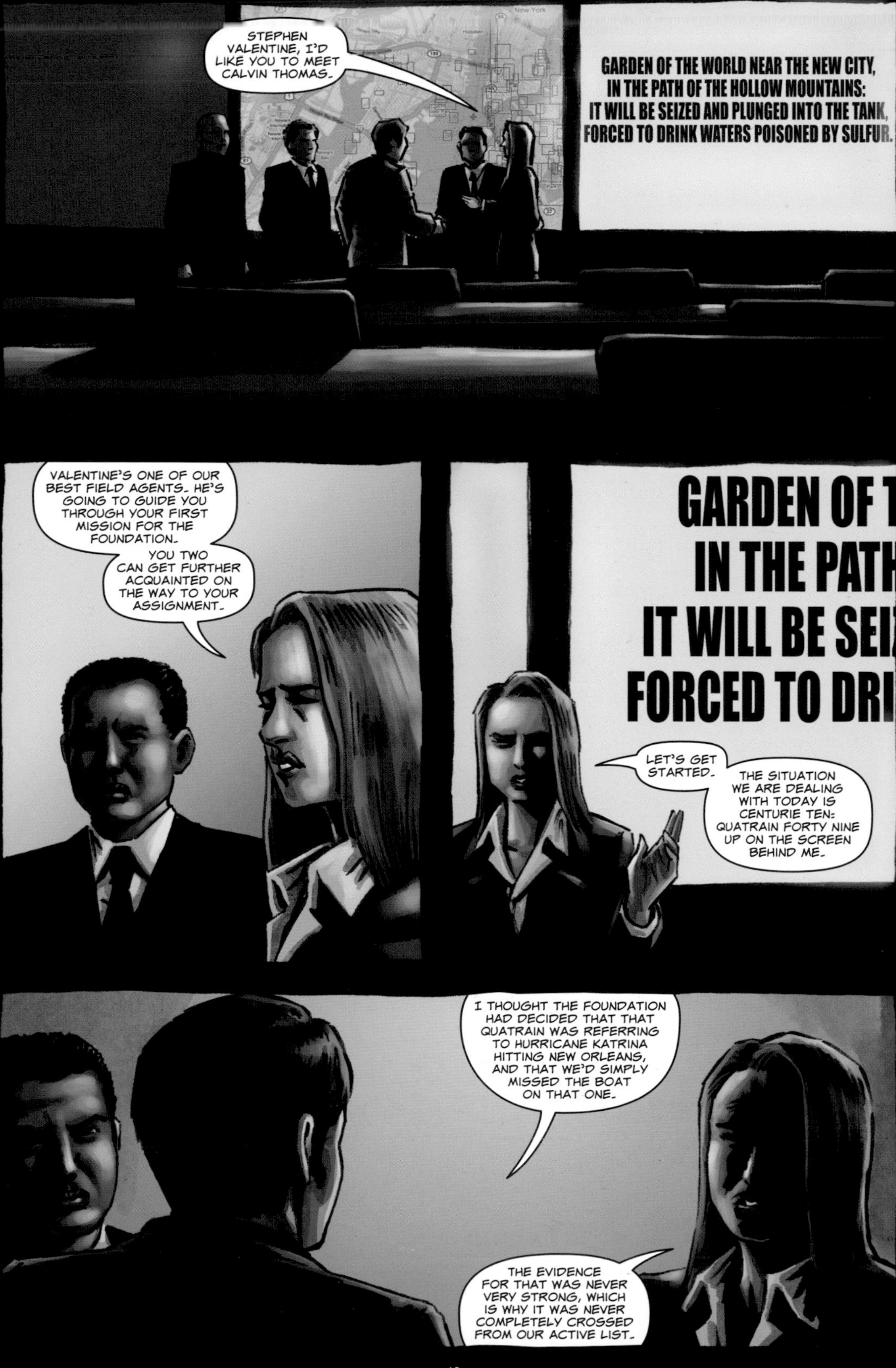
STEPHEN VALENTINE, I'D LIKE YOU TO MEET CALVIN THOMAS.
GARDEN OF THE WORLD NEAR THE NEW CITY, IN THE PATH OF THE HOLLOW MOUNTAINS: IT WILL BE SEIZED AND PLUNGED INTO THE TANK, FORCED TO DRINK WATERS POISONED BY SULFUR.
VALENTINE'S ONE OF OUR BEST FIELD AGENTS. HE'S GOING TO GUIDE YOU THROUGH YOUR FIRST MISSION FOR THE FOUNDATION.
YOU TWO CAN GET FURTHER ACQUAINTED ON THE WAY TO YOUR ASSIGNMENT.
GARDEN OF T
IN THE PATH
IT WILL BE SEI
FORCED TO DRI
LET'S GET STARTED.
THE SITUATION WE ARE DEALING WITH TODAY IS CENTURIE TEN: QUATRAIN FORTY NINE UP ON THE SCREEN BEHIND ME.
I THOUGHT THE FOUNDATION HAD DECIDED THAT THAT QUATRAIN WAS REFERRING TO HURRICANE KATRINA HITTING NEW ORLEANS, AND THAT WE'D SIMPLY MISSED THE BOAT ON THAT ONE.
THE EVIDENCE FOR THAT WAS NEVER VERY STRONG, WHICH IS WHY IT WAS NEVER COMPLETELY CROSSED FROM OUR ACTIVE LIST.

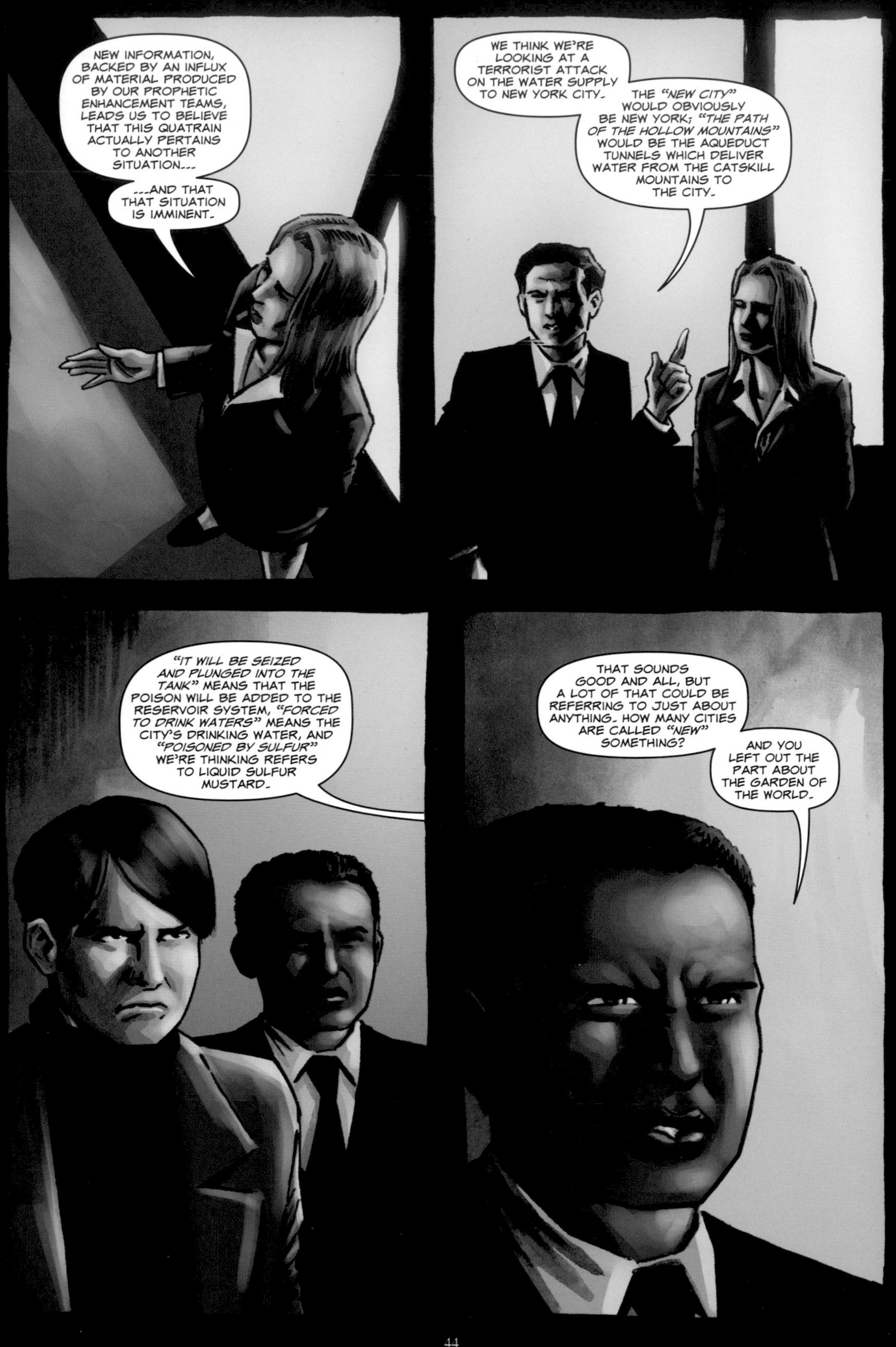
NEW INFORMATION, BACKED BY AN INFLUX OF MATERIAL PRODUCED BY OUR PROPHETIC ENHANCEMENT TEAMS, LEADS US TO BELIEVE THAT THIS QUATRAIN ACTUALLY PERTAINS TO ANOTHER SITUATION...
...AND THAT THAT SITUATION IS IMMINENT.
WE THINK WE'RE LOOKING AT A TERRORIST ATTACK ON THE WATER SUPPLY TO NEW YORK CITY.
THE *"NEW CITY"* WOULD OBVIOUSLY BE NEW YORK; *"THE PATH OF THE HOLLOW MOUNTAINS"* WOULD BE THE AQUEDUCT TUNNELS WHICH DELIVER WATER FROM THE CATSKILL MOUNTAINS TO THE CITY.
"IT WILL BE SEIZED AND PLUNGED INTO THE TANK" MEANS THAT THE POISON WILL BE ADDED TO THE RESERVOIR SYSTEM, *"FORCED TO DRINK WATERS"* MEANS THE CITY'S DRINKING WATER, AND *"POISONED BY SULFUR"* WE'RE THINKING REFERS TO LIQUID SULFUR MUSTARD.
THAT SOUNDS GOOD AND ALL, BUT A LOT OF THAT COULD BE REFERRING TO JUST ABOUT ANYTHING. HOW MANY CITIES ARE CALLED "NEW" SOMETHING?
AND YOU LEFT OUT THE PART ABOUT THE GARDEN OF THE WORLD.

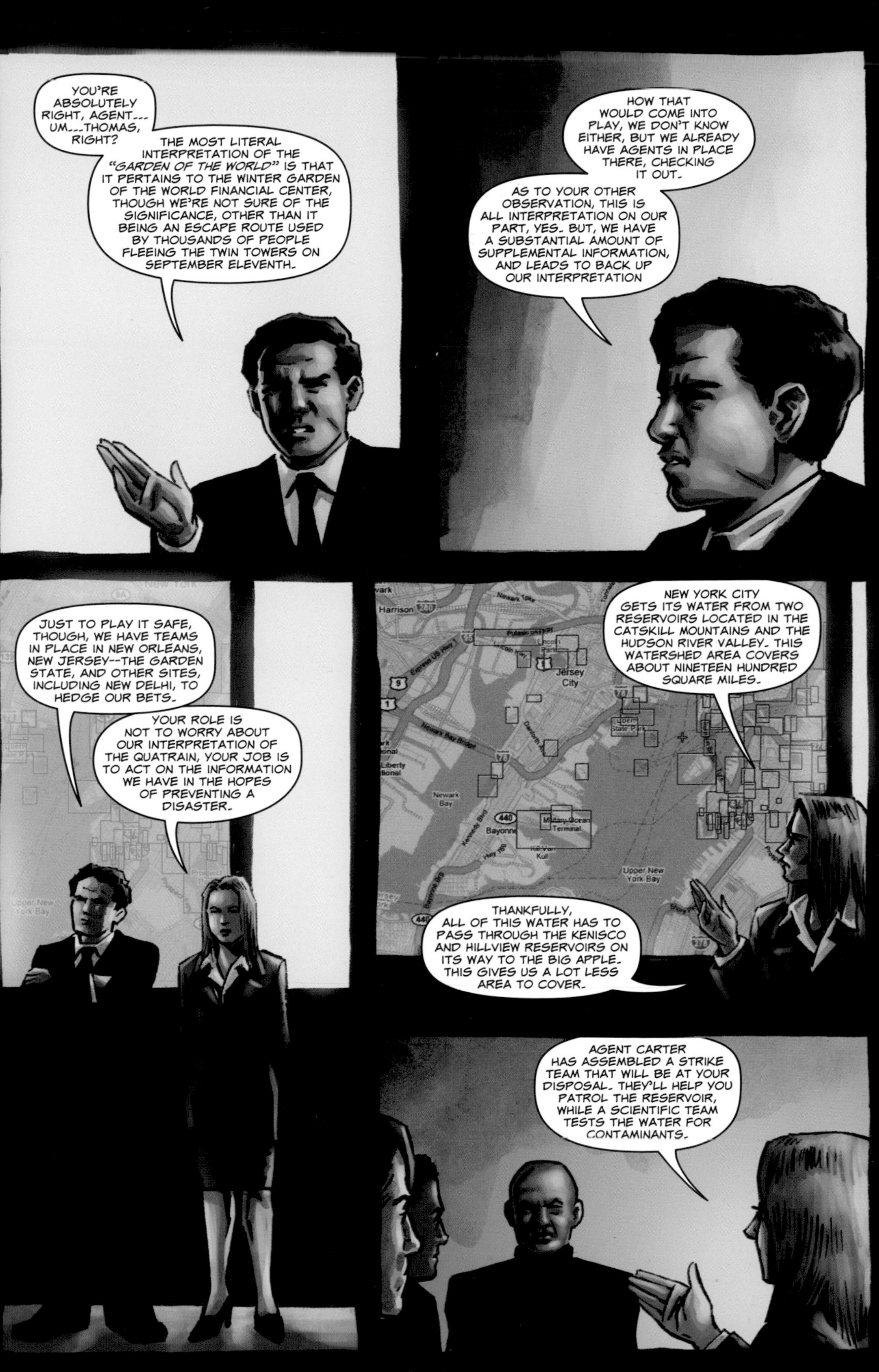
YOU'RE ABSOLUTELY RIGHT, AGENT... UM...THOMAS, RIGHT?
THE MOST LITERAL INTERPRETATION OF THE *"GARDEN OF THE WORLD"* IS THAT IT PERTAINS TO THE WINTER GARDEN OF THE WORLD FINANCIAL CENTER, THOUGH WE'RE NOT SURE OF THE SIGNIFICANCE, OTHER THAN IT BEING AN ESCAPE ROUTE USED BY THOUSANDS OF PEOPLE FLEEING THE TWIN TOWERS ON SEPTEMBER ELEVENTH.
HOW THAT WOULD COME INTO PLAY, WE DON'T KNOW EITHER, BUT WE ALREADY HAVE AGENTS IN PLACE THERE, CHECKING IT OUT.
AS TO YOUR OTHER OBSERVATION, THIS IS ALL INTERPRETATION ON OUR PART, YES. BUT, WE HAVE A SUBSTANTIAL AMOUNT OF SUPPLEMENTAL INFORMATION, AND LEADS TO BACK UP OUR INTERPRETATION
JUST TO PLAY IT SAFE, THOUGH, WE HAVE TEAMS IN PLACE IN NEW ORLEANS, NEW JERSEY--THE GARDEN STATE, AND OTHER SITES, INCLUDING NEW DELHI, TO HEDGE OUR BETS.
YOUR ROLE IS NOT TO WORRY ABOUT OUR INTERPRETATION OF THE QUATRAIN, YOUR JOB IS TO ACT ON THE INFORMATION WE HAVE IN THE HOPES OF PREVENTING A DISASTER.
Harrison
Jersey City
Newark Bay
Bayonne
Upper New York Bay
NEW YORK CITY GETS ITS WATER FROM TWO RESERVOIRS LOCATED IN THE CATSKILL MOUNTAINS AND THE HUDSON RIVER VALLEY. THIS WATERSHED AREA COVERS ABOUT NINETEEN HUNDRED SQUARE MILES.
THANKFULLY, ALL OF THIS WATER HAS TO PASS THROUGH THE KENISCO AND HILLVIEW RESERVOIRS ON ITS WAY TO THE BIG APPLE. THIS GIVES US A LOT LESS AREA TO COVER.
AGENT CARTER HAS ASSEMBLED A STRIKE TEAM THAT WILL BE AT YOUR DISPOSAL. THEY'LL HELP YOU PATROL THE RESERVOIR, WHILE A SCIENTIFIC TEAM TESTS THE WATER FOR CONTAMINANTS.

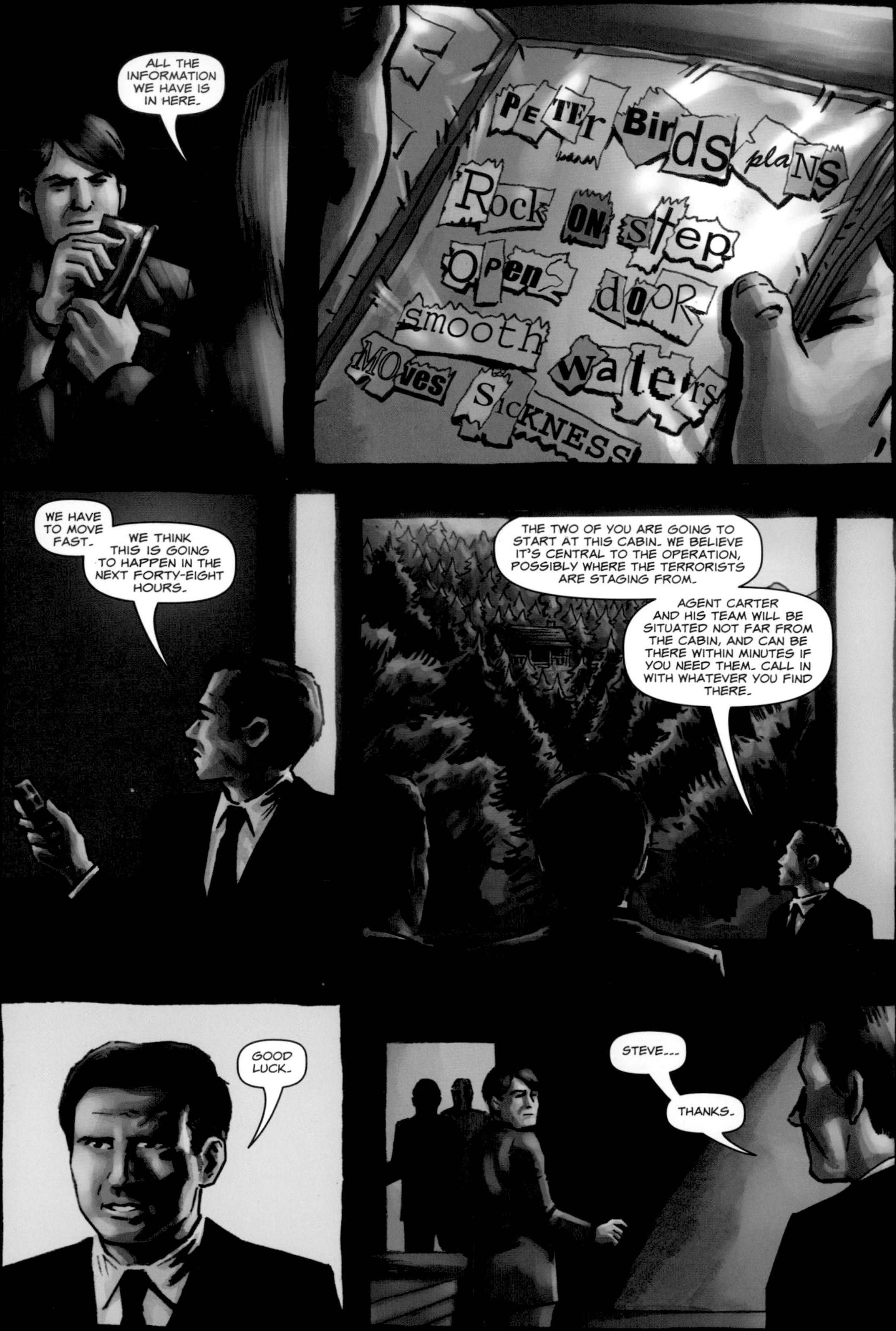
ALL THE INFORMATION WE HAVE IS IN HERE.
PETER BirdS plaNS
Rock ON step
Open door
smooth waters
MOves SickNESS
WE HAVE TO MOVE FAST.
WE THINK THIS IS GOING TO HAPPEN IN THE NEXT FORTY-EIGHT HOURS.
THE TWO OF YOU ARE GOING TO START AT THIS CABIN. WE BELIEVE IT'S CENTRAL TO THE OPERATION, POSSIBLY WHERE THE TERRORISTS ARE STAGING FROM.
AGENT CARTER AND HIS TEAM WILL BE SITUATED NOT FAR FROM THE CABIN, AND CAN BE THERE WITHIN MINUTES IF YOU NEED THEM. CALL IN WITH WHATEVER YOU FIND THERE.
GOOD LUCK.
STEVE...
THANKS.

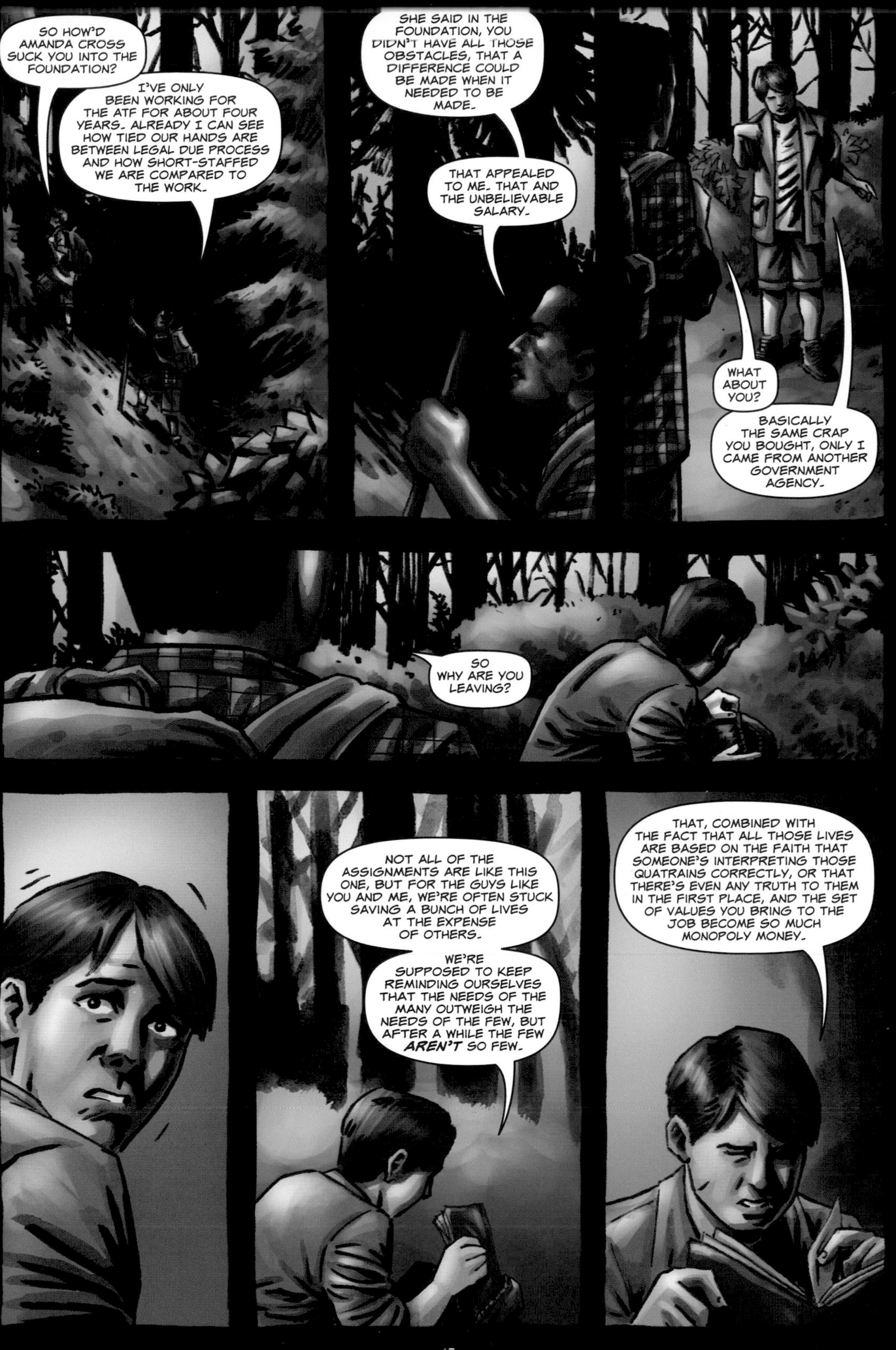
SO HOW'D AMANDA CROSS SUCK YOU INTO THE FOUNDATION?
I'VE ONLY BEEN WORKING FOR THE ATF FOR ABOUT FOUR YEARS. ALREADY I CAN SEE HOW TIED OUR HANDS ARE BETWEEN LEGAL DUE PROCESS AND HOW SHORT-STAFFED WE ARE COMPARED TO THE WORK.
SHE SAID IN THE FOUNDATION, YOU DIDN'T HAVE ALL THOSE OBSTACLES, THAT A DIFFERENCE COULD BE MADE WHEN IT NEEDED TO BE MADE.
THAT APPEALED TO ME. THAT AND THE UNBELIEVABLE SALARY.
WHAT ABOUT YOU?
BASICALLY THE SAME CRAP YOU BOUGHT, ONLY I CAME FROM ANOTHER GOVERNMENT AGENCY.
SO WHY ARE YOU LEAVING?
NOT ALL OF THE ASSIGNMENTS ARE LIKE THIS ONE, BUT FOR THE GUYS LIKE YOU AND ME, WE'RE OFTEN STUCK SAVING A BUNCH OF LIVES AT THE EXPENSE OF OTHERS.
WE'RE SUPPOSED TO KEEP REMINDING OURSELVES THAT THE NEEDS OF THE MANY OUTWEIGH THE NEEDS OF THE FEW, BUT AFTER A WHILE THE FEW ***AREN'T*** SO FEW.
THAT, COMBINED WITH THE FACT THAT ALL THOSE LIVES ARE BASED ON THE FAITH THAT SOMEONE'S INTERPRETING THOSE QUATRAINS CORRECTLY, OR THAT THERE'S EVEN ANY TRUTH TO THEM IN THE FIRST PLACE, AND THE SET OF VALUES YOU BRING TO THE JOB BECOME SO MUCH MONOPOLY MONEY.

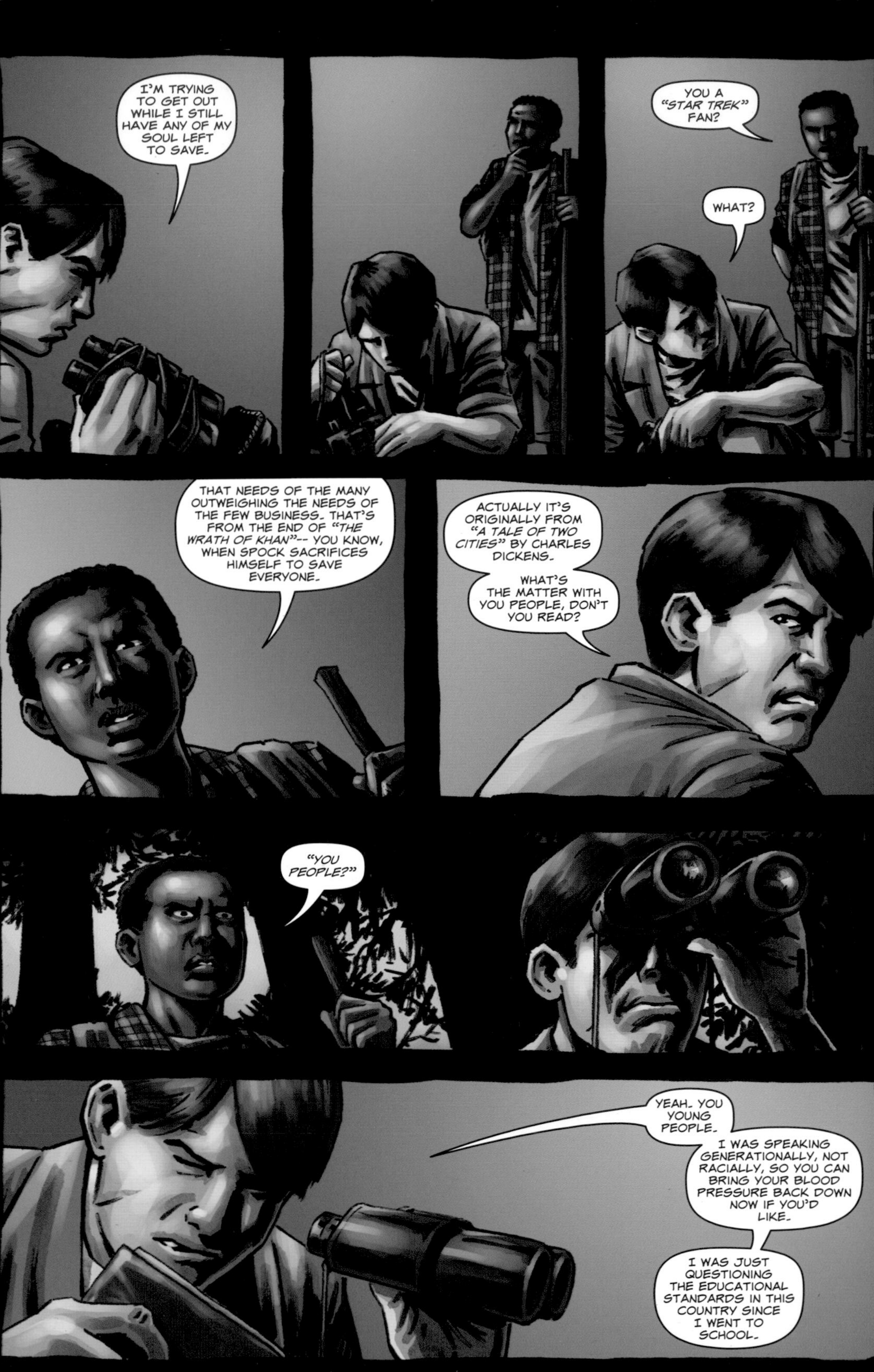
I'M TRYING TO GET OUT WHILE I STILL HAVE ANY OF MY SOUL LEFT TO SAVE.
YOU A "STAR TREK" FAN?
WHAT?
THAT NEEDS OF THE MANY OUTWEIGHING THE NEEDS OF THE FEW BUSINESS. THAT'S FROM THE END OF "THE WRATH OF KHAN"-- YOU KNOW, WHEN SPOCK SACRIFICES HIMSELF TO SAVE EVERYONE.
ACTUALLY IT'S ORIGINALLY FROM "A TALE OF TWO CITIES" BY CHARLES DICKENS.
WHAT'S THE MATTER WITH YOU PEOPLE, DON'T YOU READ?
"YOU PEOPLE?"
YEAH. YOU YOUNG PEOPLE.
I WAS SPEAKING GENERATIONALLY, NOT RACIALLY, SO YOU CAN BRING YOUR BLOOD PRESSURE BACK DOWN NOW IF YOU'D LIKE.
I WAS JUST QUESTIONING THE EDUCATIONAL STANDARDS IN THIS COUNTRY SINCE I WENT TO SCHOOL.

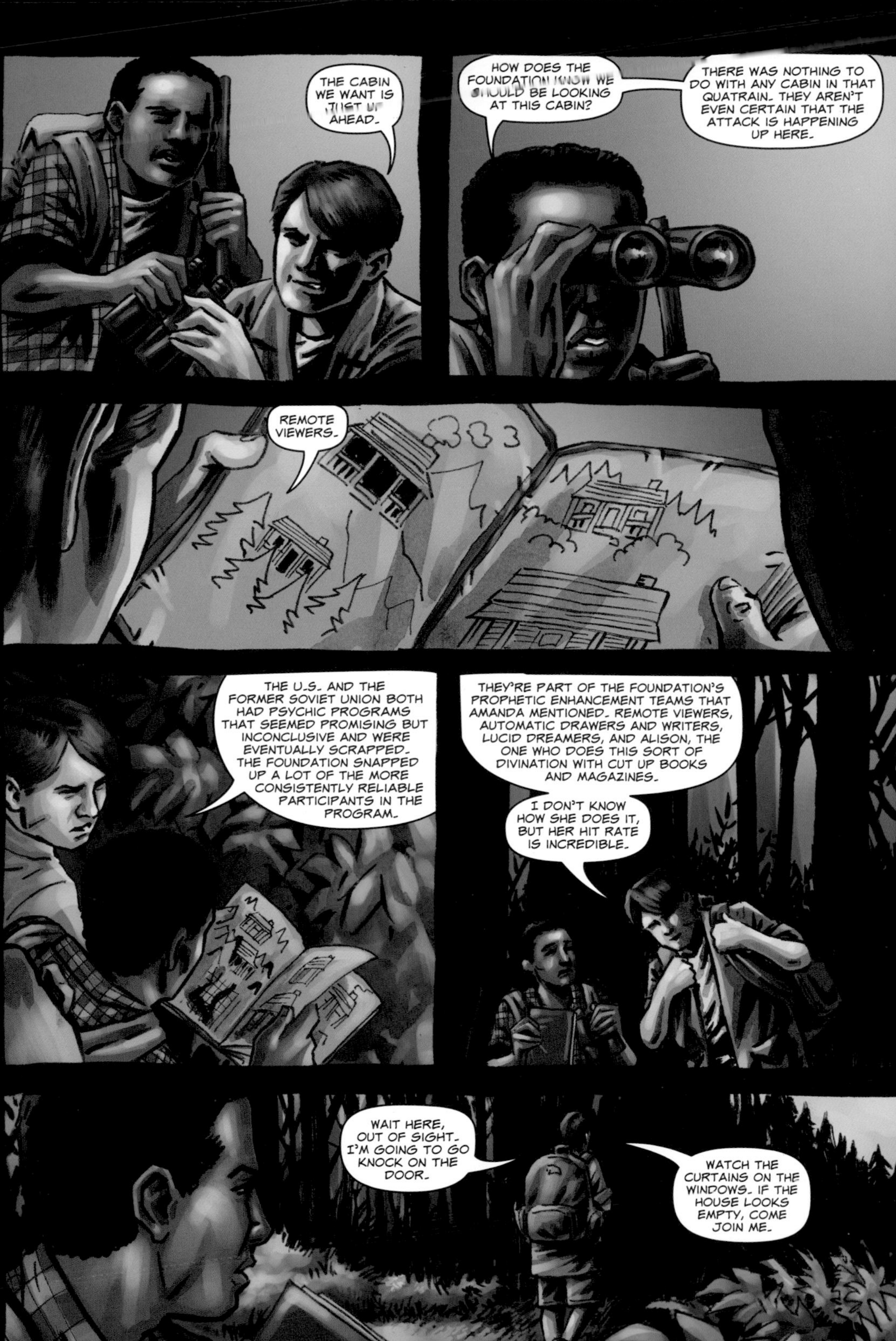
THE CABIN WE WANT IS JUST UP AHEAD.
HOW DOES THE FOUNDATION KNOW WE SHOULD BE LOOKING AT THIS CABIN?
THERE WAS NOTHING TO DO WITH ANY CABIN IN THAT QUATRAIN. THEY AREN'T EVEN CERTAIN THAT THE ATTACK IS HAPPENING UP HERE.
REMOTE VIEWERS.
THE U.S. AND THE FORMER SOVIET UNION BOTH HAD PSYCHIC PROGRAMS THAT SEEMED PROMISING BUT INCONCLUSIVE AND WERE EVENTUALLY SCRAPPED. THE FOUNDATION SNAPPED UP A LOT OF THE MORE CONSISTENTLY RELIABLE PARTICIPANTS IN THE PROGRAM.
THEY'RE PART OF THE FOUNDATION'S PROPHETIC ENHANCEMENT TEAMS THAT AMANDA MENTIONED. REMOTE VIEWERS, AUTOMATIC DRAWERS AND WRITERS, LUCID DREAMERS, AND ALISON, THE ONE WHO DOES THIS SORT OF DIVINATION WITH CUT UP BOOKS AND MAGAZINES.
I DON'T KNOW HOW SHE DOES IT, BUT HER HIT RATE IS INCREDIBLE.
WAIT HERE, OUT OF SIGHT. I'M GOING TO GO KNOCK ON THE DOOR.
WATCH THE CURTAINS ON THE WINDOWS. IF THE HOUSE LOOKS EMPTY, COME JOIN ME.

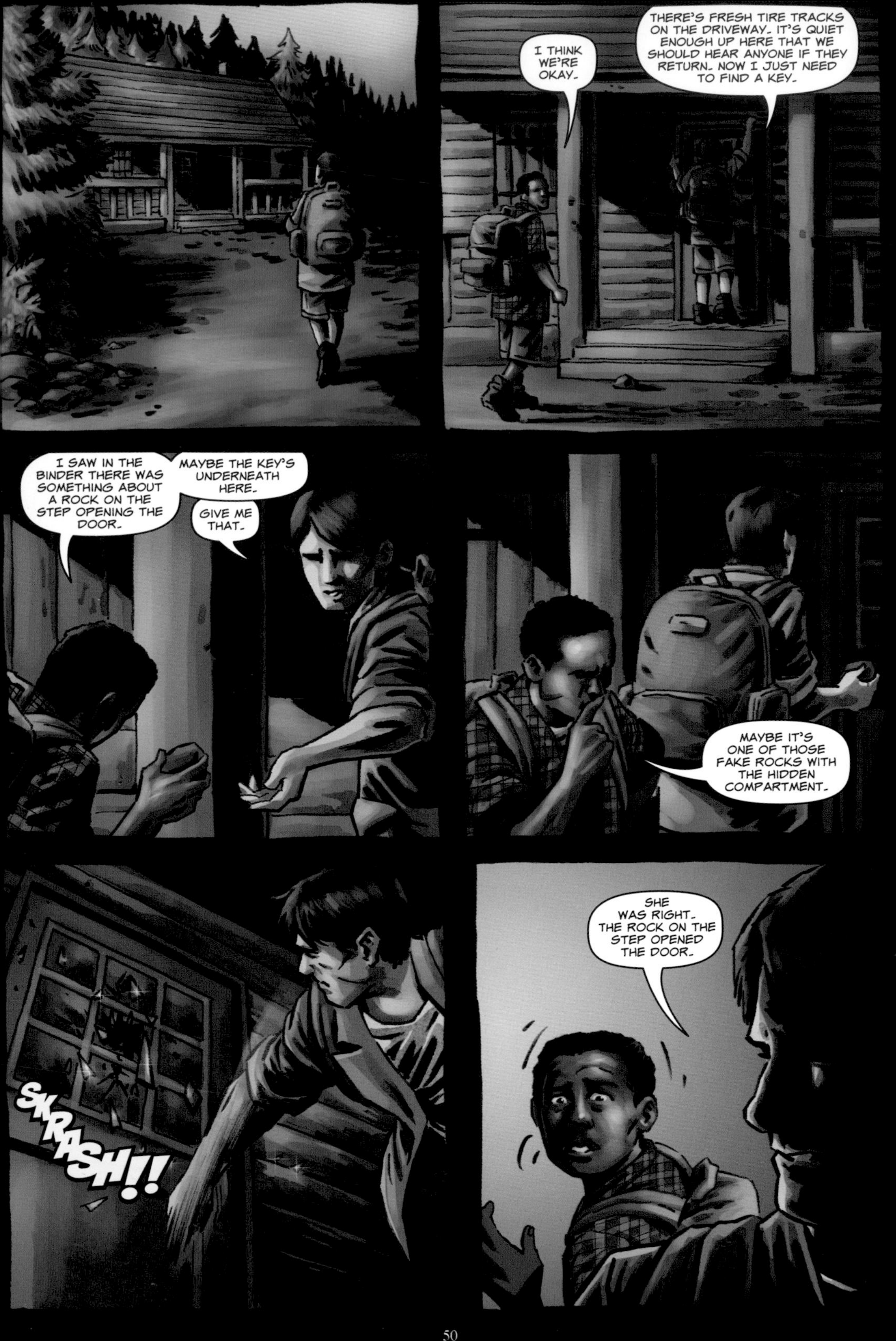
I THINK WE'RE OKAY.
THERE'S FRESH TIRE TRACKS ON THE DRIVEWAY. IT'S QUIET ENOUGH UP HERE THAT WE SHOULD HEAR ANYONE IF THEY RETURN. NOW I JUST NEED TO FIND A KEY.
I SAW IN THE BINDER THERE WAS SOMETHING ABOUT A ROCK ON THE STEP OPENING THE DOOR.
MAYBE THE KEY'S UNDERNEATH HERE.
GIVE ME THAT.
MAYBE IT'S ONE OF THOSE FAKE ROCKS WITH THE HIDDEN COMPARTMENT.
SKRASH!!
SHE WAS RIGHT. THE ROCK ON THE STEP OPENED THE DOOR.

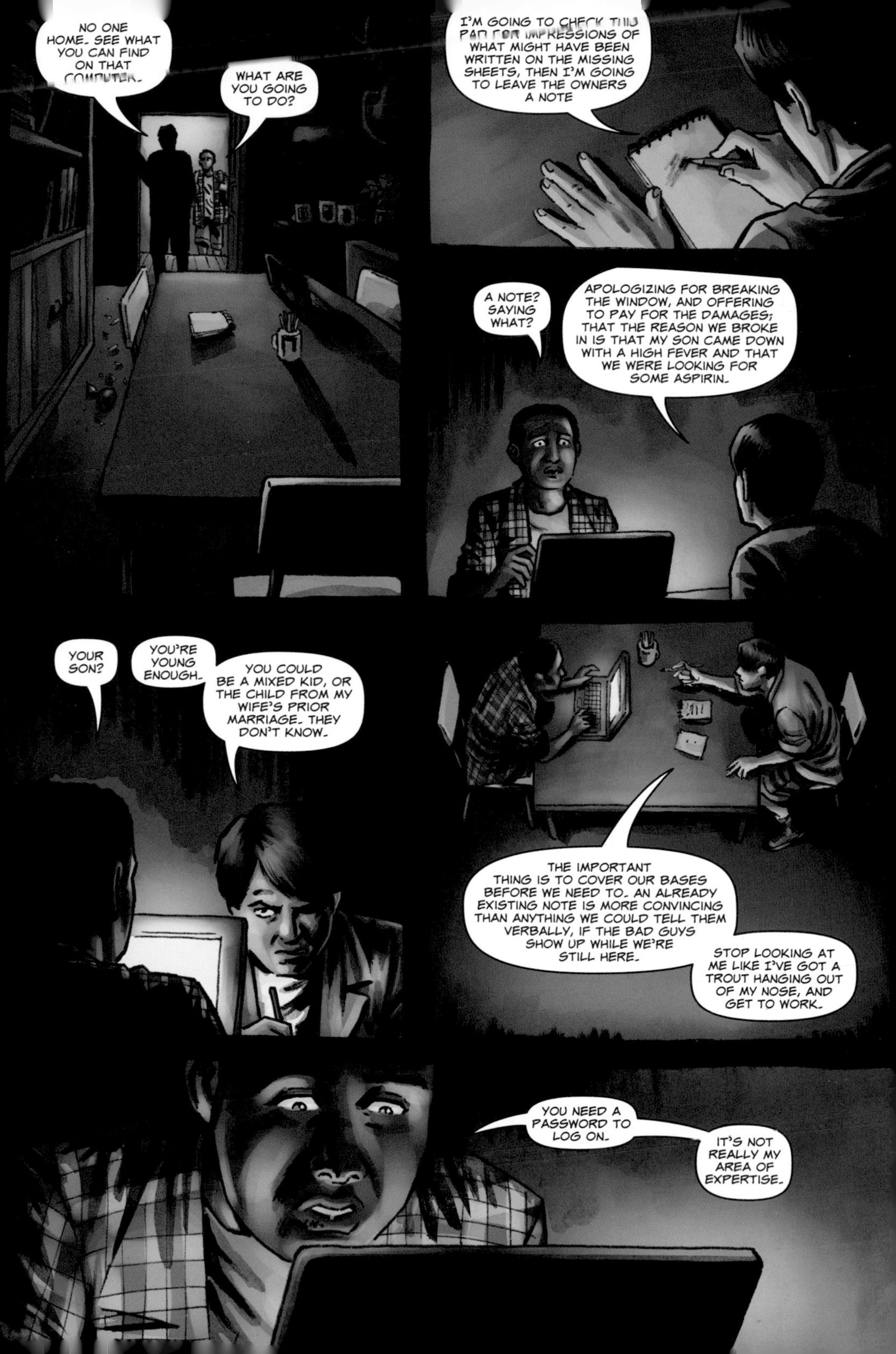

NO ONE HOME. SEE WHAT YOU CAN FIND ON THAT COMPUTER.
WHAT ARE YOU GOING TO DO?
I'M GOING TO CHECK THIS PAD FOR IMPRESSIONS OF WHAT MIGHT HAVE BEEN WRITTEN ON THE MISSING SHEETS, THEN I'M GOING TO LEAVE THE OWNERS A NOTE
A NOTE? SAYING WHAT?
APOLOGIZING FOR BREAKING THE WINDOW, AND OFFERING TO PAY FOR THE DAMAGES; THAT THE REASON WE BROKE IN IS THAT MY SON CAME DOWN WITH A HIGH FEVER AND THAT WE WERE LOOKING FOR SOME ASPIRIN.
YOUR SON?
YOU'RE YOUNG ENOUGH.
YOU COULD BE A MIXED KID, OR THE CHILD FROM MY WIFE'S PRIOR MARRIAGE. THEY DON'T KNOW.
THE IMPORTANT THING IS TO COVER OUR BASES BEFORE WE NEED TO. AN ALREADY EXISTING NOTE IS MORE CONVINCING THAN ANYTHING WE COULD TELL THEM VERBALLY, IF THE BAD GUYS SHOW UP WHILE WE'RE STILL HERE.
STOP LOOKING AT ME LIKE I'VE GOT A TROUT HANGING OUT OF MY NOSE, AND GET TO WORK.
YOU NEED A PASSWORD TO LOG ON.
IT'S NOT REALLY MY AREA OF EXPERTISE.

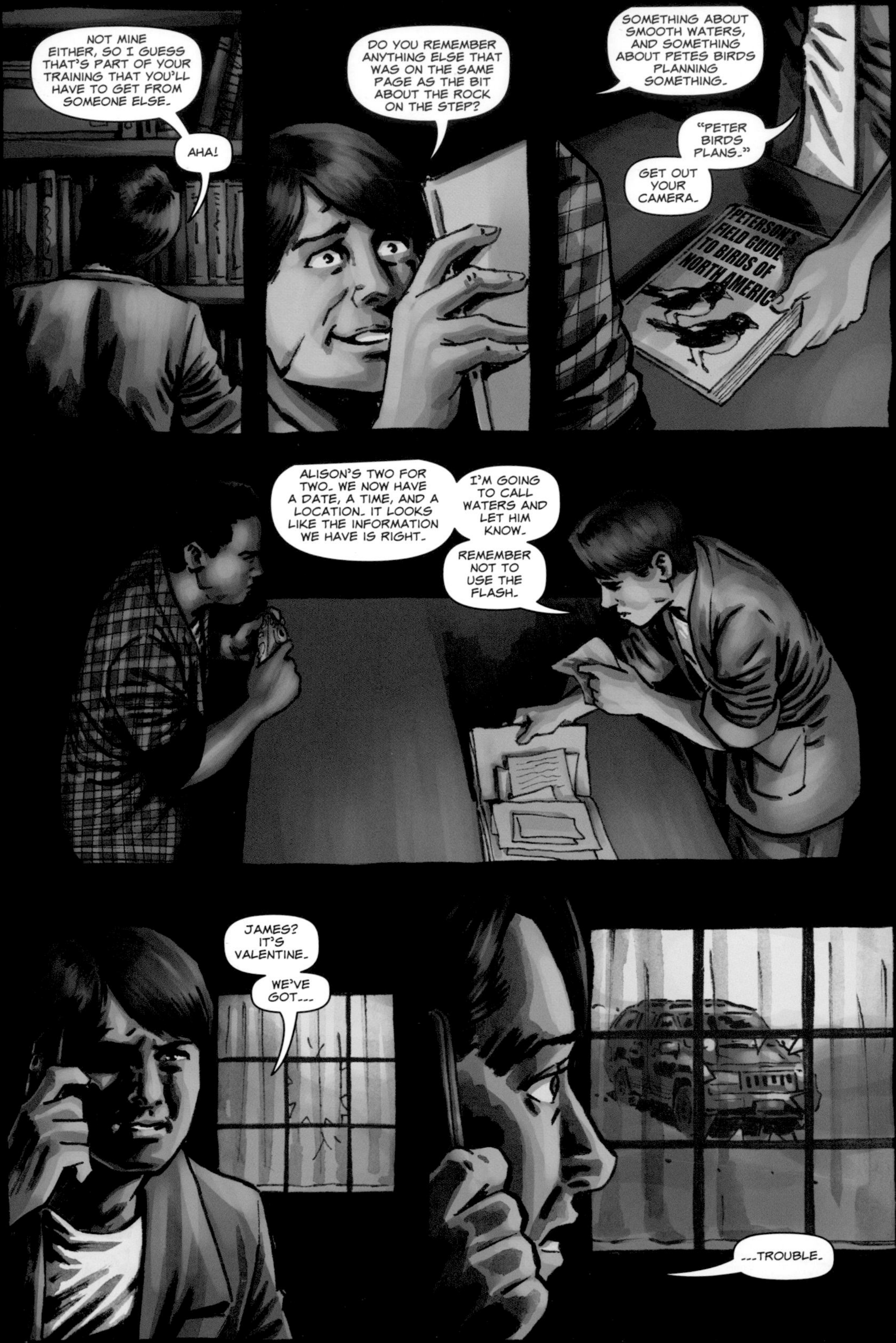
NOT MINE EITHER, SO I GUESS THAT'S PART OF YOUR TRAINING THAT YOU'LL HAVE TO GET FROM SOMEONE ELSE.
AHA!
DO YOU REMEMBER ANYTHING ELSE THAT WAS ON THE SAME PAGE AS THE BIT ABOUT THE ROCK ON THE STEP?
SOMETHING ABOUT SMOOTH WATERS, AND SOMETHING ABOUT PETES BIRDS PLANNING SOMETHING.
"PETER BIRDS PLANS."
GET OUT YOUR CAMERA.
PETERSON'S FIELD GUIDE TO BIRDS OF NORTH AMERIC
ALISON'S TWO FOR TWO. WE NOW HAVE A DATE, A TIME, AND A LOCATION. IT LOOKS LIKE THE INFORMATION WE HAVE IS RIGHT.
I'M GOING TO CALL WATERS AND LET HIM KNOW.
REMEMBER NOT TO USE THE FLASH.
JAMES? IT'S VALENTINE.
WE'VE GOT...
...TROUBLE.

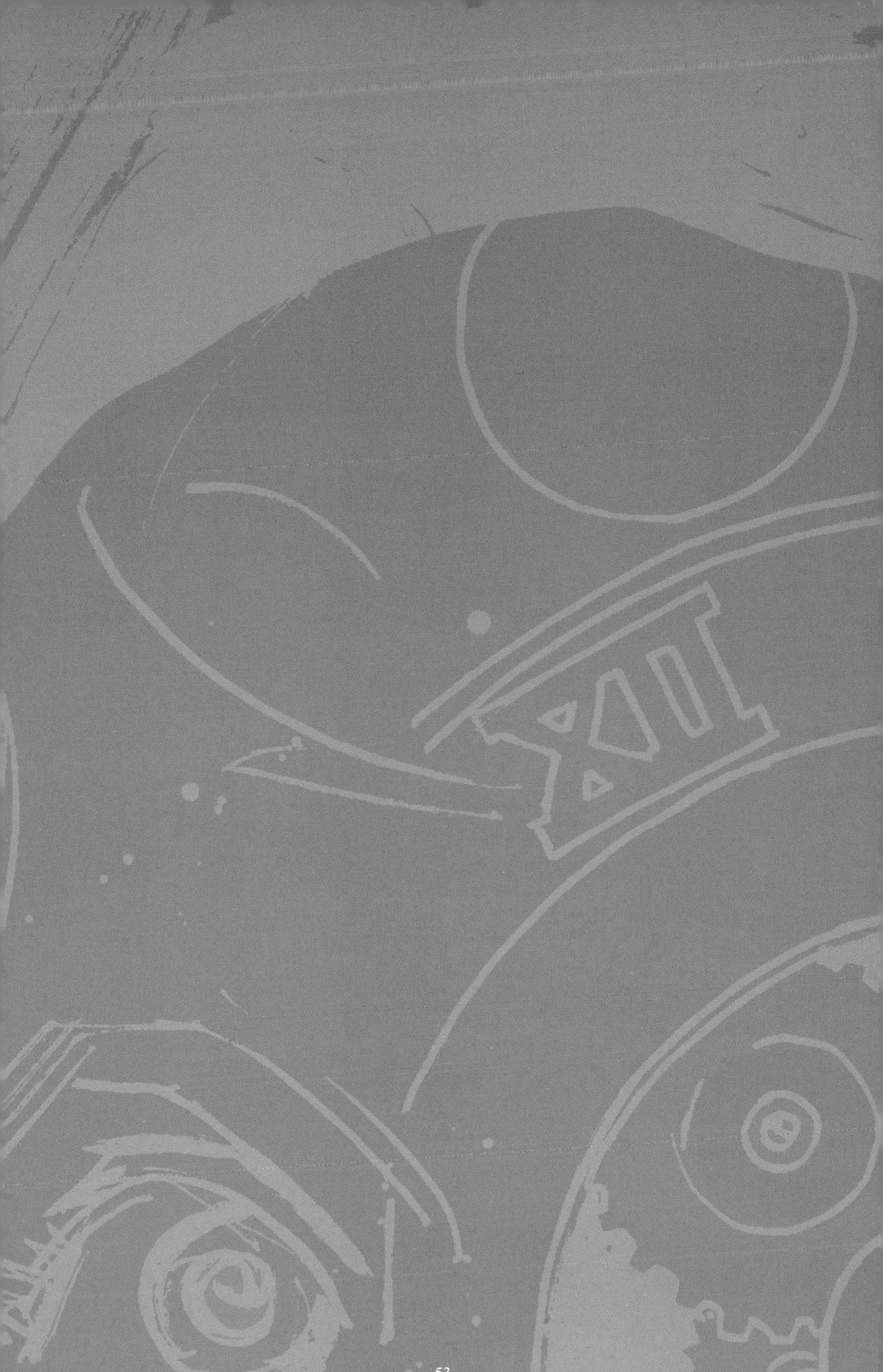
XII

Chapter Three

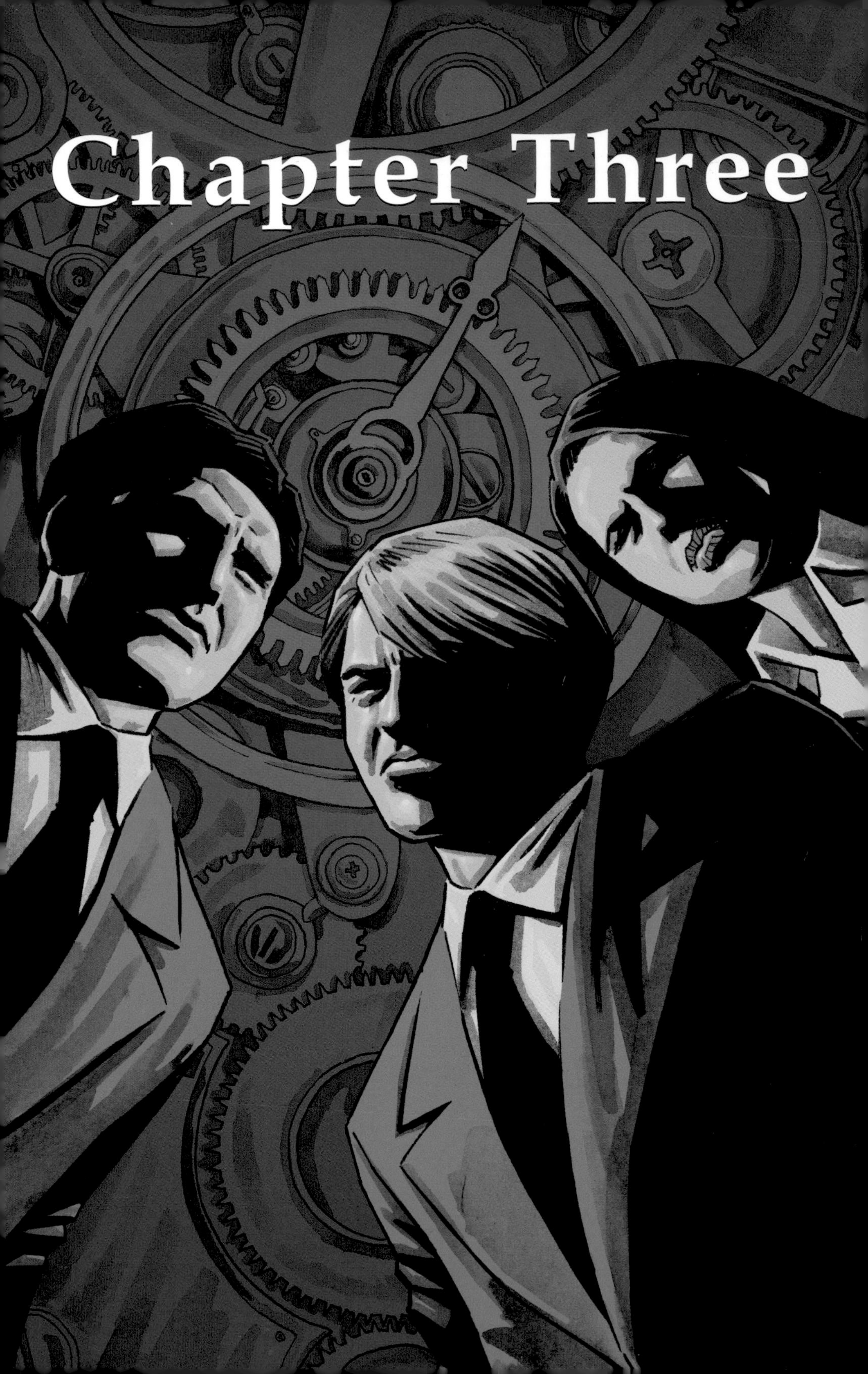

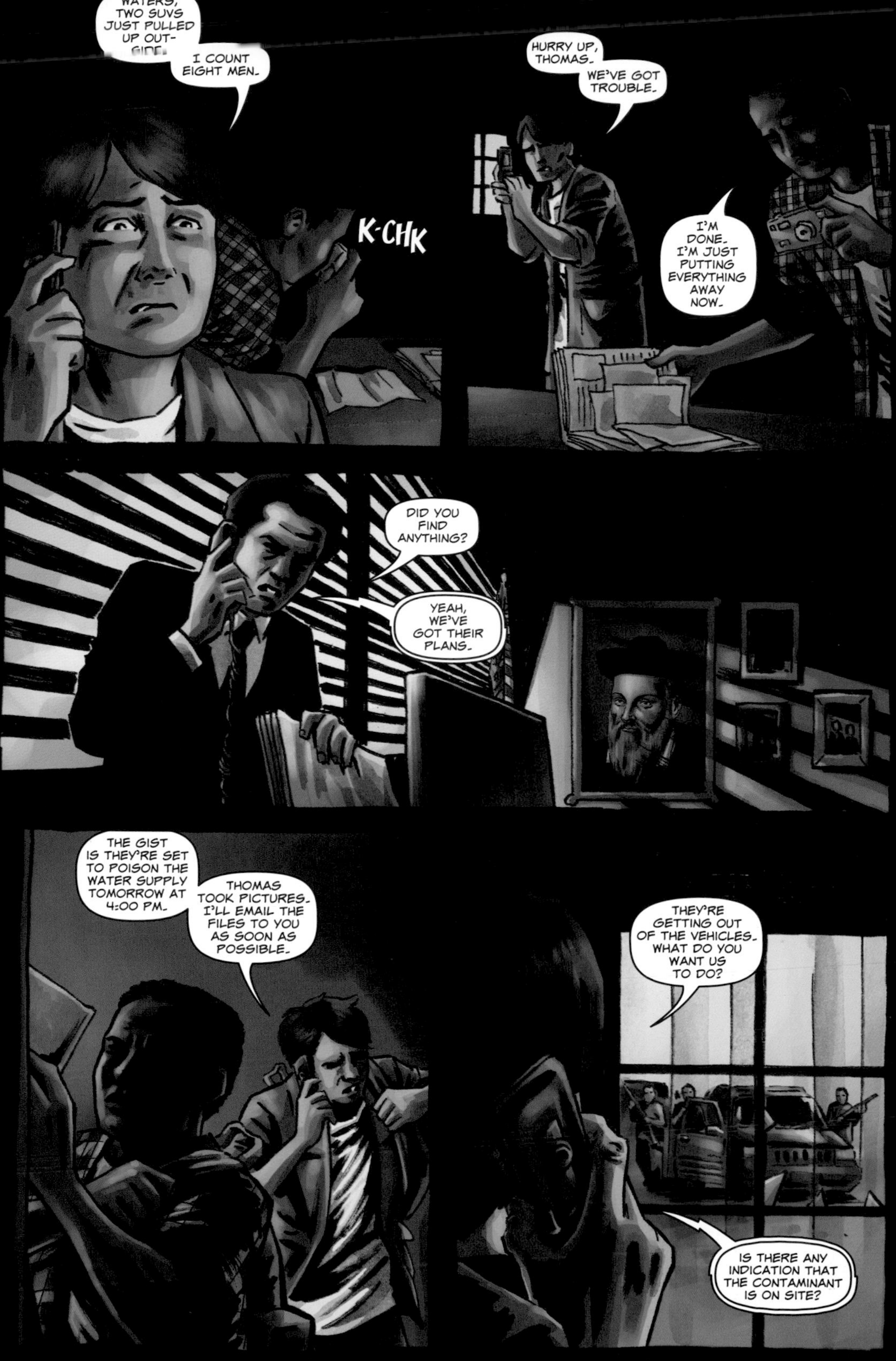
WATERS, TWO SUVS JUST PULLED UP OUT-SIDE.
I COUNT EIGHT MEN.
K-CHK
HURRY UP, THOMAS.
WE'VE GOT TROUBLE.
I'M DONE. I'M JUST PUTTING EVERYTHING AWAY NOW.
DID YOU FIND ANYTHING?
YEAH, WE'VE GOT THEIR PLANS.
THE GIST IS THEY'RE SET TO POISON THE WATER SUPPLY TOMORROW AT 4:00 PM.
THOMAS TOOK PICTURES. I'LL EMAIL THE FILES TO YOU AS SOON AS POSSIBLE.
THEY'RE GETTING OUT OF THE VEHICLES. WHAT DO YOU WANT US TO DO?
IS THERE ANY INDICATION THAT THE CONTAMINANT IS ON SITE?

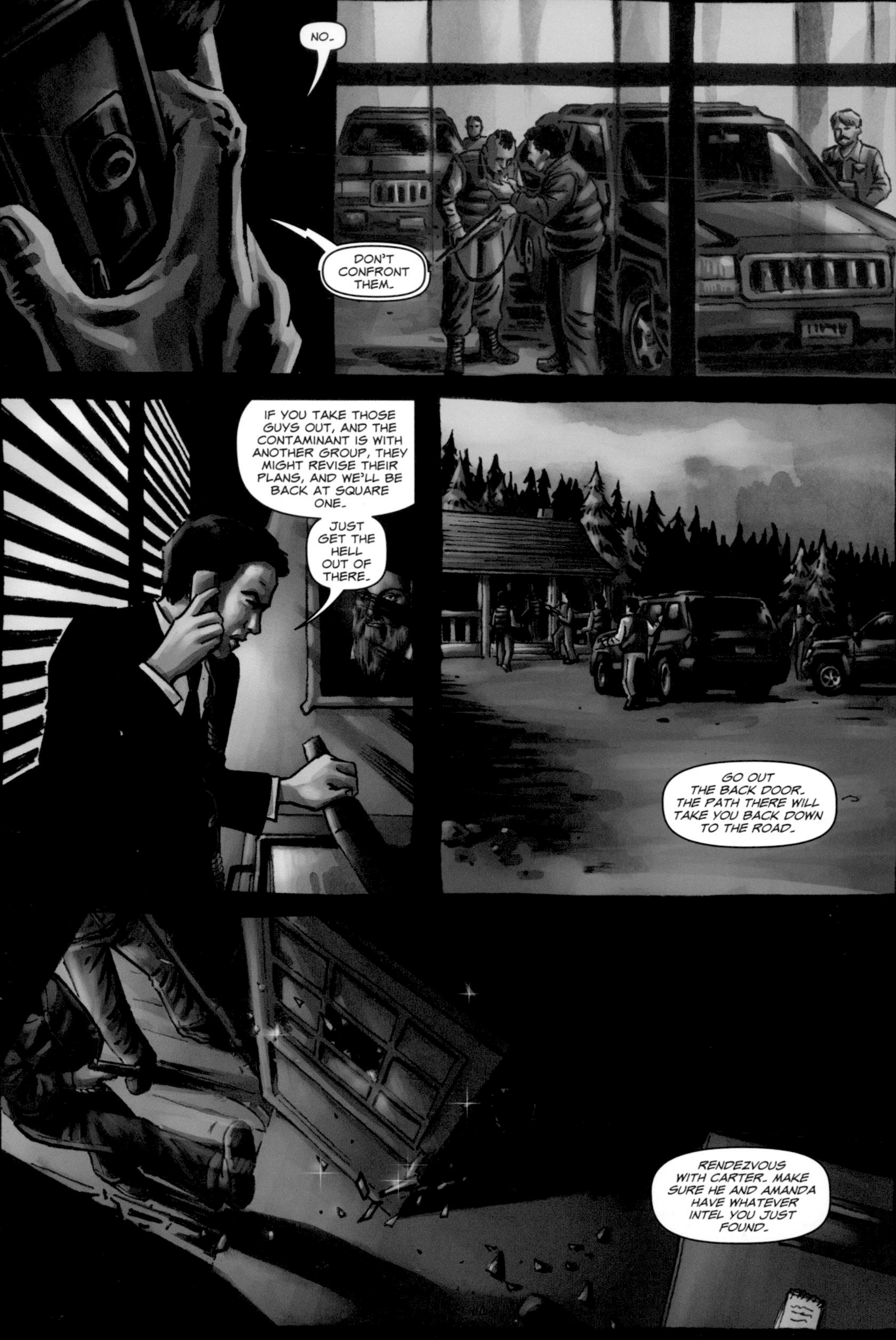
NO.
DON'T CONFRONT THEM.
IF YOU TAKE THOSE GUYS OUT, AND THE CONTAMINANT IS WITH ANOTHER GROUP, THEY MIGHT REVISE THEIR PLANS, AND WE'LL BE BACK AT SQUARE ONE.
JUST GET THE HELL OUT OF THERE.
GO OUT THE BACK DOOR. THE PATH THERE WILL TAKE YOU BACK DOWN TO THE ROAD.
RENDEZVOUS WITH CARTER. MAKE SURE HE AND AMANDA HAVE WHATEVER INTEL YOU JUST FOUND.

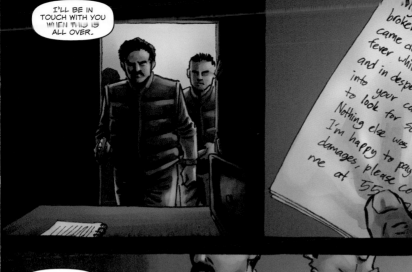

I'LL BE IN TOUCH WITH YOU WHEN THIS IS ALL OVER.

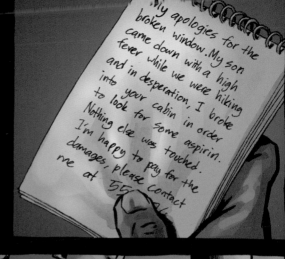

My apologies for the broken window. My son came down with a high fever while we were hiking and in desperation, I broke into your cabin in order to look for some aspirin. Nothing else was touched. I'm happy to pay for the damages, please contact me at 55...

WAIT A MINUTE. WHAT ARE YOU TALKING ABOUT, MIKE?

AFTER THIS IS OVER? WHERE ARE YOU GOING?

I HAVE TO GO INTO NEW YORK CITY. THE VICE-PRESIDENT AND SECRETARY OF DEFENSE ARE ATTENDING A CHARITY EVENT. I'LL BE OVERSEEING SECURITY.

THE TIMING IS NOT CONVENIENT, BUT MY MOONLIGHTING JOB IS HOW I GET A LOT OF MY INTEL.

DEET DEET DEET

IT DOESN'T SOUND LIKE YOU'LL NEED ME ANYWAY. YOU KNOW WHEN AND WHERE THE BAD GUYS ARE GOING TO BE.

ROUNDING THEM UP SHOULD BE A PIECE OF CAKE.

LISTEN, I'VE GOT TO GO. SOMEONE'S TRYING TO REACH ME ON MY CELL.

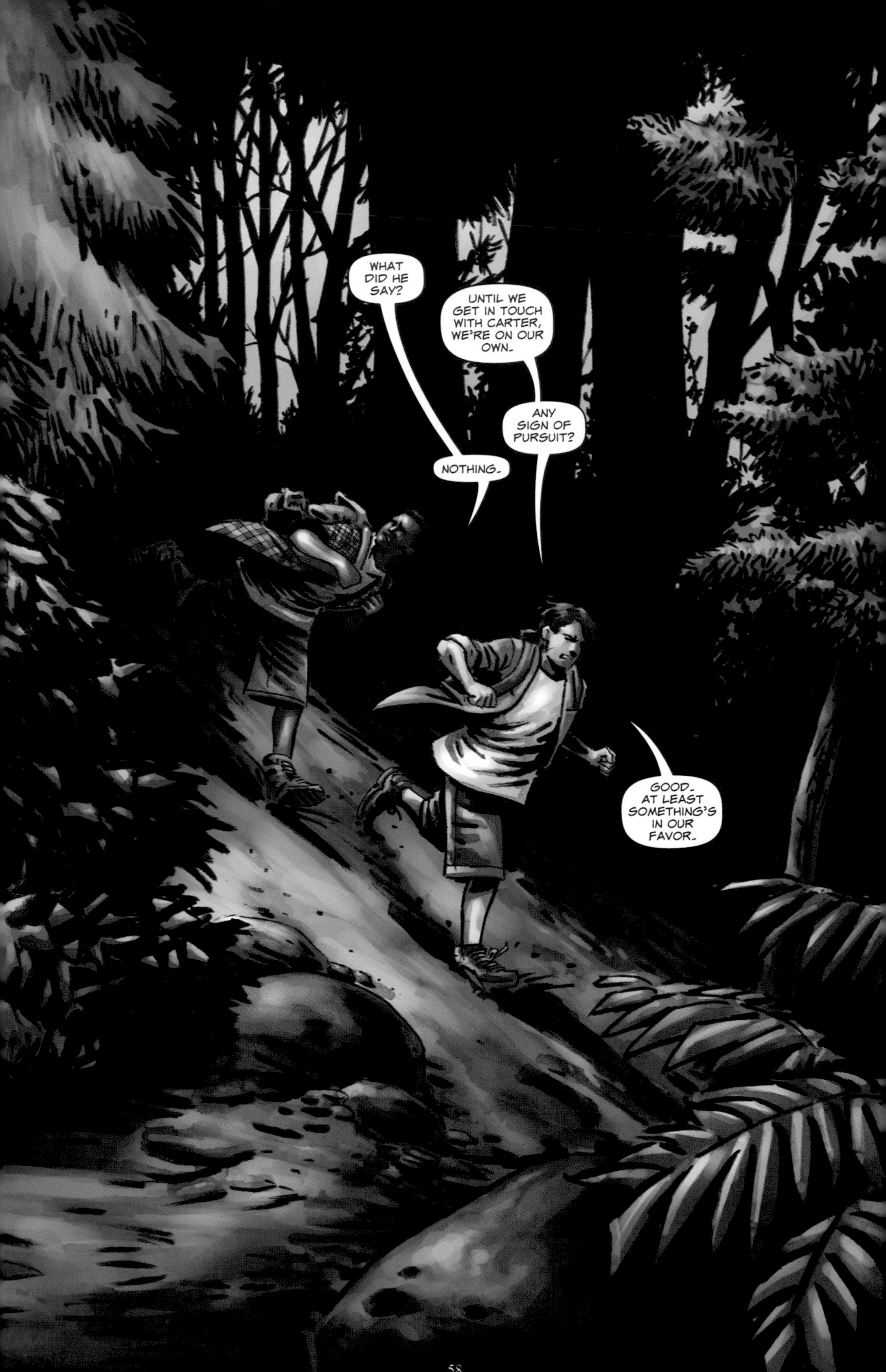
WHAT DID HE SAY?
UNTIL WE GET IN TOUCH WITH CARTER, WE'RE ON OUR OWN.
ANY SIGN OF PURSUIT?
NOTHING.
GOOD. AT LEAST SOMETHING'S IN OUR FAVOR.

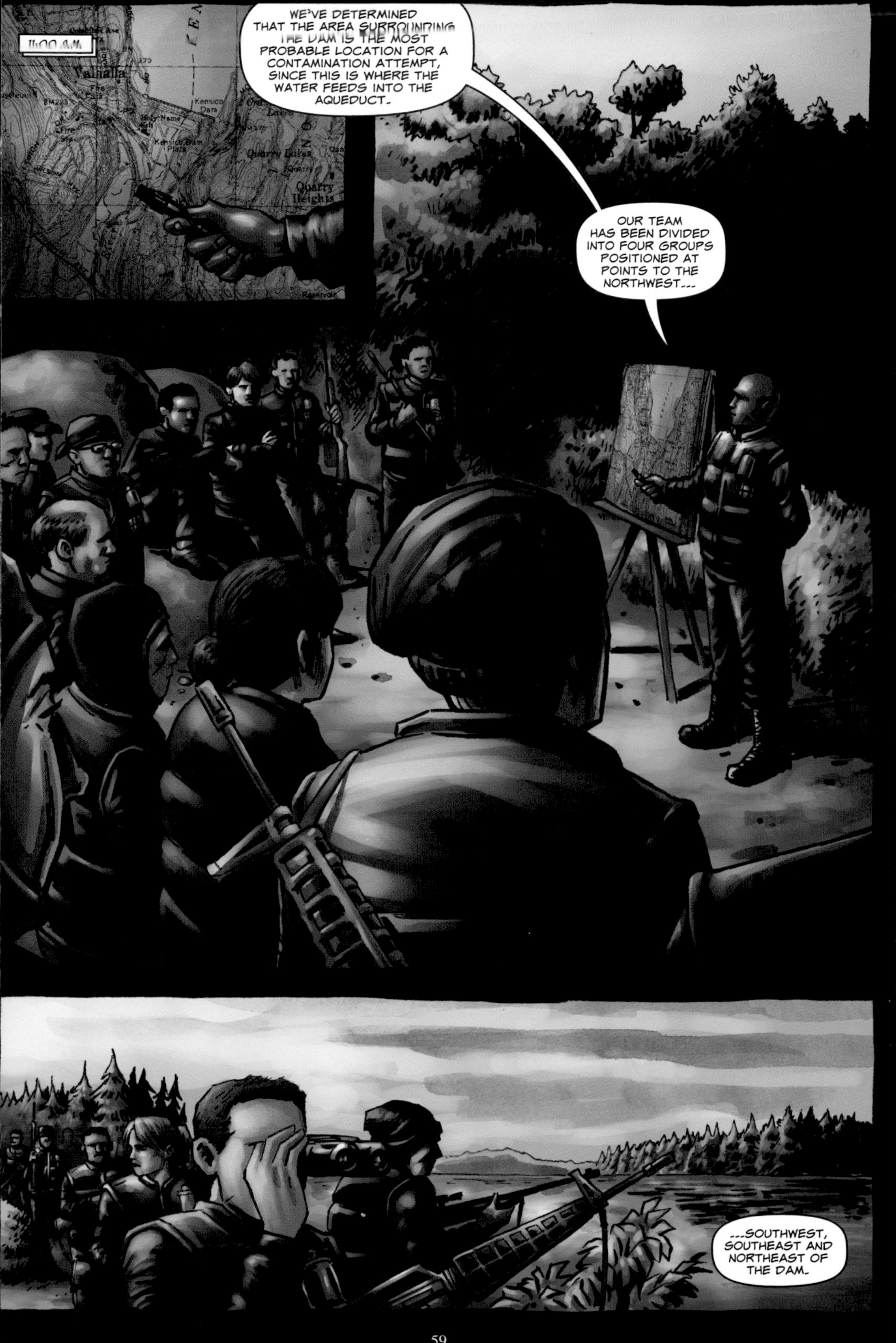
11:00 A.M.
WE'VE DETERMINED THAT THE AREA SURROUNDING THE DAM IS THE MOST PROBABLE LOCATION FOR A CONTAMINATION ATTEMPT, SINCE THIS IS WHERE THE WATER FEEDS INTO THE AQUEDUCT.
OUR TEAM HAS BEEN DIVIDED INTO FOUR GROUPS POSITIONED AT POINTS TO THE NORTHWEST...
...SOUTHWEST, SOUTHEAST AND NORTHEAST OF THE DAM.

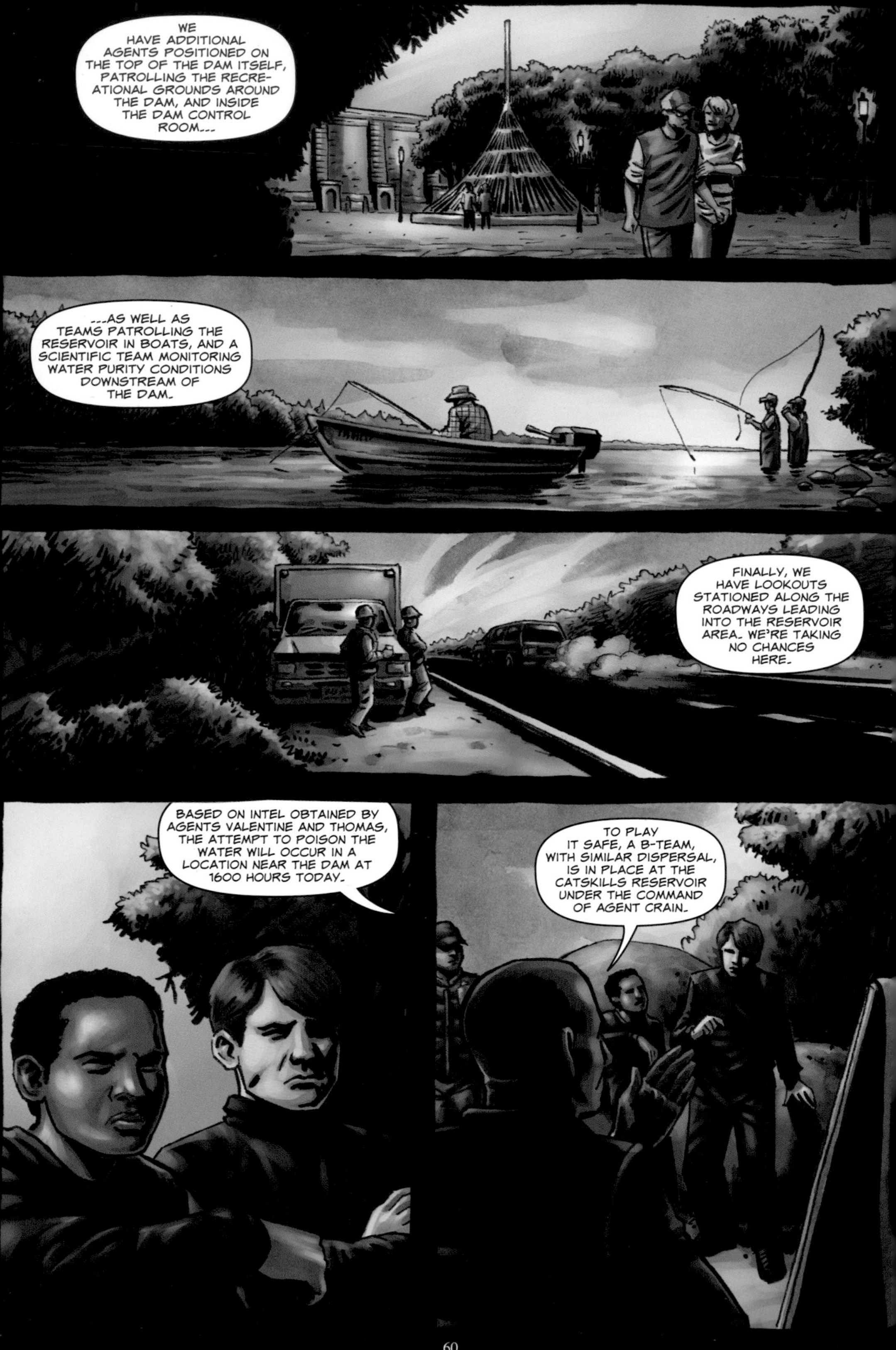
WE HAVE ADDITIONAL AGENTS POSITIONED ON THE TOP OF THE DAM ITSELF, PATROLLING THE RECRE- ATIONAL GROUNDS AROUND THE DAM, AND INSIDE THE DAM CONTROL ROOM...
...AS WELL AS TEAMS PATROLLING THE RESERVOIR IN BOATS, AND A SCIENTIFIC TEAM MONITORING WATER PURITY CONDITIONS DOWNSTREAM OF THE DAM.
FINALLY, WE HAVE LOOKOUTS STATIONED ALONG THE ROADWAYS LEADING INTO THE RESERVOIR AREA. WE'RE TAKING NO CHANCES HERE.
BASED ON INTEL OBTAINED BY AGENTS VALENTINE AND THOMAS, THE ATTEMPT TO POISON THE WATER WILL OCCUR IN A LOCATION NEAR THE DAM AT 1600 HOURS TODAY.
TO PLAY IT SAFE, A B-TEAM, WITH SIMILAR DISPERSAL, IS IN PLACE AT THE CATSKILLS RESERVOIR UNDER THE COMMAND OF AGENT CRAIN.

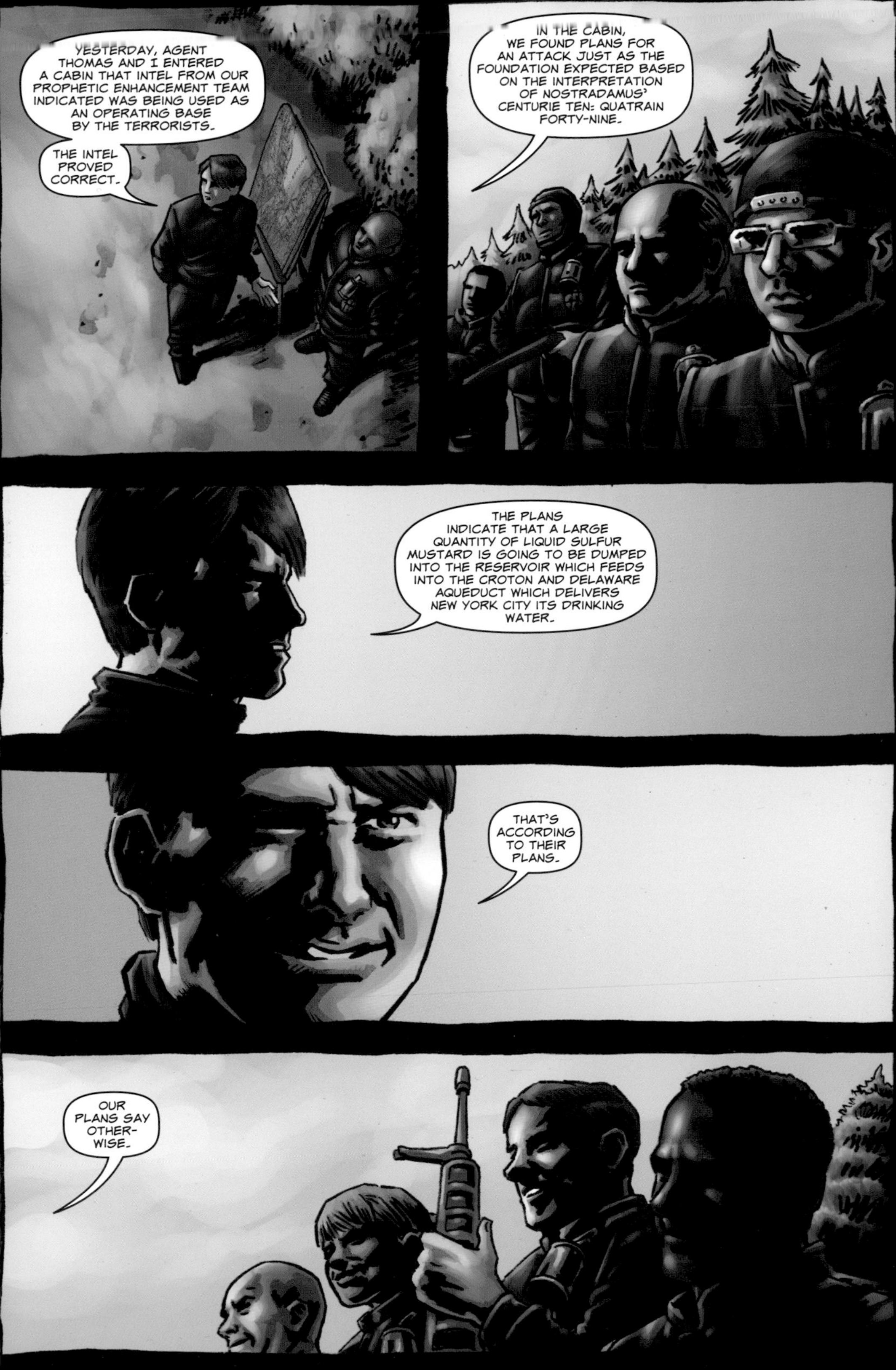

YESTERDAY, AGENT THOMAS AND I ENTERED A CABIN THAT INTEL FROM OUR PROPHETIC ENHANCEMENT TEAM INDICATED WAS BEING USED AS AN OPERATING BASE BY THE TERRORISTS.
THE INTEL PROVED CORRECT.
IN THE CABIN, WE FOUND PLANS FOR AN ATTACK JUST AS THE FOUNDATION EXPECTED BASED ON THE INTERPRETATION OF NOSTRADAMUS' CENTURIE TEN: QUATRAIN FORTY-NINE.
THE PLANS INDICATE THAT A LARGE QUANTITY OF LIQUID SULFUR MUSTARD IS GOING TO BE DUMPED INTO THE RESERVOIR WHICH FEEDS INTO THE CROTON AND DELAWARE AQUEDUCT WHICH DELIVERS NEW YORK CITY ITS DRINKING WATER.
THAT'S ACCORDING TO THEIR PLANS.
OUR PLANS SAY OTHER-WISE.

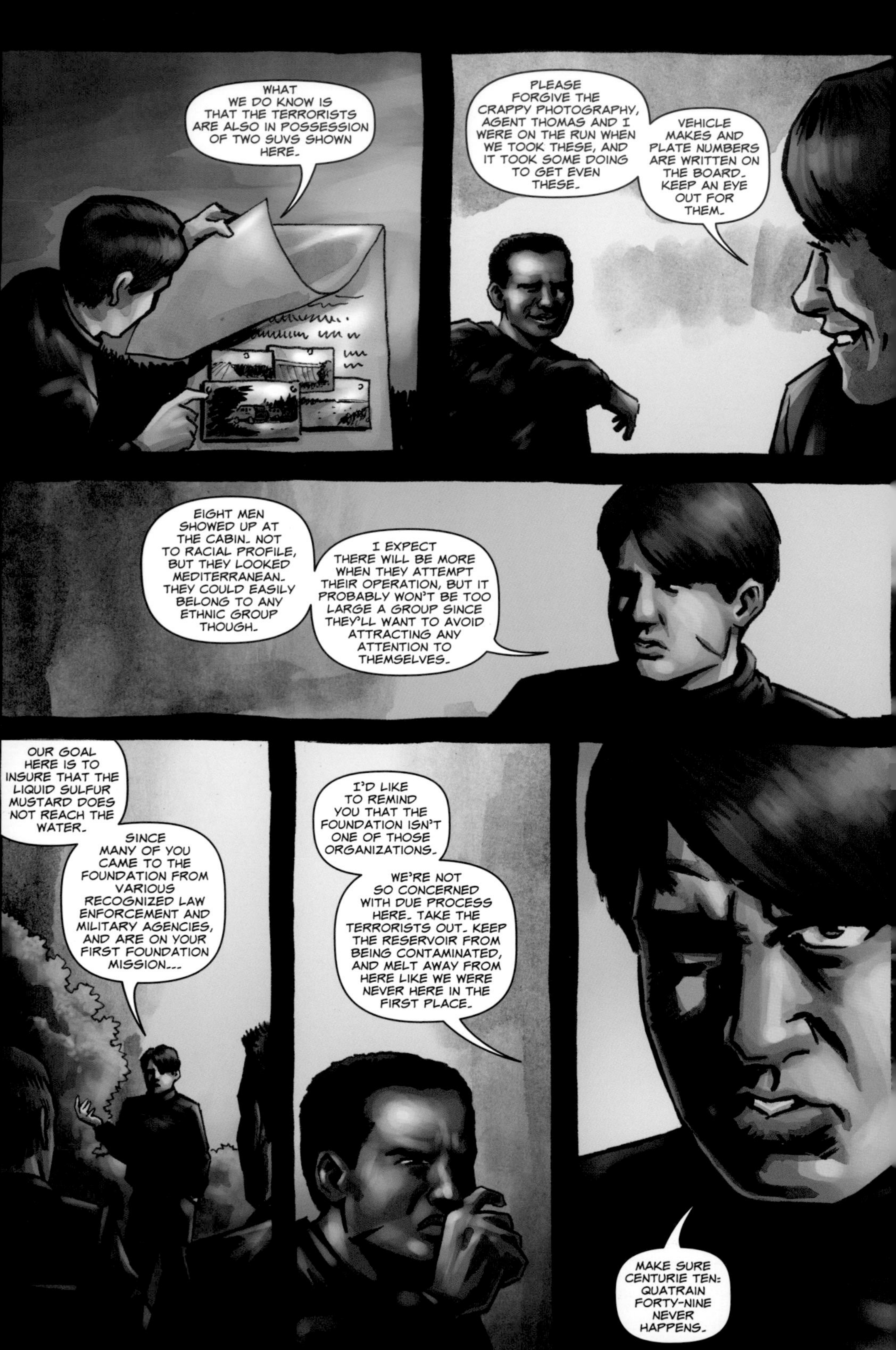
WHAT WE DO KNOW IS THAT THE TERRORISTS ARE ALSO IN POSSESSION OF TWO SUVS SHOWN HERE.
PLEASE FORGIVE THE CRAPPY PHOTOGRAPHY, AGENT THOMAS AND I WERE ON THE RUN WHEN WE TOOK THESE, AND IT TOOK SOME DOING TO GET EVEN THESE.
VEHICLE MAKES AND PLATE NUMBERS ARE WRITTEN ON THE BOARD. KEEP AN EYE OUT FOR THEM.
EIGHT MEN SHOWED UP AT THE CABIN. NOT TO RACIAL PROFILE, BUT THEY LOOKED MEDITERRANEAN. THEY COULD EASILY BELONG TO ANY ETHNIC GROUP THOUGH.
I EXPECT THERE WILL BE MORE WHEN THEY ATTEMPT THEIR OPERATION, BUT IT PROBABLY WON'T BE TOO LARGE A GROUP SINCE THEY'LL WANT TO AVOID ATTRACTING ANY ATTENTION TO THEMSELVES.
OUR GOAL HERE IS TO INSURE THAT THE LIQUID SULFUR MUSTARD DOES NOT REACH THE WATER.
SINCE MANY OF YOU CAME TO THE FOUNDATION FROM VARIOUS RECOGNIZED LAW ENFORCEMENT AND MILITARY AGENCIES, AND ARE ON YOUR FIRST FOUNDATION MISSION...
I'D LIKE TO REMIND YOU THAT THE FOUNDATION ISN'T ONE OF THOSE ORGANIZATIONS.
WE'RE NOT SO CONCERNED WITH DUE PROCESS HERE. TAKE THE TERRORISTS OUT. KEEP THE RESERVOIR FROM BEING CONTAMINATED, AND MELT AWAY FROM HERE LIKE WE WERE NEVER HERE IN THE FIRST PLACE.
MAKE SURE CENTURIE TEN: QUATRAIN FORTY-NINE NEVER HAPPENS.

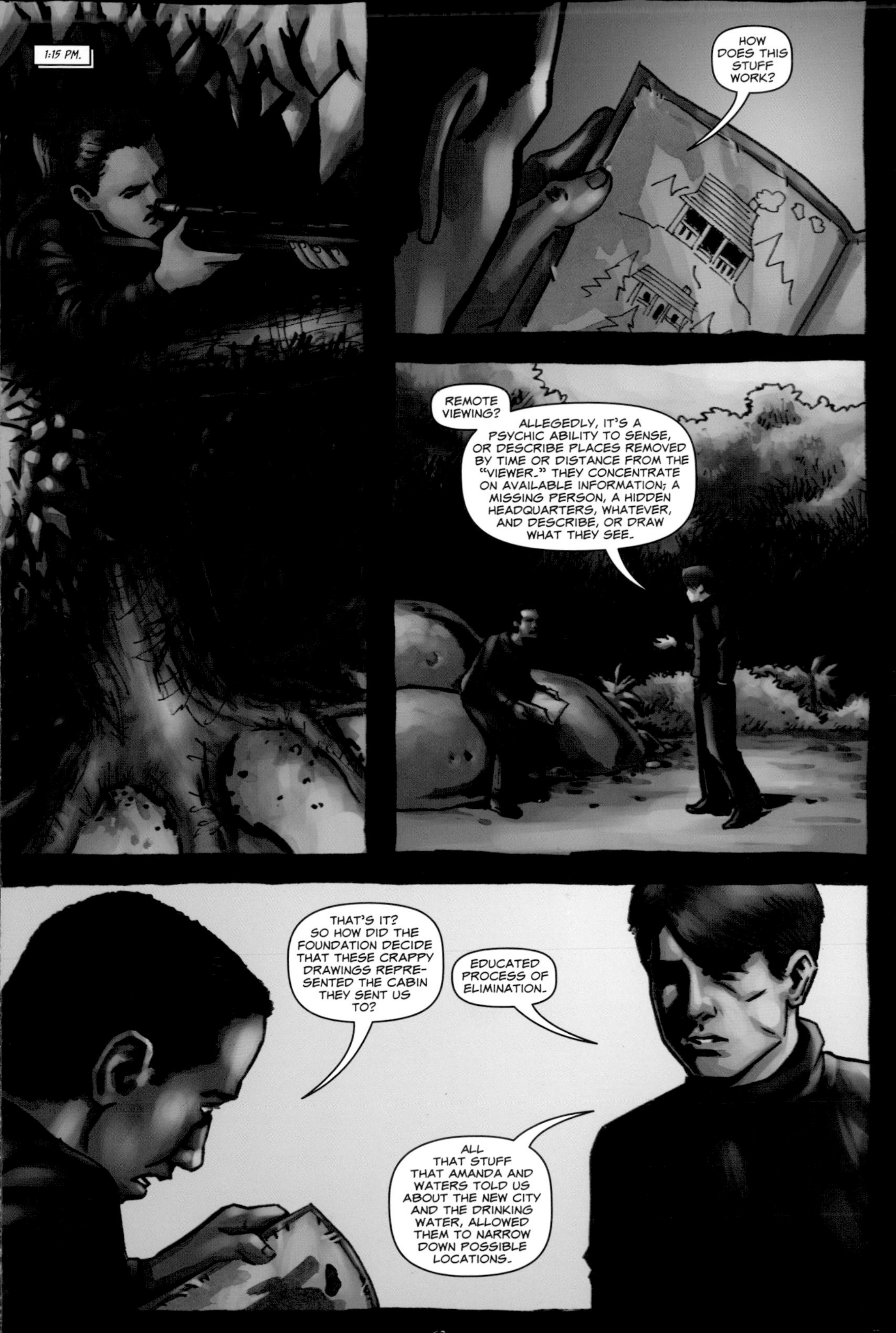
1:15 PM.
HOW DOES THIS STUFF WORK?
REMOTE VIEWING?
ALLEGEDLY, IT'S A PSYCHIC ABILITY TO SENSE, OR DESCRIBE PLACES REMOVED BY TIME OR DISTANCE FROM THE "VIEWER." THEY CONCENTRATE ON AVAILABLE INFORMATION; A MISSING PERSON, A HIDDEN HEADQUARTERS, WHATEVER, AND DESCRIBE, OR DRAW WHAT THEY SEE.
THAT'S IT? SO HOW DID THE FOUNDATION DECIDE THAT THESE CRAPPY DRAWINGS REPRESENTED THE CABIN THEY SENT US TO?
EDUCATED PROCESS OF ELIMINATION.
ALL THAT STUFF THAT AMANDA AND WATERS TOLD US ABOUT THE NEW CITY AND THE DRINKING WATER, ALLOWED THEM TO NARROW DOWN POSSIBLE LOCATIONS.

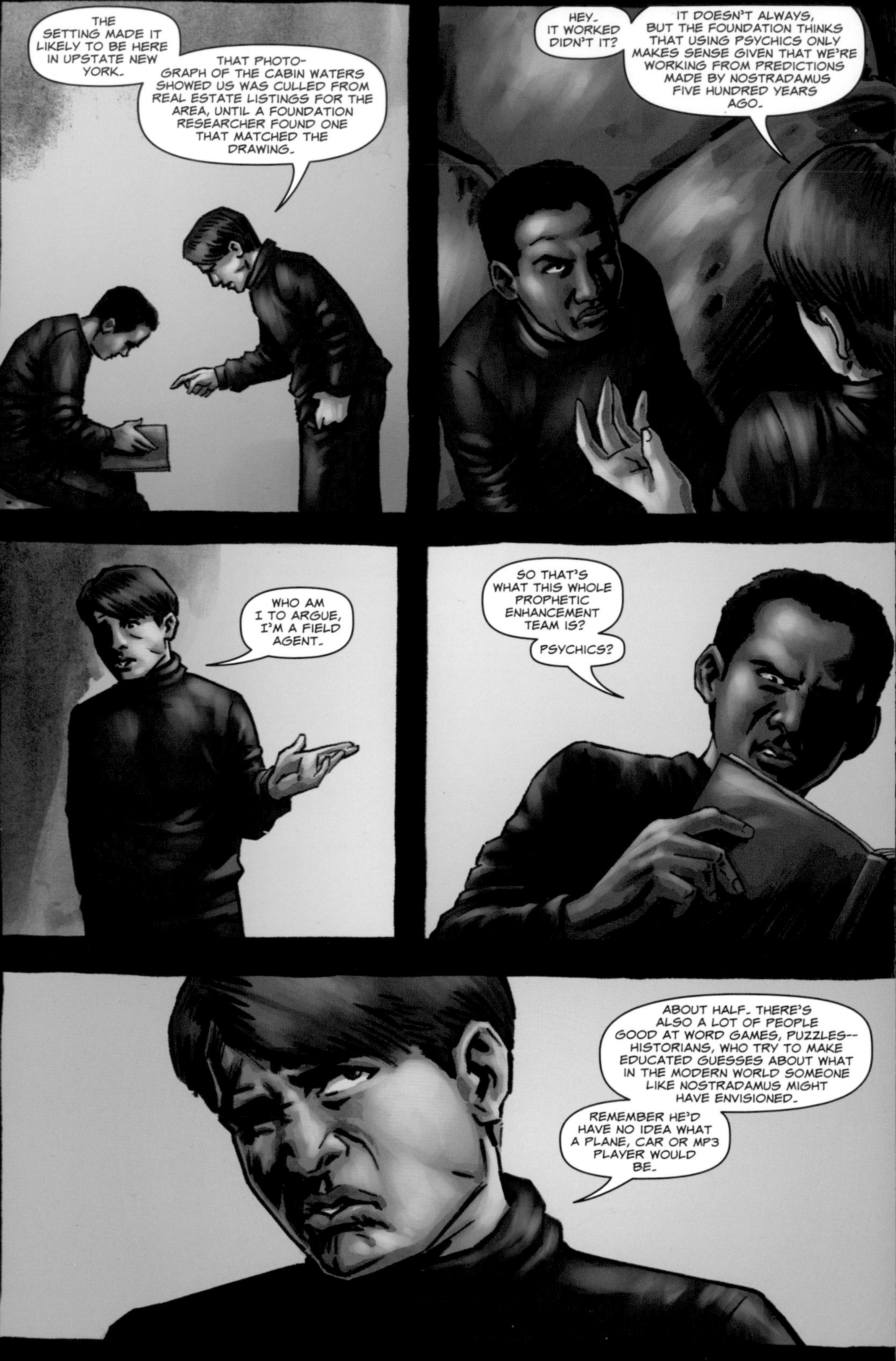
THE SETTING MADE IT LIKELY TO BE HERE IN UPSTATE NEW YORK.
THAT PHOTOGRAPH OF THE CABIN WATERS SHOWED US WAS CULLED FROM REAL ESTATE LISTINGS FOR THE AREA, UNTIL A FOUNDATION RESEARCHER FOUND ONE THAT MATCHED THE DRAWING.
HEY. IT WORKED DIDN'T IT?
IT DOESN'T ALWAYS, BUT THE FOUNDATION THINKS THAT USING PSYCHICS ONLY MAKES SENSE GIVEN THAT WE'RE WORKING FROM PREDICTIONS MADE BY NOSTRADAMUS FIVE HUNDRED YEARS AGO.
WHO AM I TO ARGUE, I'M A FIELD AGENT.
SO THAT'S WHAT THIS WHOLE PROPHETIC ENHANCEMENT TEAM IS?
PSYCHICS?
ABOUT HALF. THERE'S ALSO A LOT OF PEOPLE GOOD AT WORD GAMES, PUZZLES--HISTORIANS, WHO TRY TO MAKE EDUCATED GUESSES ABOUT WHAT IN THE MODERN WORLD SOMEONE LIKE NOSTRADAMUS MIGHT HAVE ENVISIONED.
REMEMBER HE'D HAVE NO IDEA WHAT A PLANE, CAR OR MP3 PLAYER WOULD BE.

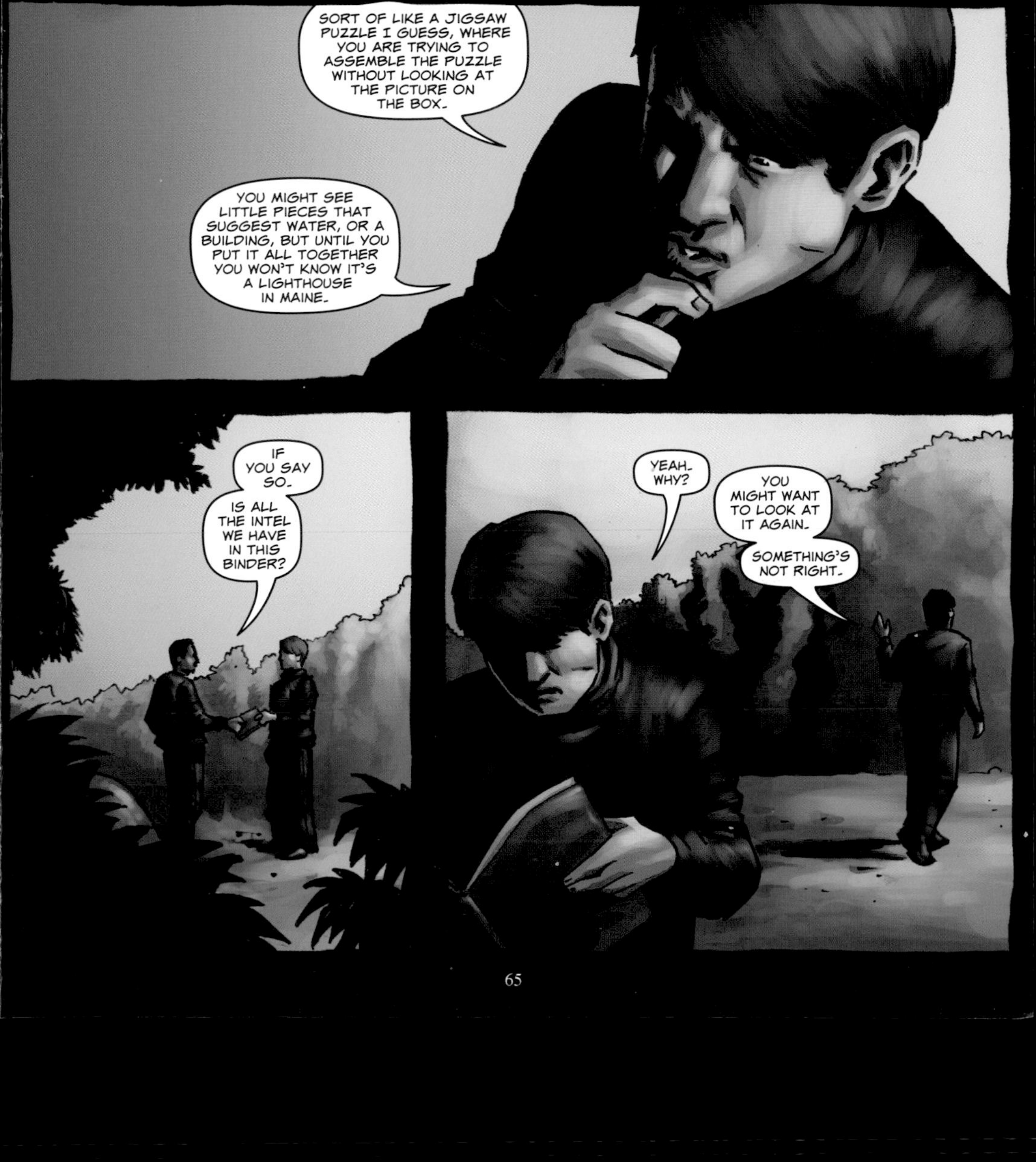
SORT OF LIKE A JIGSAW PUZZLE I GUESS, WHERE YOU ARE TRYING TO ASSEMBLE THE PUZZLE WITHOUT LOOKING AT THE PICTURE ON THE BOX.
YOU MIGHT SEE LITTLE PIECES THAT SUGGEST WATER, OR A BUILDING, BUT UNTIL YOU PUT IT ALL TOGETHER YOU WON'T KNOW IT'S A LIGHTHOUSE IN MAINE.
IF YOU SAY SO.
IS ALL THE INTEL WE HAVE IN THIS BINDER?
YEAH. WHY?
YOU MIGHT WANT TO LOOK AT IT AGAIN.
SOMETHING'S NOT RIGHT.

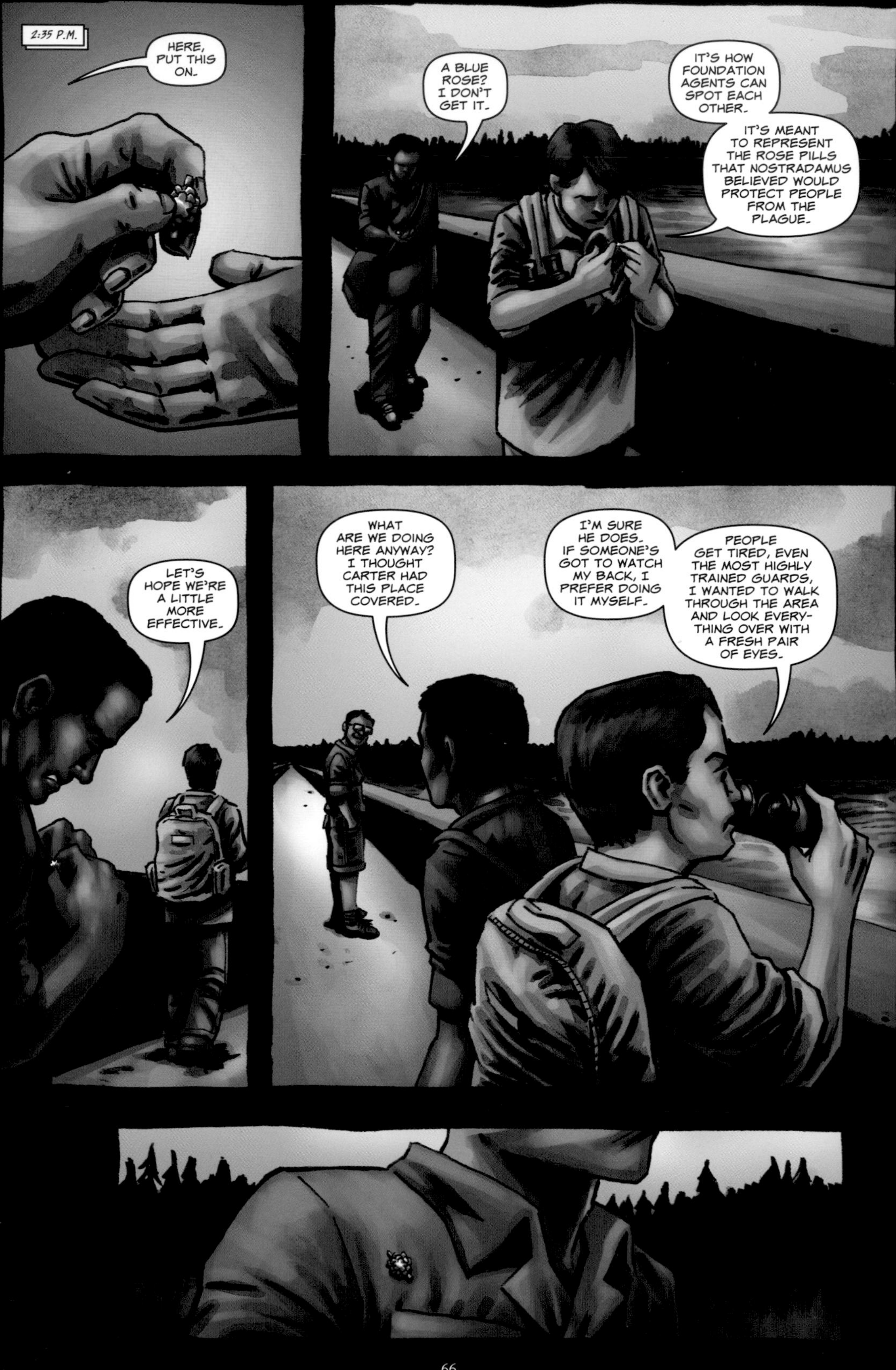
2:35 P.M.
HERE, PUT THIS ON.
A BLUE ROSE? I DON'T GET IT.
IT'S HOW FOUNDATION AGENTS CAN SPOT EACH OTHER.
IT'S MEANT TO REPRESENT THE ROSE PILLS THAT NOSTRADAMUS BELIEVED WOULD PROTECT PEOPLE FROM THE PLAGUE.
LET'S HOPE WE'RE A LITTLE MORE EFFECTIVE.
WHAT ARE WE DOING HERE ANYWAY? I THOUGHT CARTER HAD THIS PLACE COVERED.
I'M SURE HE DOES. IF SOMEONE'S GOT TO WATCH MY BACK, I PREFER DOING IT MYSELF.
PEOPLE GET TIRED, EVEN THE MOST HIGHLY TRAINED GUARDS, I WANTED TO WALK THROUGH THE AREA AND LOOK EVERYTHING OVER WITH A FRESH PAIR OF EYES.

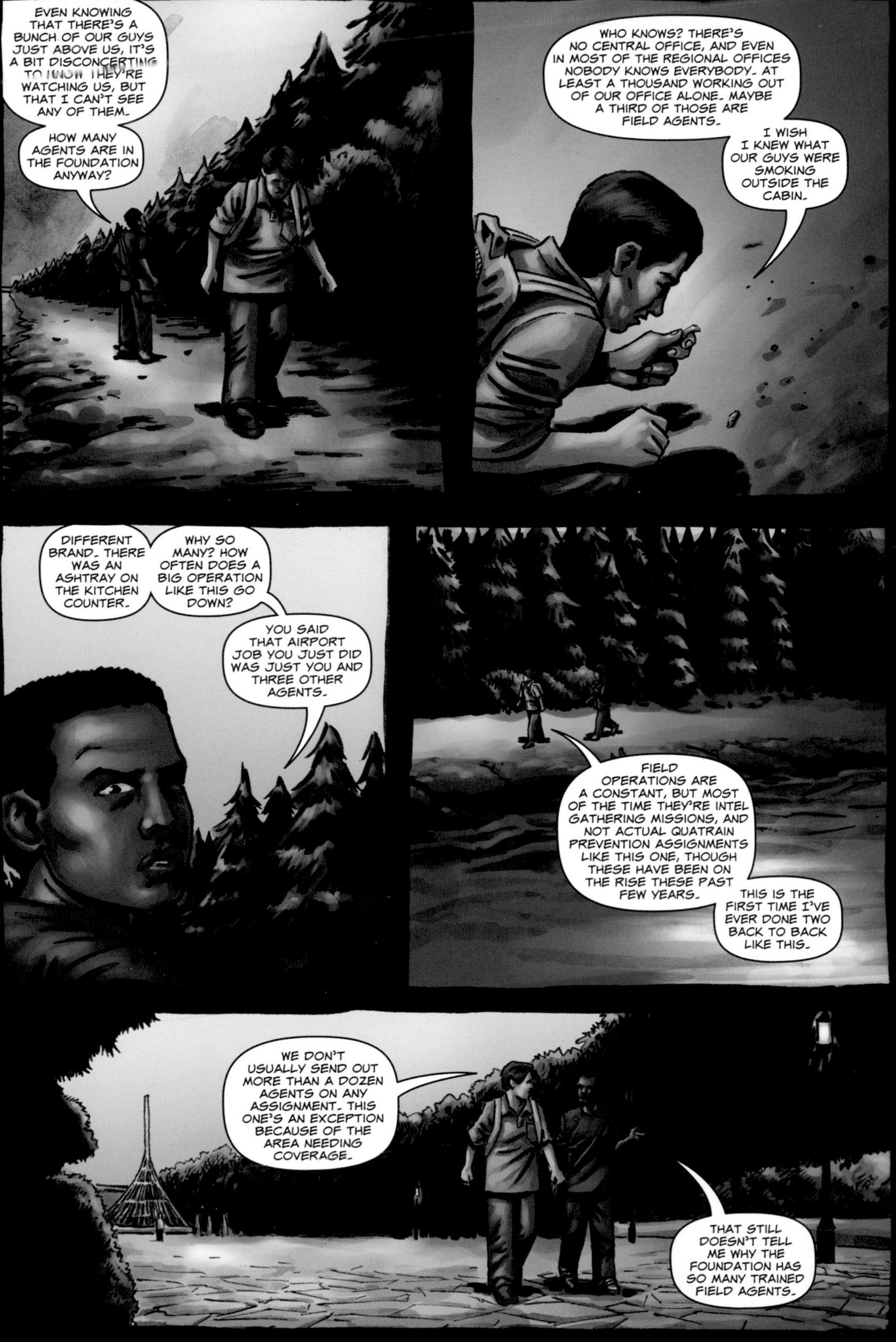

EVEN KNOWING THAT THERE'S A BUNCH OF OUR GUYS JUST ABOVE US, IT'S A BIT DISCONCERTING TO KNOW THEY'RE WATCHING US, BUT THAT I CAN'T SEE ANY OF THEM.
HOW MANY AGENTS ARE IN THE FOUNDATION ANYWAY?
WHO KNOWS? THERE'S NO CENTRAL OFFICE, AND EVEN IN MOST OF THE REGIONAL OFFICES NOBODY KNOWS EVERYBODY. AT LEAST A THOUSAND WORKING OUT OF OUR OFFICE ALONE. MAYBE A THIRD OF THOSE ARE FIELD AGENTS.
I WISH I KNEW WHAT OUR GUYS WERE SMOKING OUTSIDE THE CABIN.
DIFFERENT BRAND. THERE WAS AN ASHTRAY ON THE KITCHEN COUNTER.
WHY SO MANY? HOW OFTEN DOES A BIG OPERATION LIKE THIS GO DOWN?
YOU SAID THAT AIRPORT JOB YOU JUST DID WAS JUST YOU AND THREE OTHER AGENTS.
FIELD OPERATIONS ARE A CONSTANT, BUT MOST OF THE TIME THEY'RE INTEL GATHERING MISSIONS, AND NOT ACTUAL QUATRAIN PREVENTION ASSIGNMENTS LIKE THIS ONE, THOUGH THESE HAVE BEEN ON THE RISE THESE PAST FEW YEARS.
THIS IS THE FIRST TIME I'VE EVER DONE TWO BACK TO BACK LIKE THIS.
WE DON'T USUALLY SEND OUT MORE THAN A DOZEN AGENTS ON ANY ASSIGNMENT. THIS ONE'S AN EXCEPTION BECAUSE OF THE AREA NEEDING COVERAGE.
THAT STILL DOESN'T TELL ME WHY THE FOUNDATION HAS SO MANY TRAINED FIELD AGENTS.

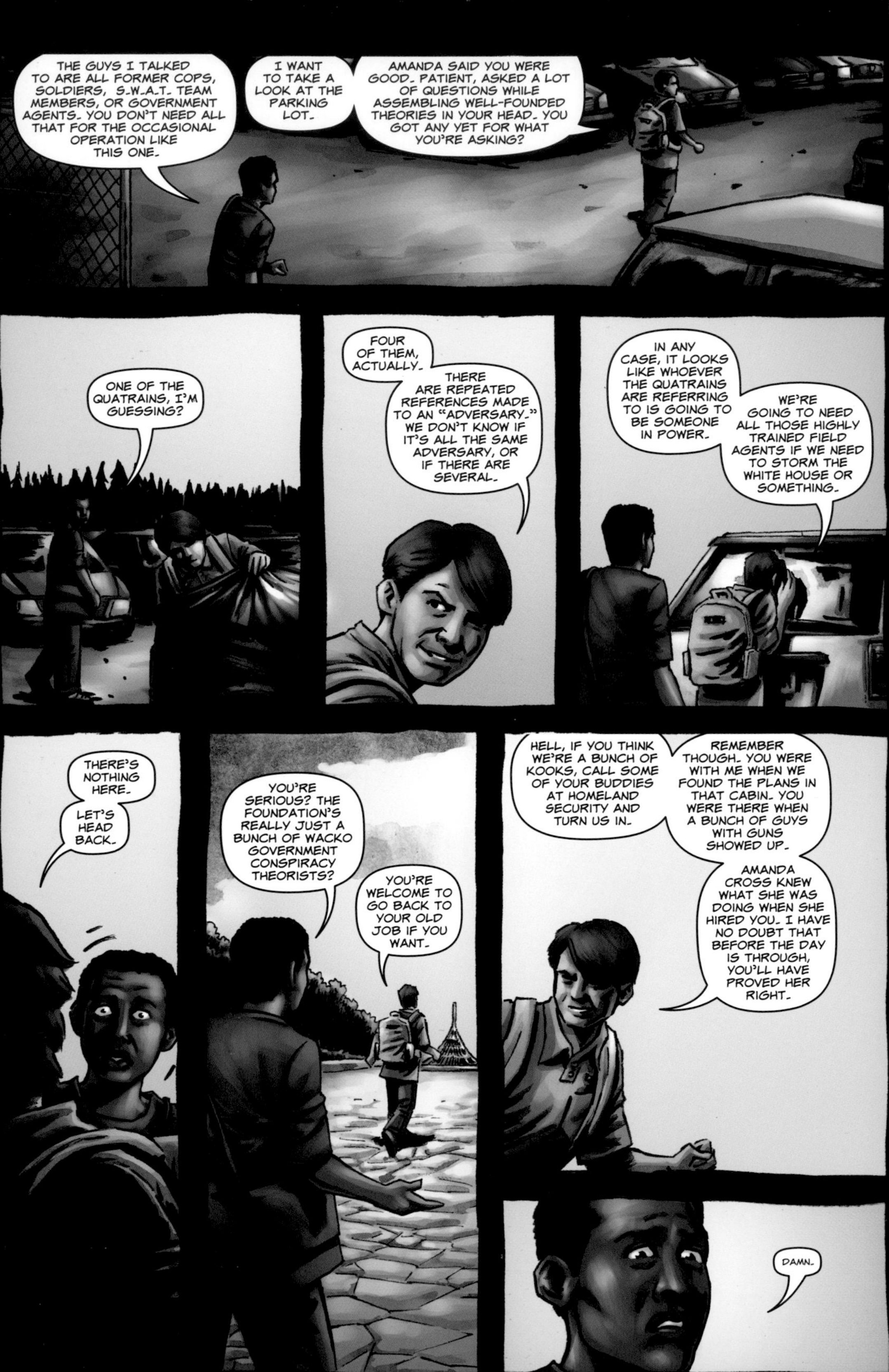
THE GUYS I TALKED TO ARE ALL FORMER COPS, SOLDIERS, S.W.A.T. TEAM MEMBERS, OR GOVERNMENT AGENTS. YOU DON'T NEED ALL THAT FOR THE OCCASIONAL OPERATION LIKE THIS ONE.
I WANT TO TAKE A LOOK AT THE PARKING LOT.
AMANDA SAID YOU WERE GOOD. PATIENT, ASKED A LOT OF QUESTIONS WHILE ASSEMBLING WELL-FOUNDED THEORIES IN YOUR HEAD. YOU GOT ANY YET FOR WHAT YOU'RE ASKING?
ONE OF THE QUATRAINS, I'M GUESSING?
FOUR OF THEM, ACTUALLY.
THERE ARE REPEATED REFERENCES MADE TO AN "ADVERSARY." WE DON'T KNOW IF IT'S ALL THE SAME ADVERSARY, OR IF THERE ARE SEVERAL.
IN ANY CASE, IT LOOKS LIKE WHOEVER THE QUATRAINS ARE REFERRING TO IS GOING TO BE SOMEONE IN POWER.
WE'RE GOING TO NEED ALL THOSE HIGHLY TRAINED FIELD AGENTS IF WE NEED TO STORM THE WHITE HOUSE OR SOMETHING.
THERE'S NOTHING HERE.
LET'S HEAD BACK.
YOU'RE SERIOUS? THE FOUNDATION'S REALLY JUST A BUNCH OF WACKO GOVERNMENT CONSPIRACY THEORISTS?
YOU'RE WELCOME TO GO BACK TO YOUR OLD JOB IF YOU WANT.
HELL, IF YOU THINK WE'RE A BUNCH OF KOOKS, CALL SOME OF YOUR BUDDIES AT HOMELAND SECURITY AND TURN US IN.
REMEMBER THOUGH. YOU WERE WITH ME WHEN WE FOUND THE PLANS IN THAT CABIN. YOU WERE THERE WHEN A BUNCH OF GUYS WITH GUNS SHOWED UP.
AMANDA CROSS KNEW WHAT SHE WAS DOING WHEN SHE HIRED YOU. I HAVE NO DOUBT THAT BEFORE THE DAY IS THROUGH, YOU'LL HAVE PROVED HER RIGHT.
DAMN.

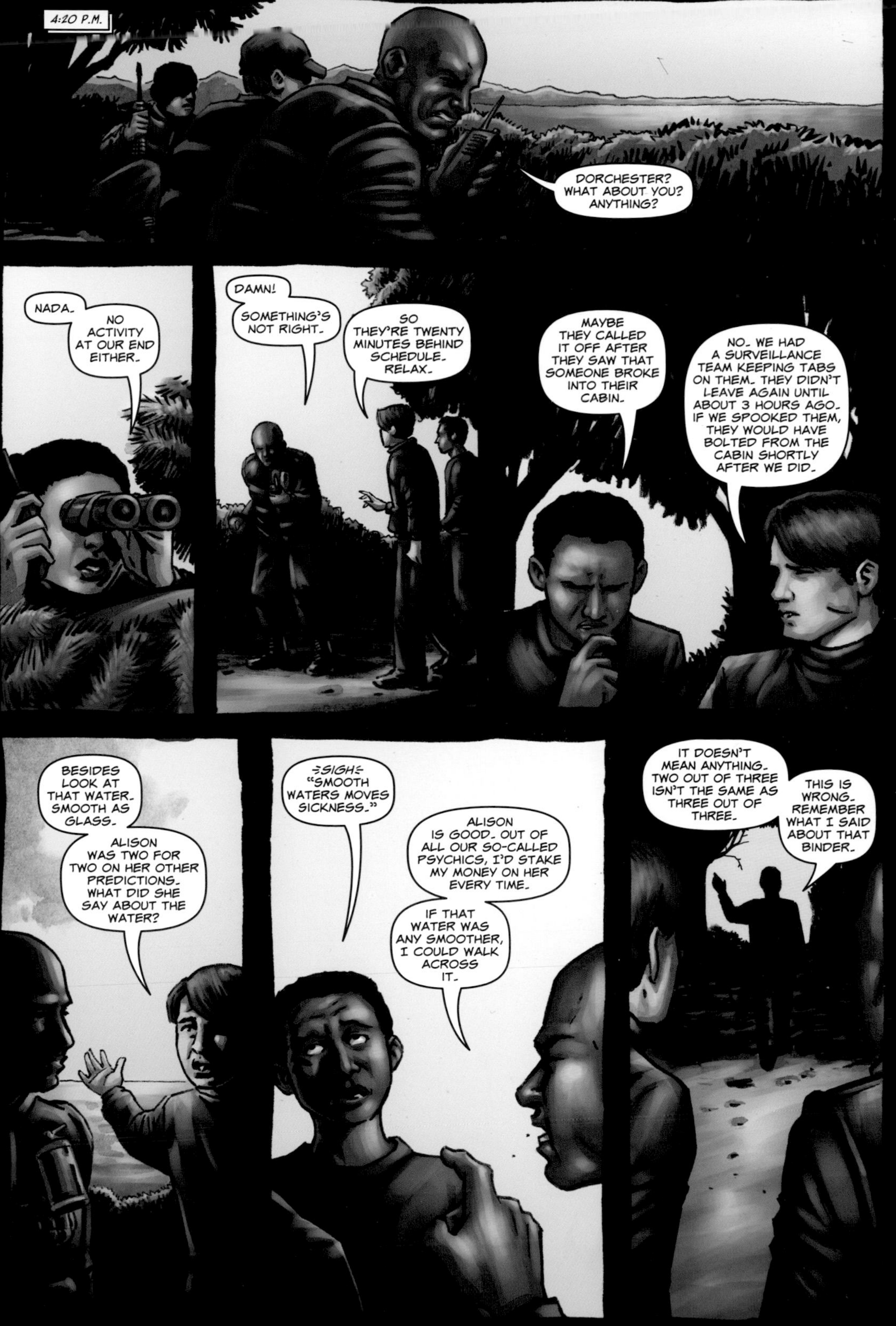
4:20 P.M.
DORCHESTER? WHAT ABOUT YOU? ANYTHING?
NADA.
NO ACTIVITY AT OUR END EITHER.
DAMN!
SOMETHING'S NOT RIGHT.
SO THEY'RE TWENTY MINUTES BEHIND SCHEDULE. RELAX.
MAYBE THEY CALLED IT OFF AFTER THEY SAW THAT SOMEONE BROKE INTO THEIR CABIN.
NO. WE HAD A SURVEILLANCE TEAM KEEPING TABS ON THEM. THEY DIDN'T LEAVE AGAIN UNTIL ABOUT 3 HOURS AGO. IF WE SPOOKED THEM, THEY WOULD HAVE BOLTED FROM THE CABIN SHORTLY AFTER WE DID.
BESIDES LOOK AT THAT WATER. SMOOTH AS GLASS.
ALISON WAS TWO FOR TWO ON HER OTHER PREDICTIONS. WHAT DID SHE SAY ABOUT THE WATER?
=SIGH= "SMOOTH WATERS MOVES SICKNESS."
ALISON IS GOOD. OUT OF ALL OUR SO-CALLED PSYCHICS, I'D STAKE MY MONEY ON HER EVERY TIME.
IF THAT WATER WAS ANY SMOOTHER, I COULD WALK ACROSS IT.
IT DOESN'T MEAN ANYTHING. TWO OUT OF THREE ISN'T THE SAME AS THREE OUT OF THREE.
THIS IS WRONG. REMEMBER WHAT I SAID ABOUT THAT BINDER.

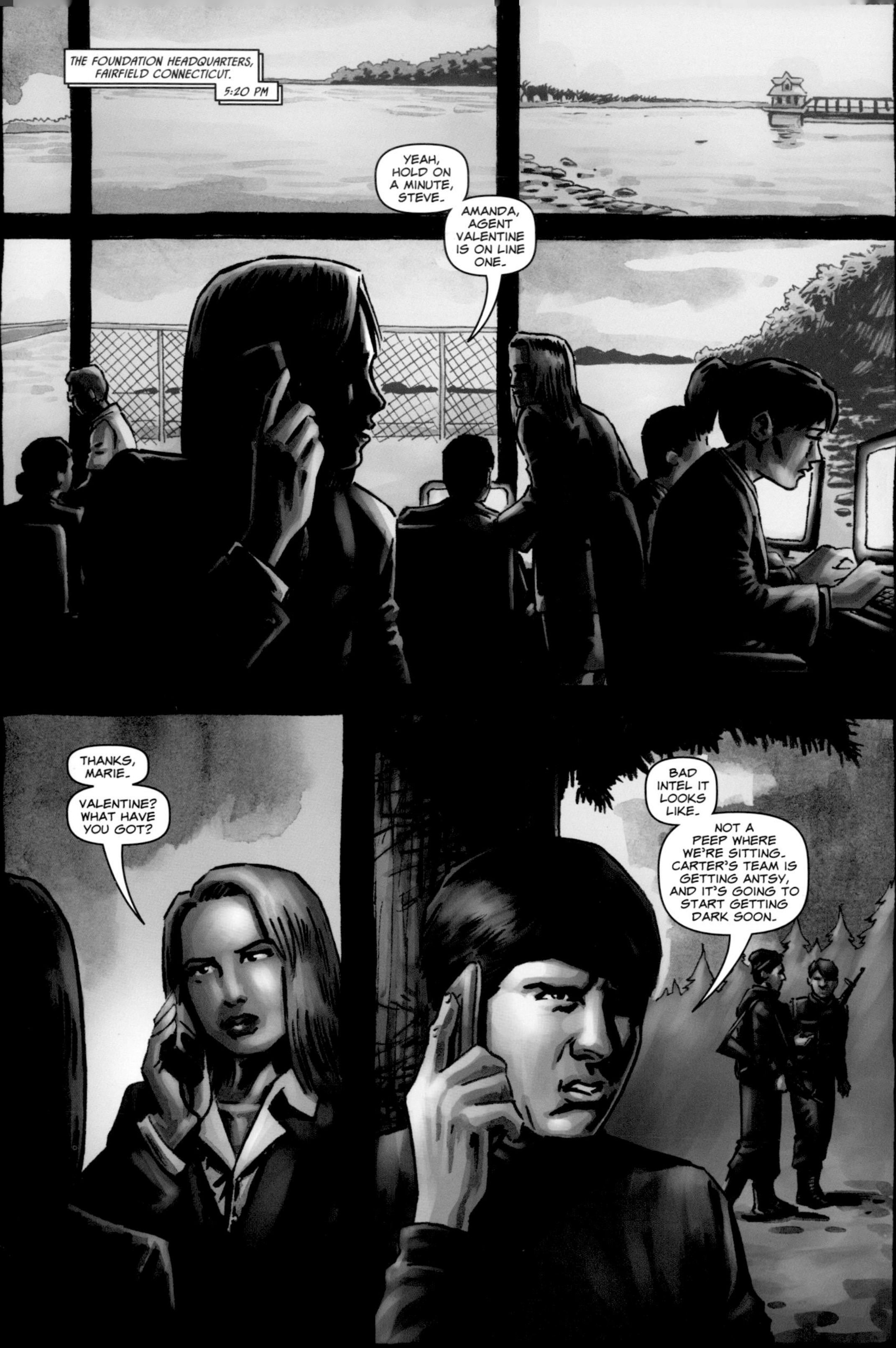
THE FOUNDATION HEADQUARTERS, FAIRFIELD CONNECTICUT.
5:20 PM
YEAH, HOLD ON A MINUTE, STEVE.
AMANDA, AGENT VALENTINE IS ON LINE ONE.
THANKS, MARIE.
VALENTINE? WHAT HAVE YOU GOT?
BAD INTEL IT LOOKS LIKE.
NOT A PEEP WHERE WE'RE SITTING. CARTER'S TEAM IS GETTING ANTSY, AND IT'S GOING TO START GETTING DARK SOON.

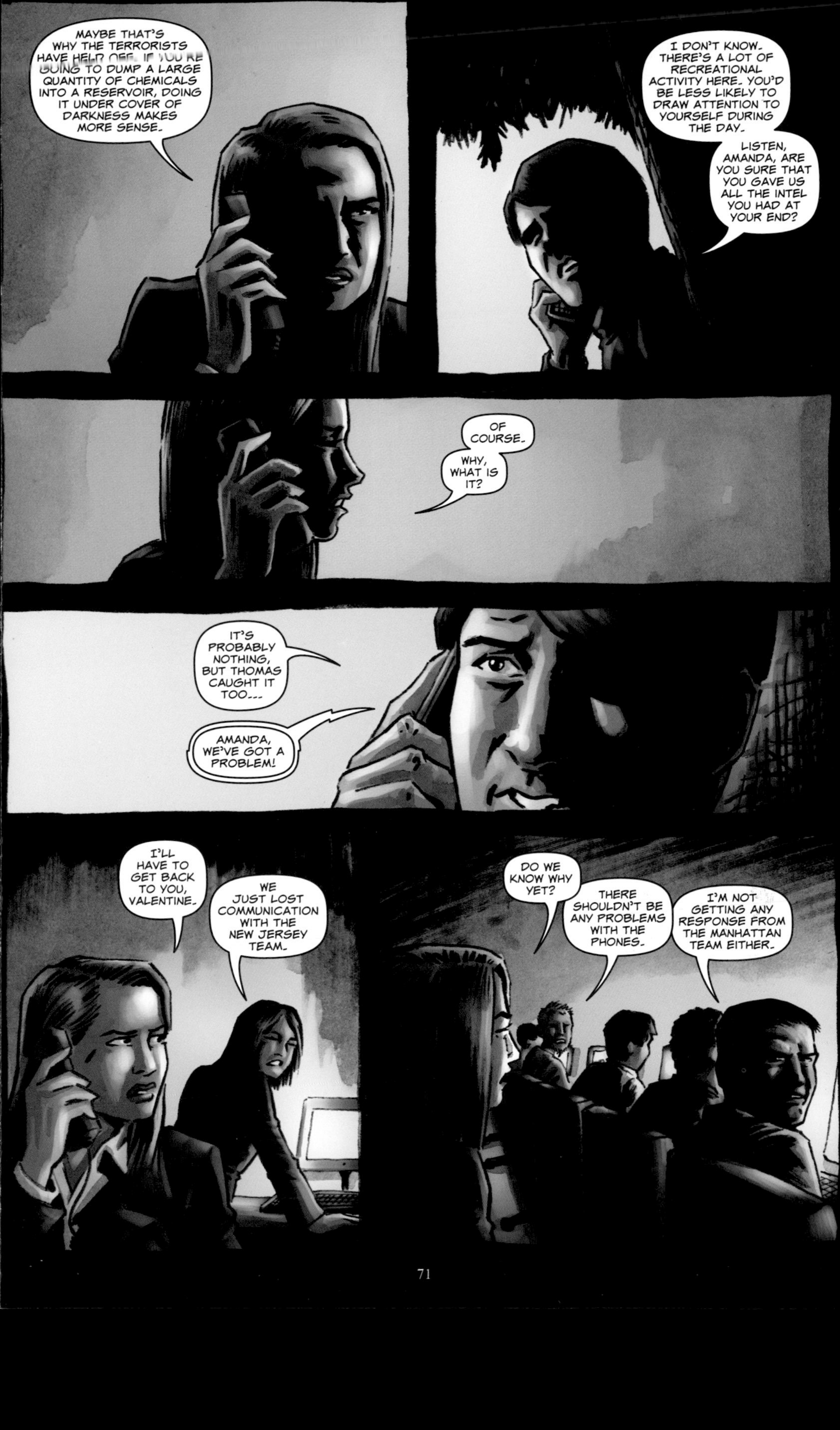
MAYBE THAT'S WHY THE TERRORISTS HAVE HELD OFF. IF YOU'RE GOING TO DUMP A LARGE QUANTITY OF CHEMICALS INTO A RESERVOIR, DOING IT UNDER COVER OF DARKNESS MAKES MORE SENSE.
I DON'T KNOW. THERE'S A LOT OF RECREATIONAL ACTIVITY HERE. YOU'D BE LESS LIKELY TO DRAW ATTENTION TO YOURSELF DURING THE DAY.
LISTEN, AMANDA, ARE YOU SURE THAT YOU GAVE US ALL THE INTEL YOU HAD AT YOUR END?
OF COURSE.
WHY, WHAT IS IT?
IT'S PROBABLY NOTHING, BUT THOMAS CAUGHT IT TOO...
AMANDA, WE'VE GOT A PROBLEM!
I'LL HAVE TO GET BACK TO YOU, VALENTINE.
WE JUST LOST COMMUNICATION WITH THE NEW JERSEY TEAM.
DO WE KNOW WHY YET?
THERE SHOULDN'T BE ANY PROBLEMS WITH THE PHONES.
I'M NOT GETTING ANY RESPONSE FROM THE MANHATTAN TEAM EITHER.

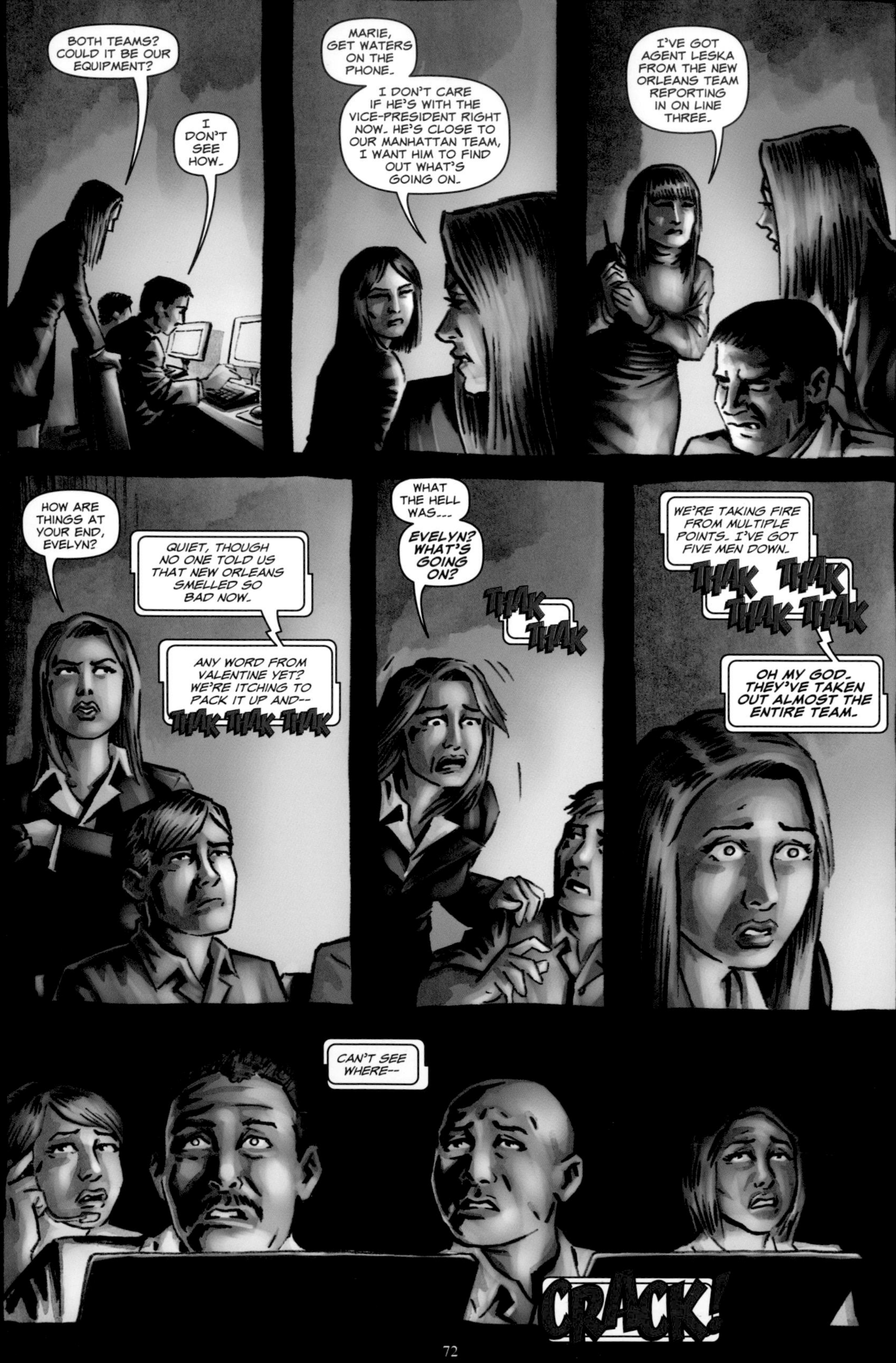
BOTH TEAMS? COULD IT BE OUR EQUIPMENT?
I DON'T SEE HOW.
MARIE, GET WATERS ON THE PHONE.
I DON'T CARE IF HE'S WITH THE VICE-PRESIDENT RIGHT NOW. HE'S CLOSE TO OUR MANHATTAN TEAM, I WANT HIM TO FIND OUT WHAT'S GOING ON.
I'VE GOT AGENT LESKA FROM THE NEW ORLEANS TEAM REPORTING IN ON LINE THREE.
HOW ARE THINGS AT YOUR END, EVELYN?
QUIET, THOUGH NO ONE TOLD US THAT NEW ORLEANS SMELLED SO BAD NOW.
ANY WORD FROM VALENTINE YET? WE'RE ITCHING TO PACK IT UP AND--
THAK THAK THAK
WHAT THE HELL WAS---
EVELYN? WHAT'S GOING ON?
THAK THAK
WE'RE TAKING FIRE FROM MULTIPLE POINTS. I'VE GOT FIVE MEN DOWN.
THAK THAK THAK THAK
OH MY GOD. THEY'VE TAKEN OUT ALMOST THE ENTIRE TEAM.
CAN'T SEE WHERE--
CRACK!

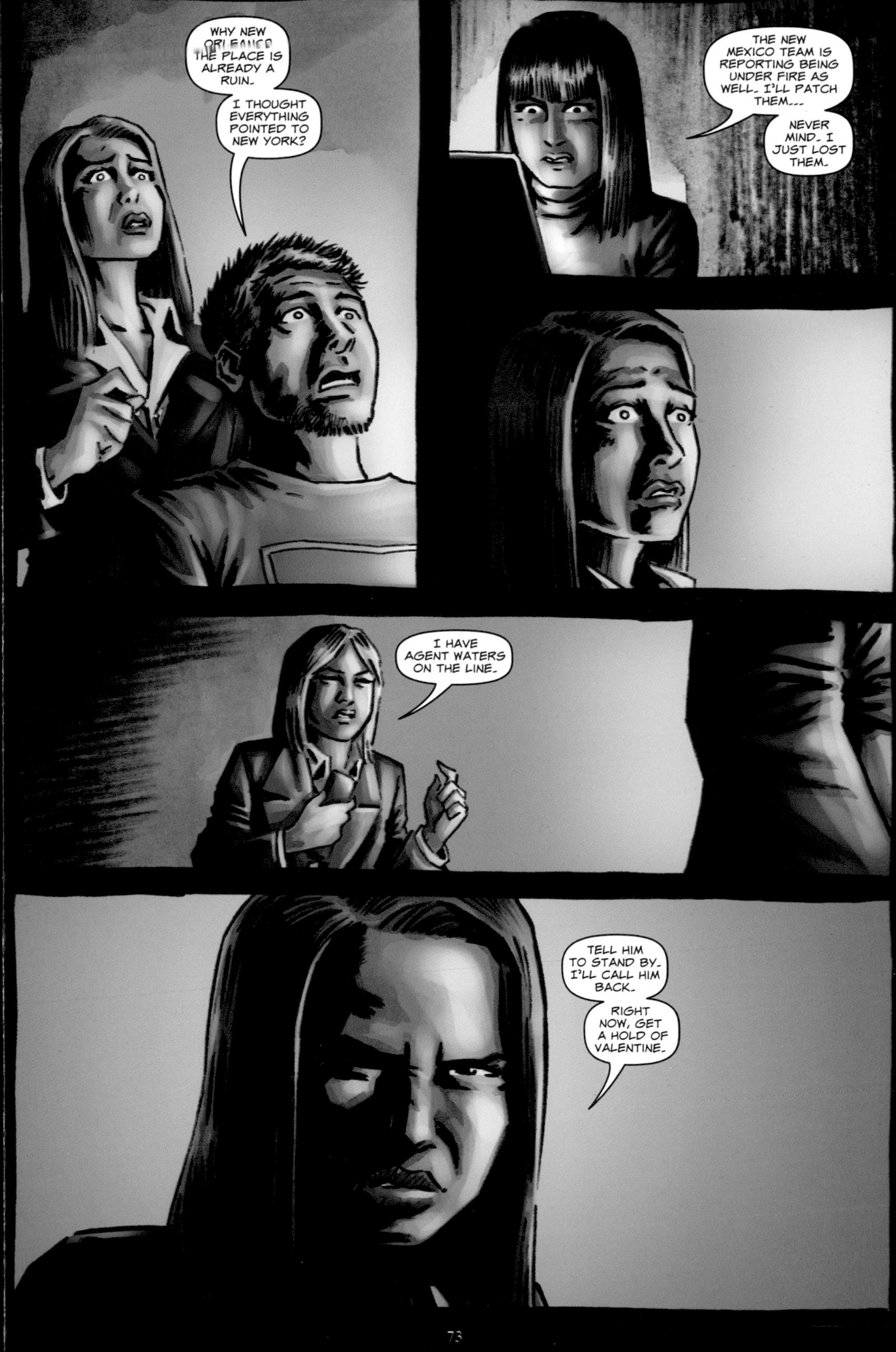

WHY NEW
THE PLACE IS ALREADY A RUIN.
I THOUGHT EVERYTHING POINTED TO NEW YORK?
THE NEW MEXICO TEAM IS REPORTING BEING UNDER FIRE AS WELL. I'LL PATCH THEM...
NEVER MIND. I JUST LOST THEM.
I HAVE AGENT WATERS ON THE LINE.
TELL HIM TO STAND BY. I'LL CALL HIM BACK.
RIGHT NOW, GET A HOLD OF VALENTINE.

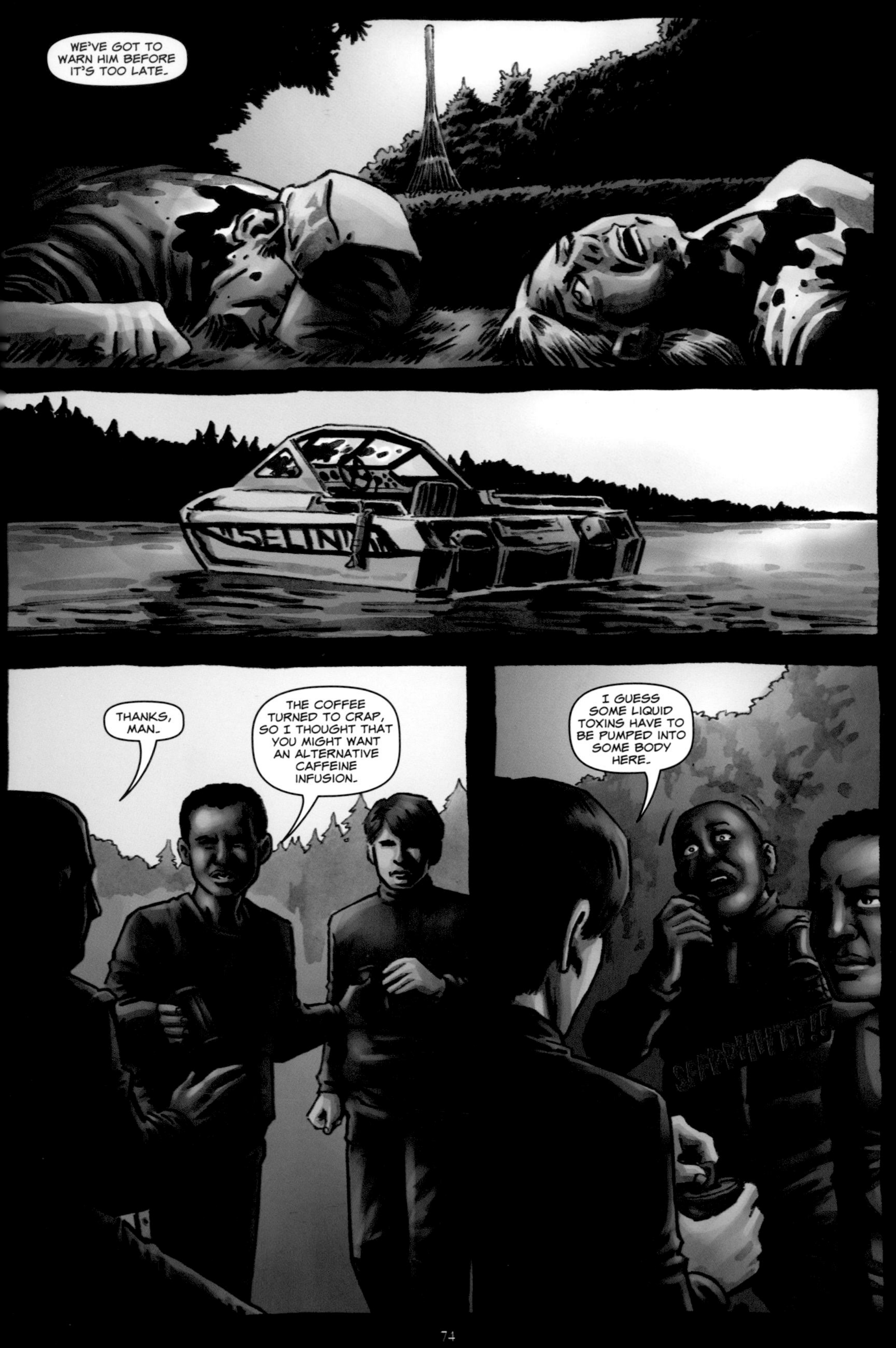
WE'VE GOT TO WARN HIM BEFORE IT'S TOO LATE.
THANKS, MAN.
THE COFFEE TURNED TO CRAP, SO I THOUGHT THAT YOU MIGHT WANT AN ALTERNATIVE CAFFEINE INFUSION.
I GUESS SOME LIQUID TOXINS HAVE TO BE PUMPED INTO SOME BODY HERE.

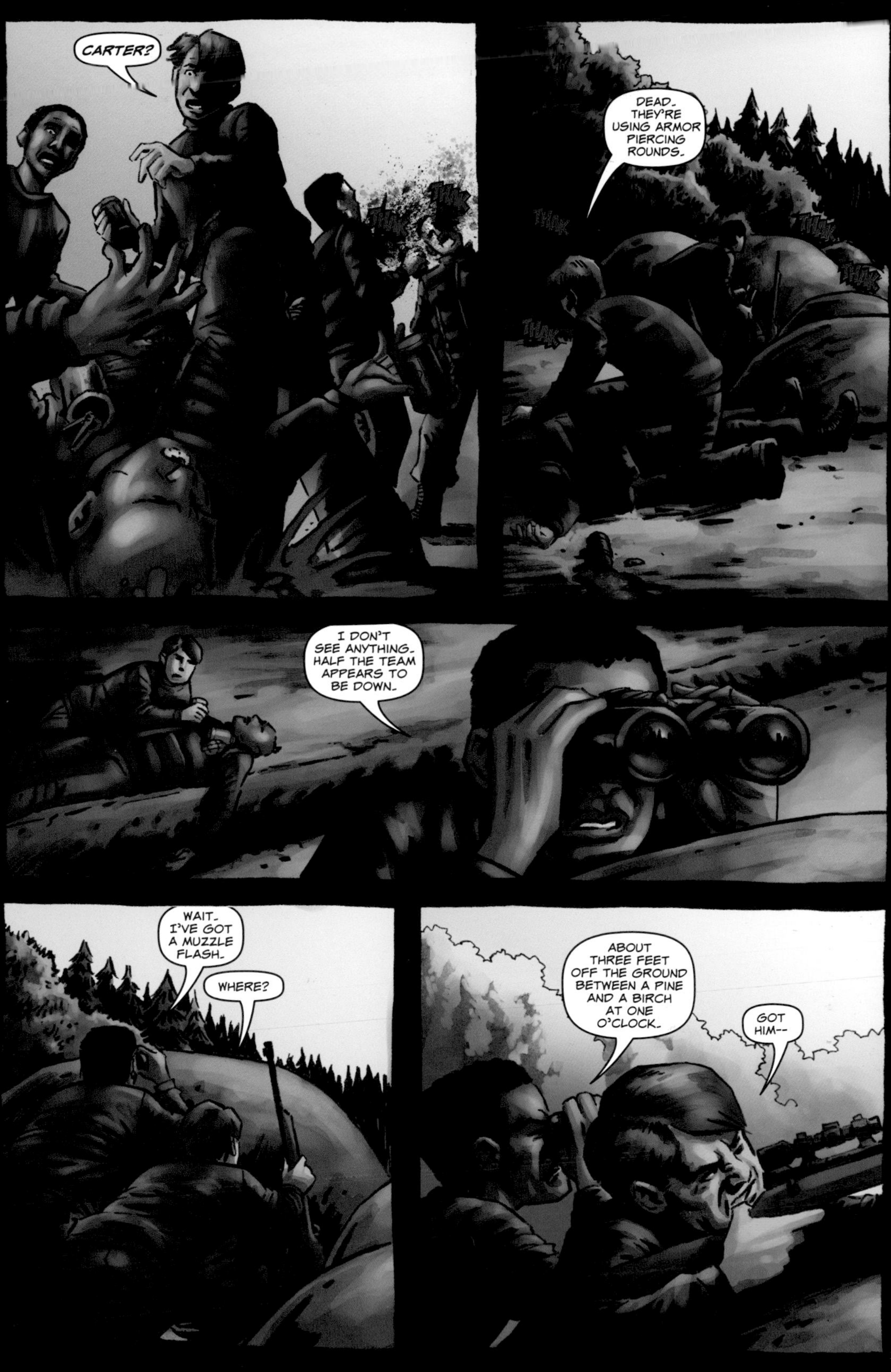
CARTER?
THAK
THAK
DEAD. THEY'RE USING ARMOR PIERCING ROUNDS.
THAK
THAK
THAK
THAK
I DON'T SEE ANYTHING. HALF THE TEAM APPEARS TO BE DOWN.
WAIT. I'VE GOT A MUZZLE FLASH.
WHERE?
ABOUT THREE FEET OFF THE GROUND BETWEEN A PINE AND A BIRCH AT ONE O'CLOCK.
GOT HIM--

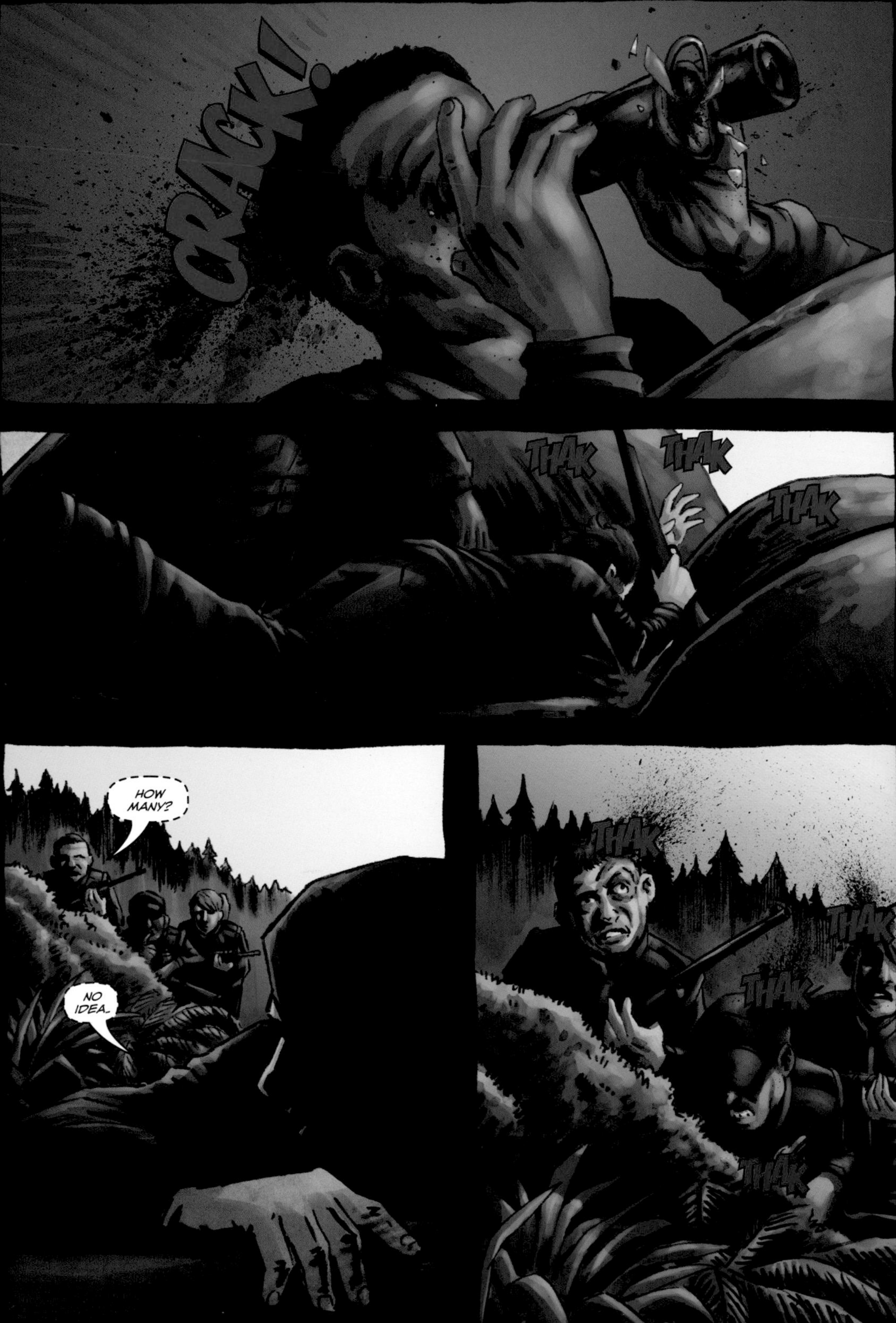
CRACK!
THAK
THAK
THAK
HOW MANY?
NO IDEA.
THAK
THAK
THAK
THAK

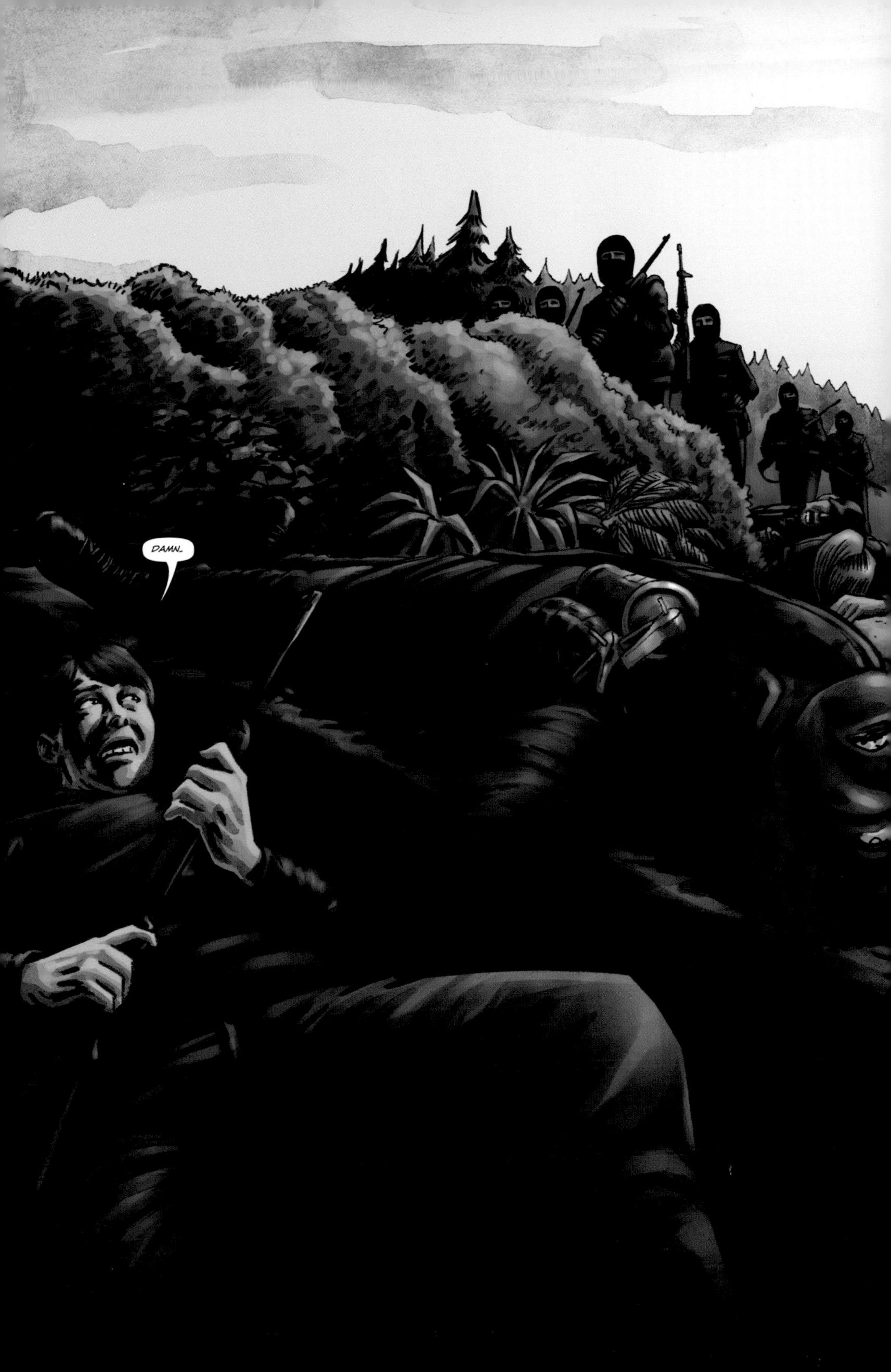
DAMN.

Chapter Four

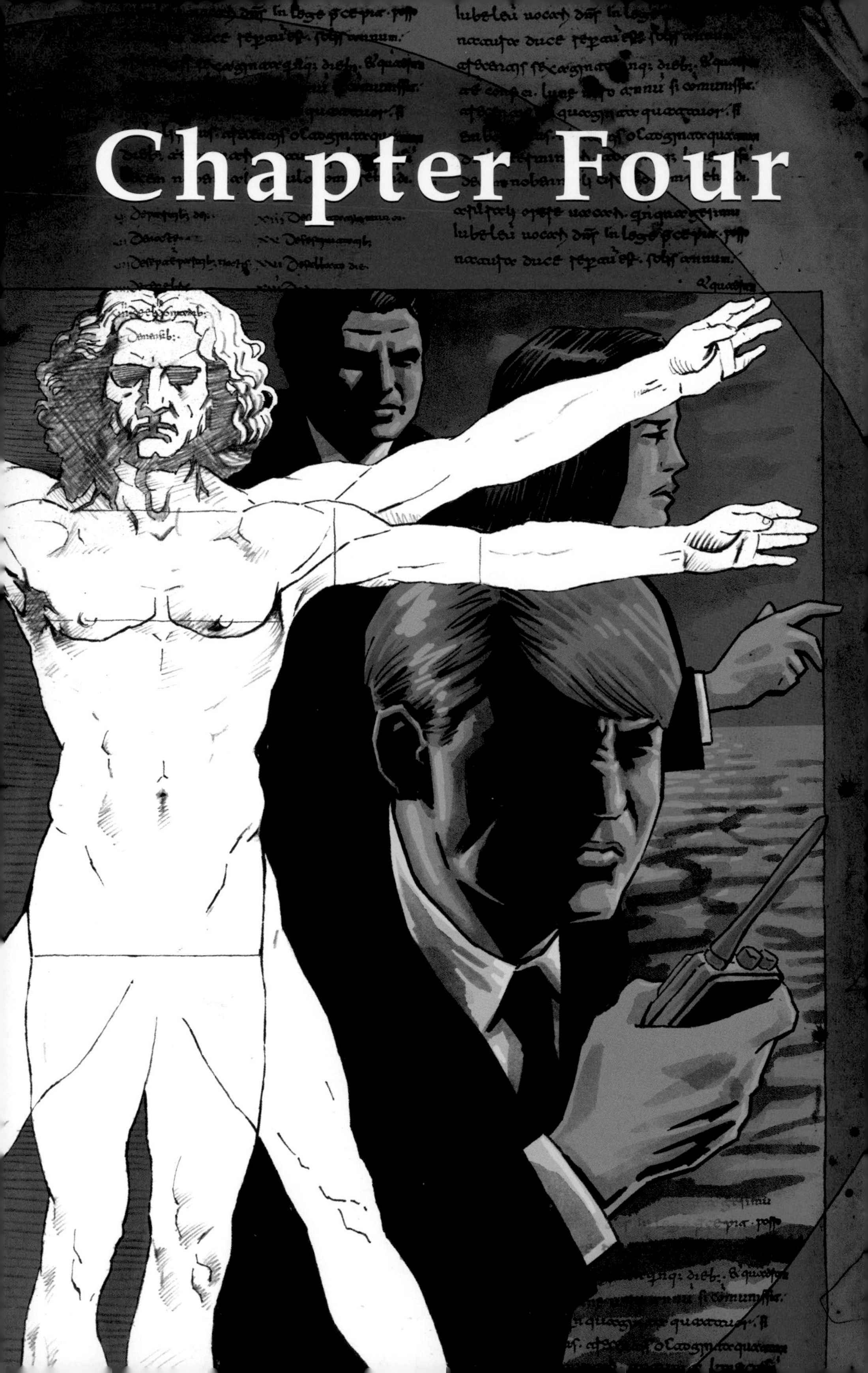

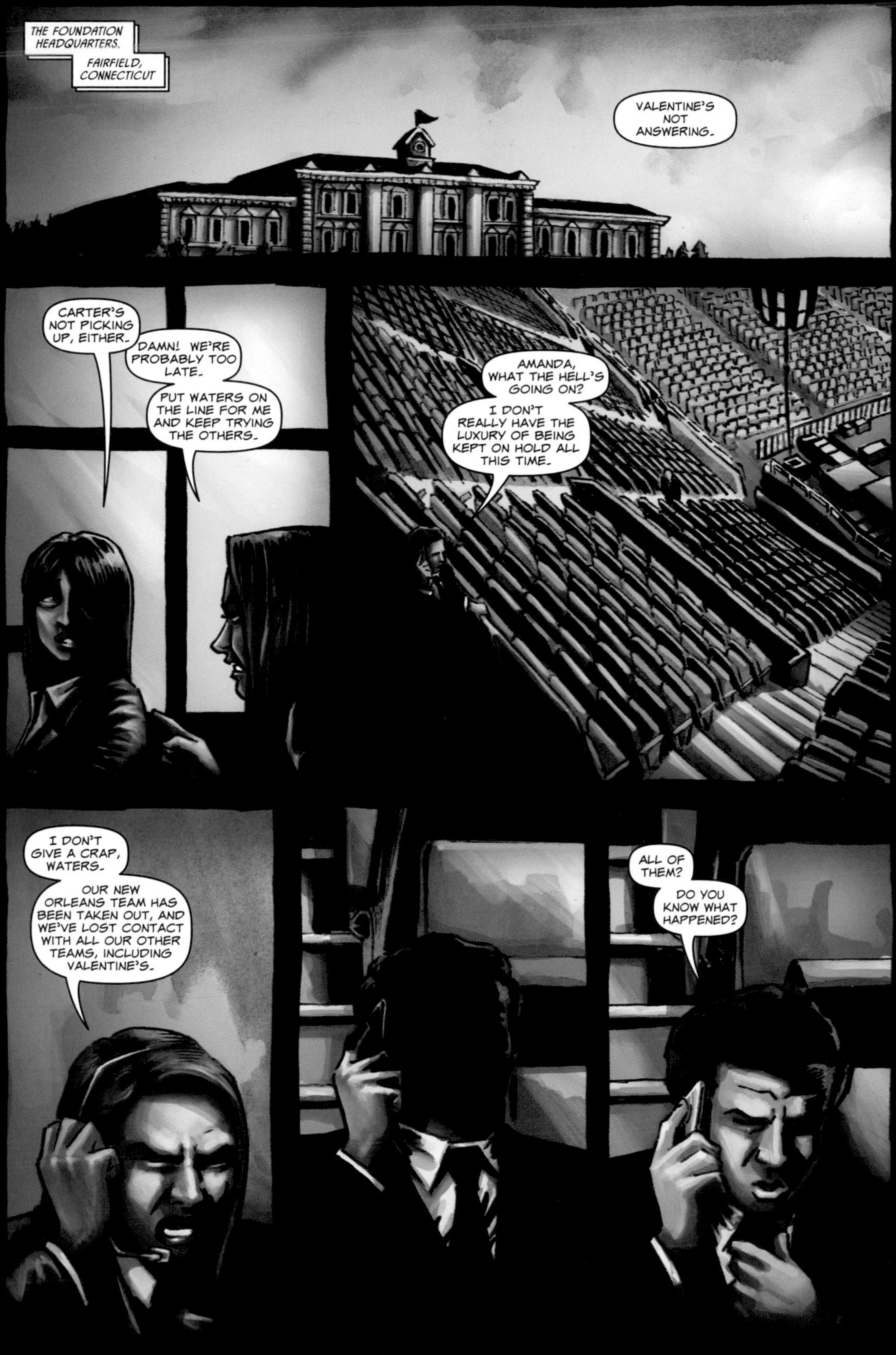
THE FOUNDATION HEADQUARTERS.
FAIRFIELD, CONNECTICUT
VALENTINE'S NOT ANSWERING.
CARTER'S NOT PICKING UP, EITHER.
DAMN! WE'RE PROBABLY TOO LATE.
PUT WATERS ON THE LINE FOR ME AND KEEP TRYING THE OTHERS.
AMANDA, WHAT THE HELL'S GOING ON?
I DON'T REALLY HAVE THE LUXURY OF BEING KEPT ON HOLD ALL THIS TIME.
I DON'T GIVE A CRAP, WATERS.
OUR NEW ORLEANS TEAM HAS BEEN TAKEN OUT, AND WE'VE LOST CONTACT WITH ALL OUR OTHER TEAMS, INCLUDING VALENTINE'S.
ALL OF THEM?
DO YOU KNOW WHAT HAPPENED?

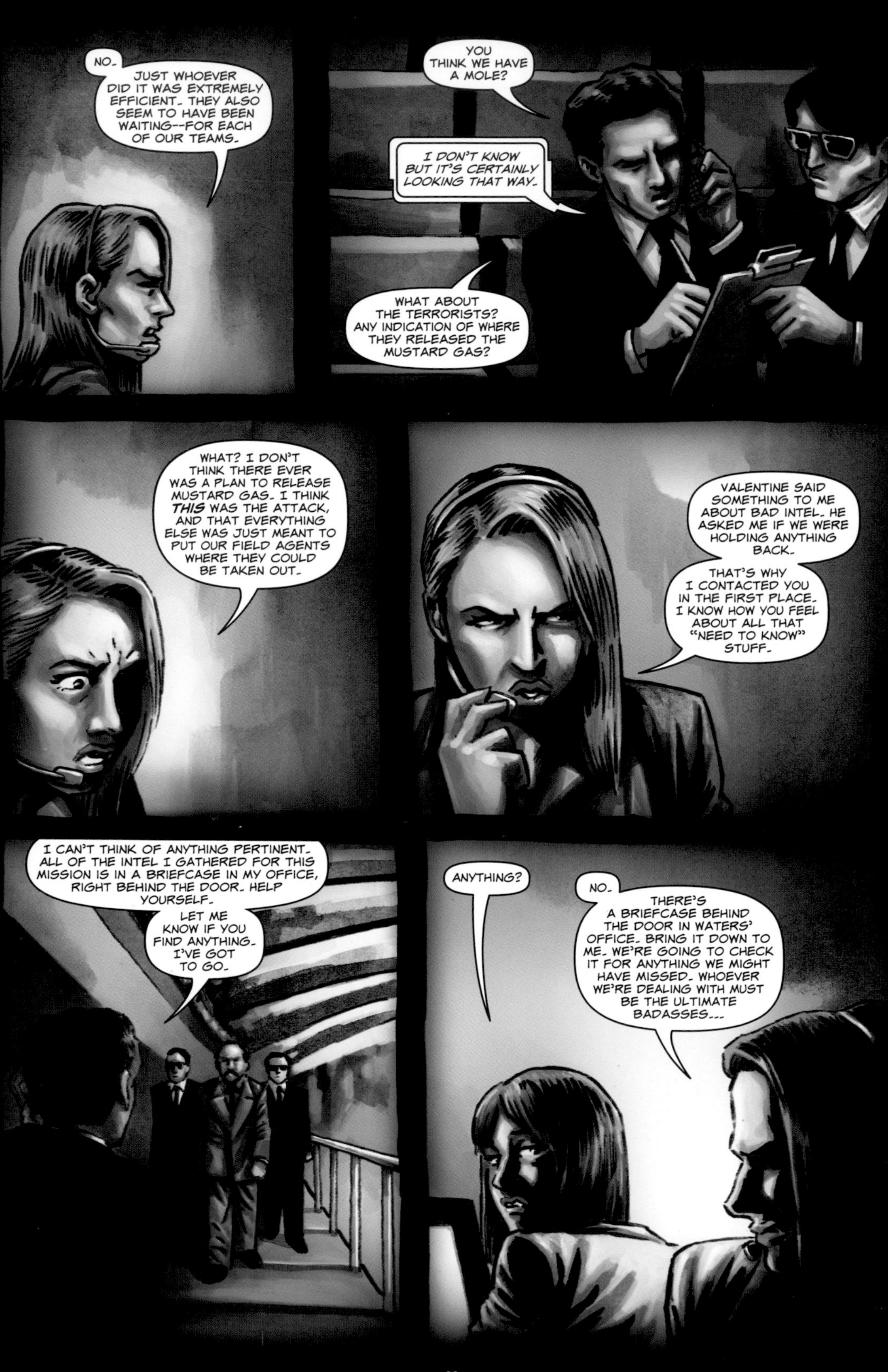
NO.
JUST WHOEVER DID IT WAS EXTREMELY EFFICIENT. THEY ALSO SEEM TO HAVE BEEN WAITING--FOR EACH OF OUR TEAMS.
YOU THINK WE HAVE A MOLE?
I DON'T KNOW BUT IT'S CERTAINLY LOOKING THAT WAY.
WHAT ABOUT THE TERRORISTS? ANY INDICATION OF WHERE THEY RELEASED THE MUSTARD GAS?
WHAT? I DON'T THINK THERE EVER WAS A PLAN TO RELEASE MUSTARD GAS. I THINK *THIS* WAS THE ATTACK, AND THAT EVERYTHING ELSE WAS JUST MEANT TO PUT OUR FIELD AGENTS WHERE THEY COULD BE TAKEN OUT.
VALENTINE SAID SOMETHING TO ME ABOUT BAD INTEL. HE ASKED ME IF WE WERE HOLDING ANYTHING BACK.
THAT'S WHY I CONTACTED YOU IN THE FIRST PLACE. I KNOW HOW YOU FEEL ABOUT ALL THAT "NEED TO KNOW" STUFF.
I CAN'T THINK OF ANYTHING PERTINENT. ALL OF THE INTEL I GATHERED FOR THIS MISSION IS IN A BRIEFCASE IN MY OFFICE, RIGHT BEHIND THE DOOR. HELP YOURSELF.
LET ME KNOW IF YOU FIND ANYTHING. I'VE GOT TO GO.
ANYTHING?
NO.
THERE'S A BRIEFCASE BEHIND THE DOOR IN WATERS' OFFICE. BRING IT DOWN TO ME. WE'RE GOING TO CHECK IT FOR ANYTHING WE MIGHT HAVE MISSED. WHOEVER WE'RE DEALING WITH MUST BE THE ULTIMATE BADASSES...

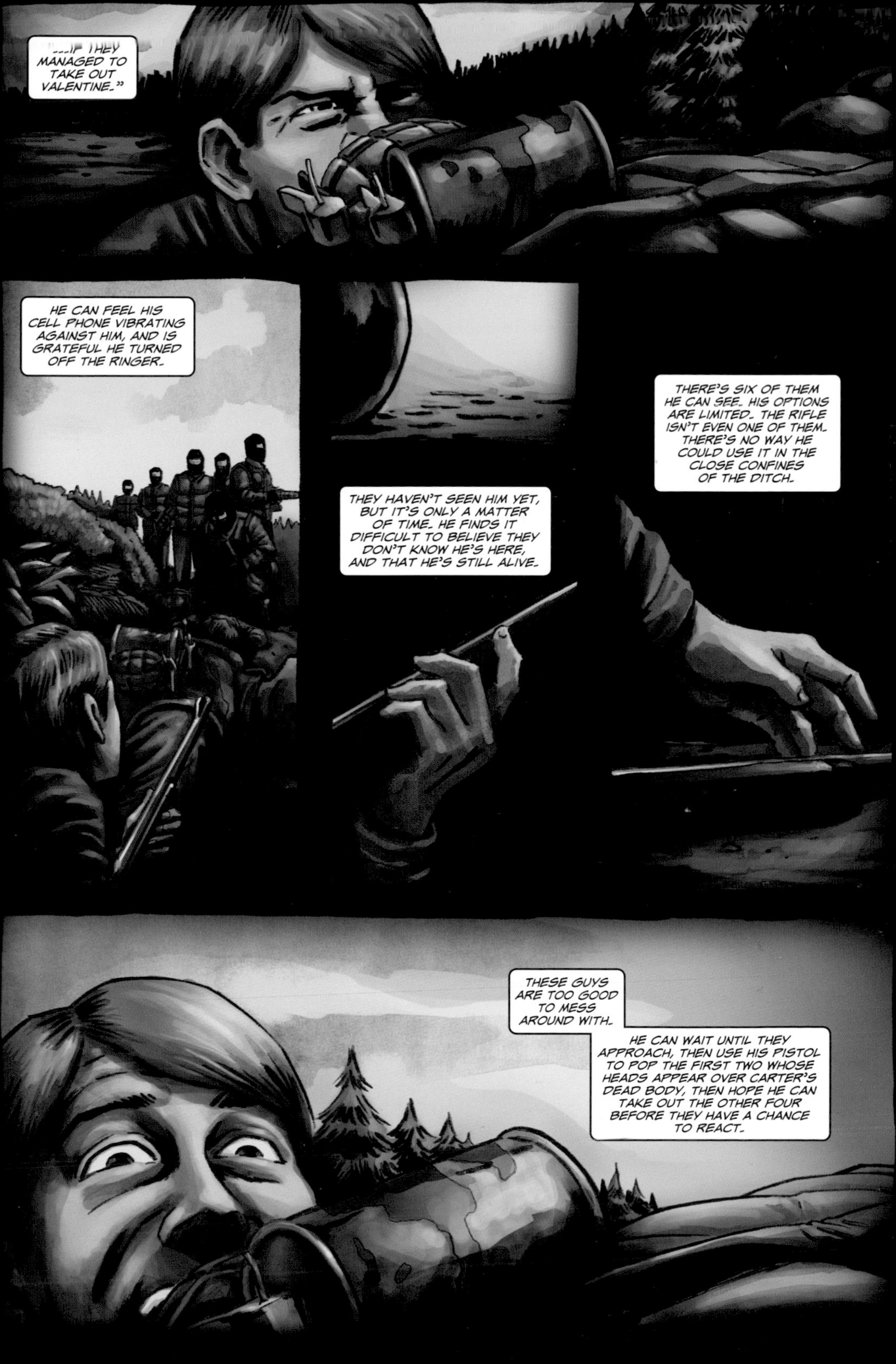
"...IF THEY MANAGED TO TAKE OUT VALENTINE."
HE CAN FEEL HIS CELL PHONE VIBRATING AGAINST HIM, AND IS GRATEFUL HE TURNED OFF THE RINGER.
THEY HAVEN'T SEEN HIM YET, BUT IT'S ONLY A MATTER OF TIME. HE FINDS IT DIFFICULT TO BELIEVE THEY DON'T KNOW HE'S HERE, AND THAT HE'S STILL ALIVE.
THERE'S SIX OF THEM HE CAN SEE. HIS OPTIONS ARE LIMITED. THE RIFLE ISN'T EVEN ONE OF THEM. THERE'S NO WAY HE COULD USE IT IN THE CLOSE CONFINES OF THE DITCH.
THESE GUYS ARE TOO GOOD TO MESS AROUND WITH.
HE CAN WAIT UNTIL THEY APPROACH, THEN USE HIS PISTOL TO POP THE FIRST TWO WHOSE HEADS APPEAR OVER CARTER'S DEAD BODY, THEN HOPE HE CAN TAKE OUT THE OTHER FOUR BEFORE THEY HAVE A CHANCE TO REACT.

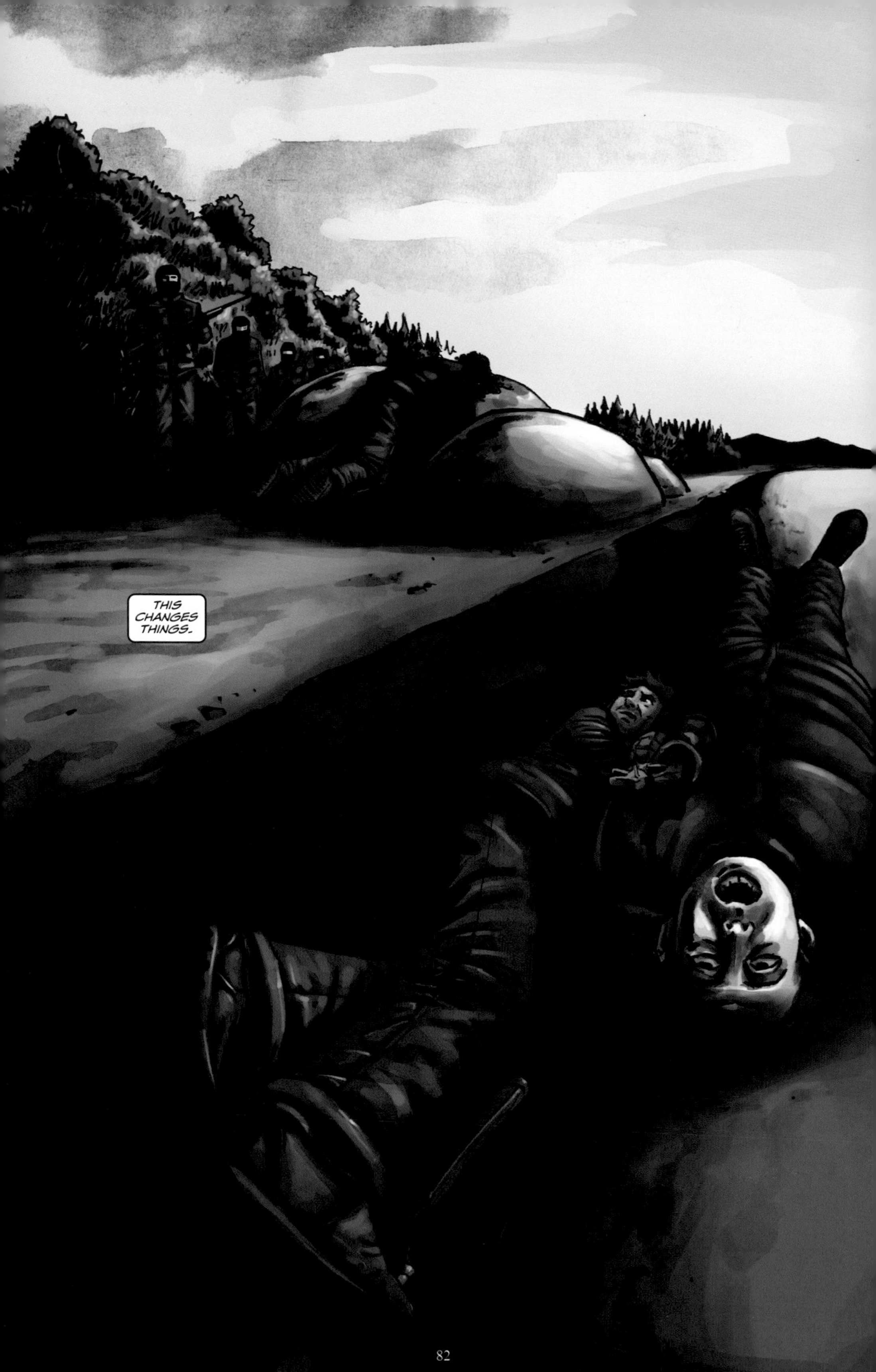
THIS CHANGES THINGS.

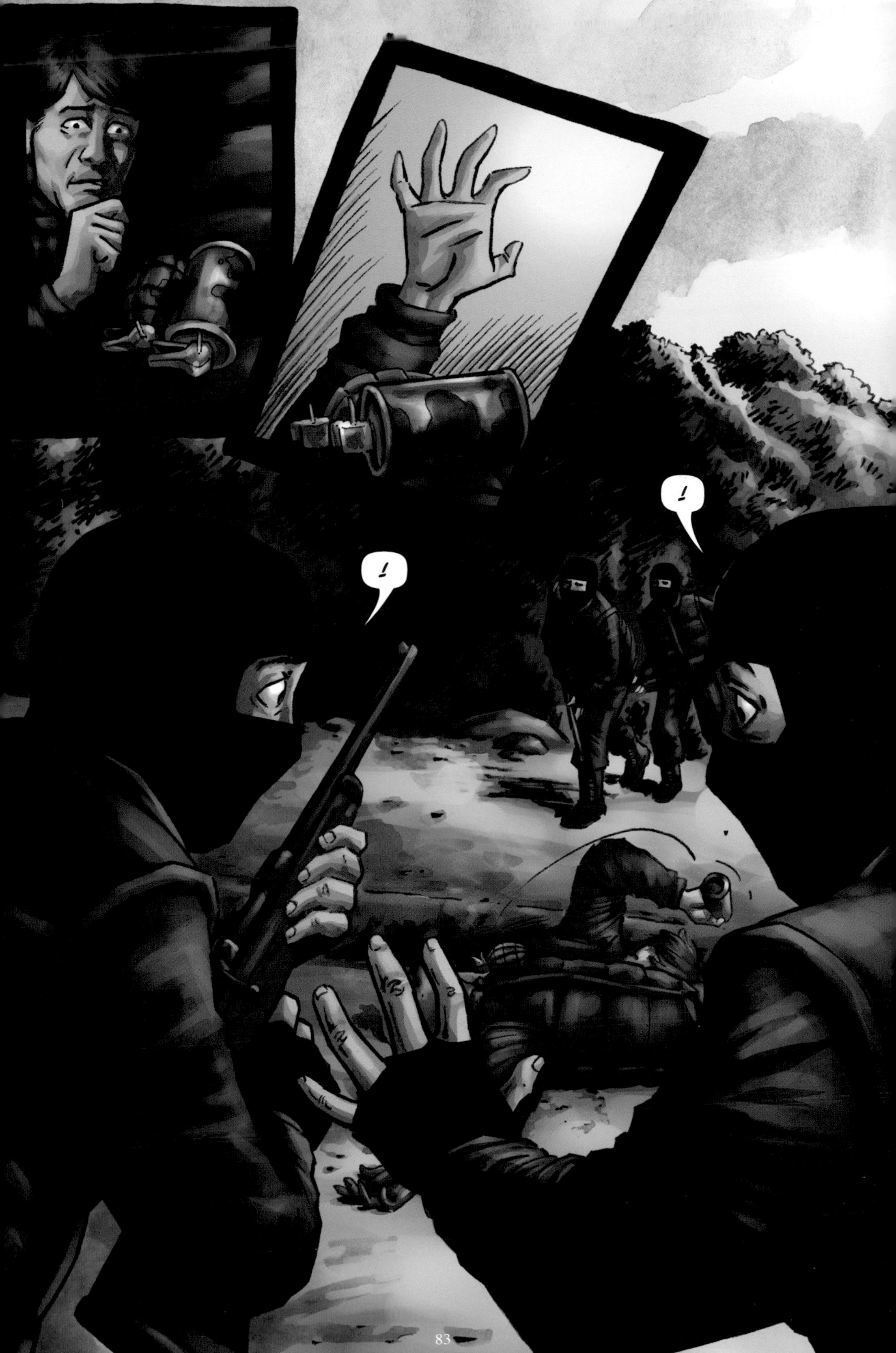
!
!

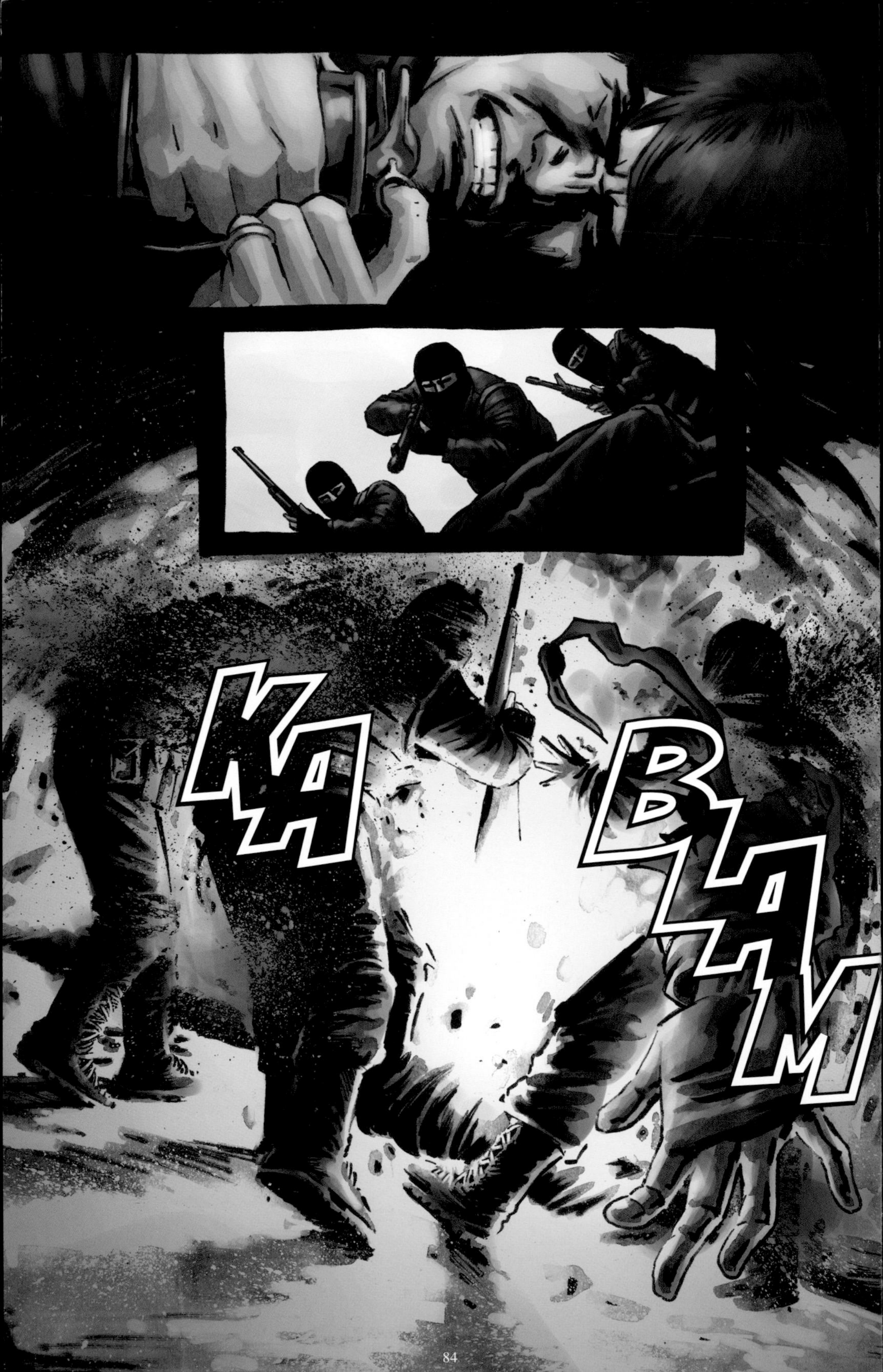
KA
BLAM

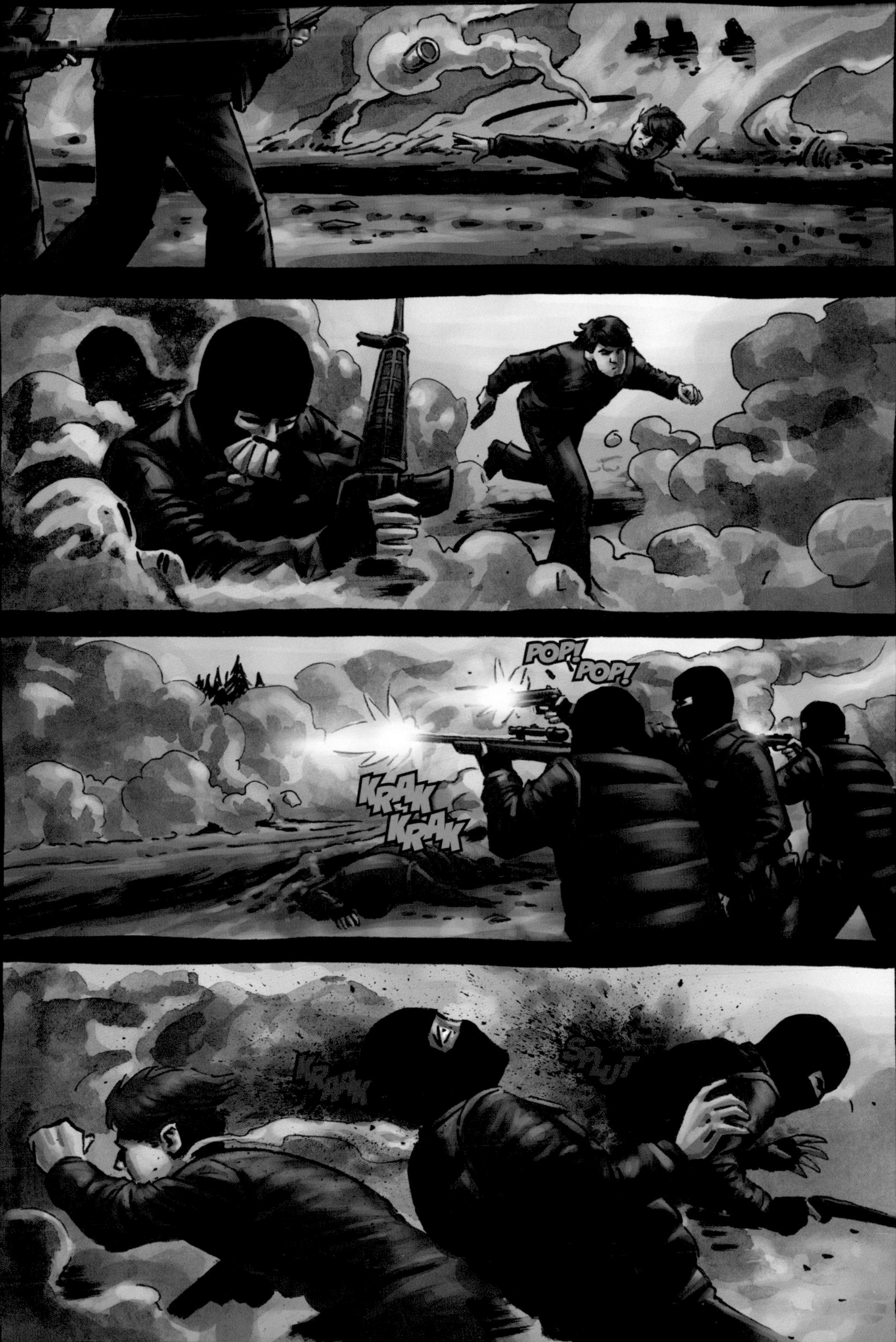
POP! POP!
KRAK KRAK
SPLUT

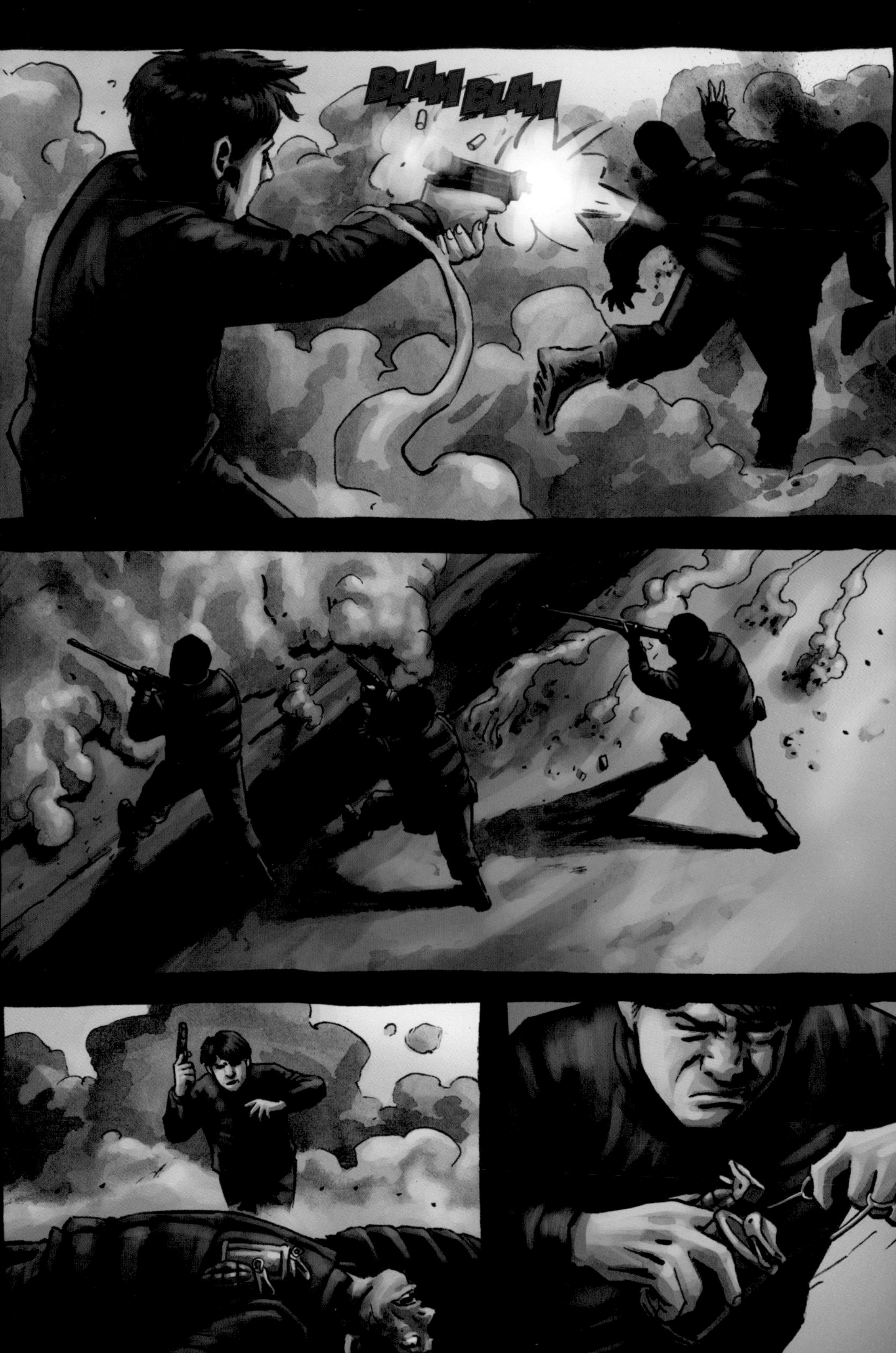
BLAM BLAM

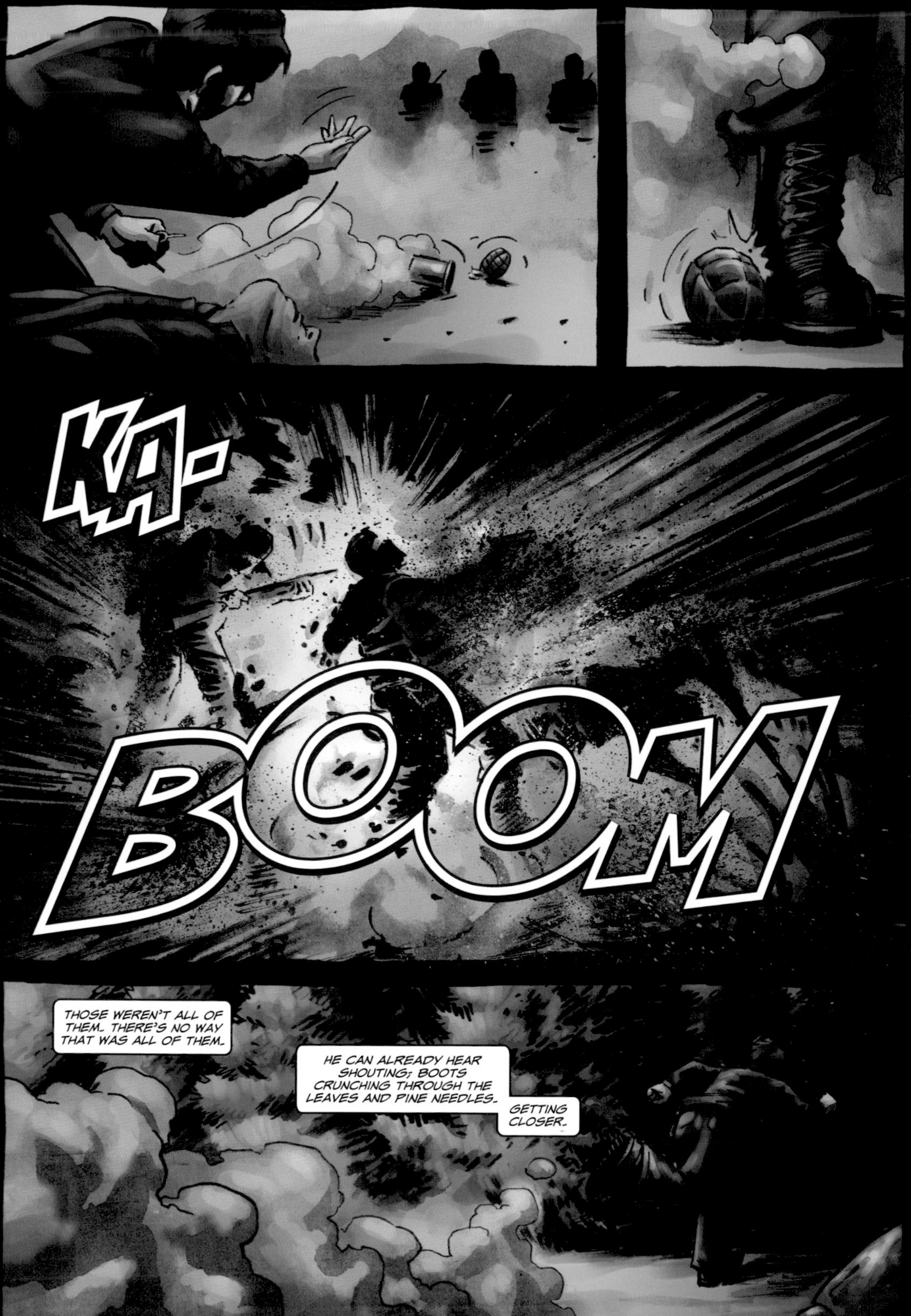
KA-
BOOM
THOSE WEREN'T ALL OF THEM. THERE'S NO WAY THAT WAS ALL OF THEM.
HE CAN ALREADY HEAR SHOUTING; BOOTS CRUNCHING THROUGH THE LEAVES AND PINE NEEDLES.
GETTING CLOSER.

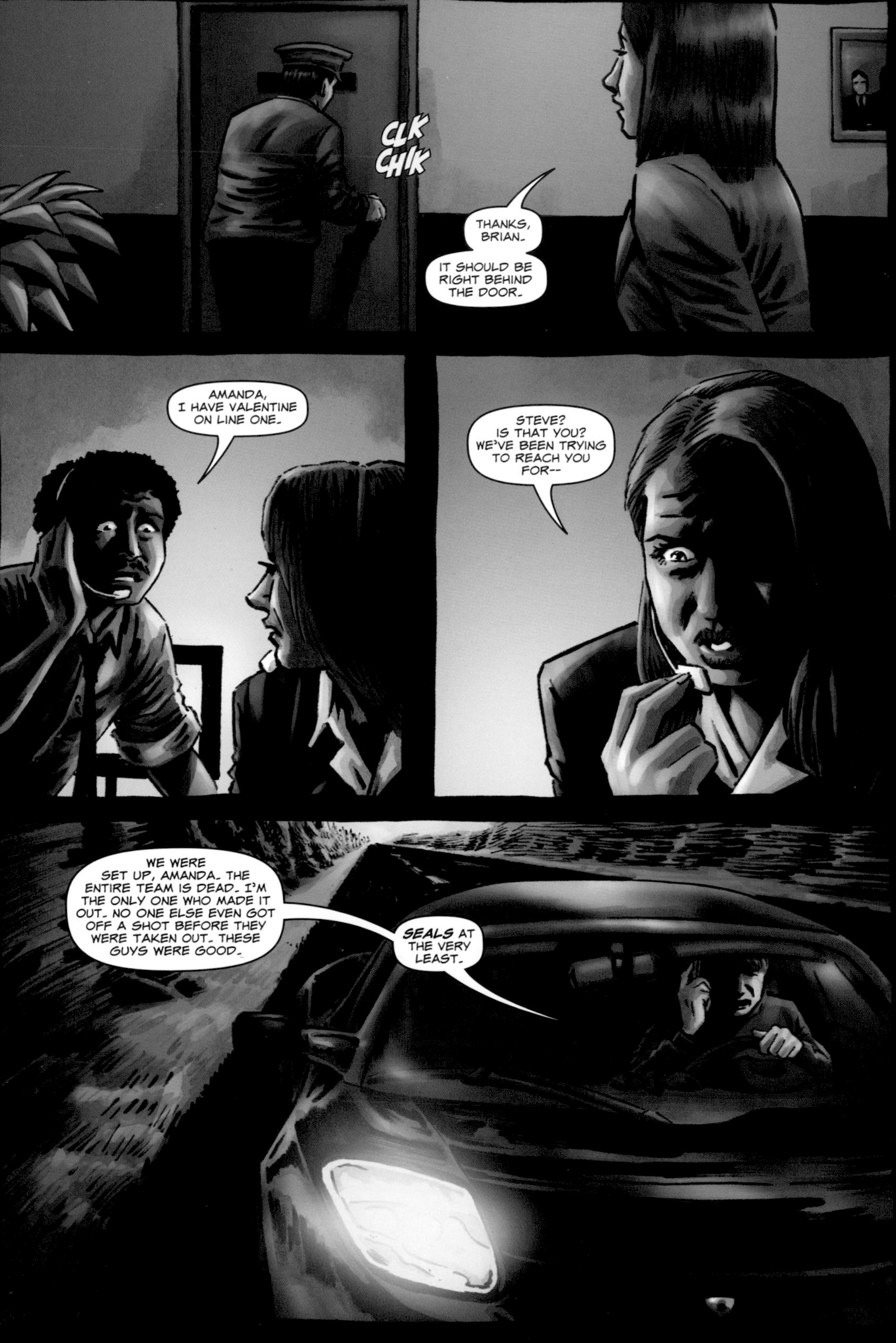
CLK
CHIK
THANKS, BRIAN.
IT SHOULD BE RIGHT BEHIND THE DOOR.
AMANDA, I HAVE VALENTINE ON LINE ONE.
STEVE? IS THAT YOU? WE'VE BEEN TRYING TO REACH YOU FOR--
WE WERE SET UP, AMANDA. THE ENTIRE TEAM IS DEAD. I'M THE ONLY ONE WHO MADE IT OUT. NO ONE ELSE EVEN GOT OFF A SHOT BEFORE THEY WERE TAKEN OUT. THESE GUYS WERE GOOD.
SEALS AT THE VERY LEAST.

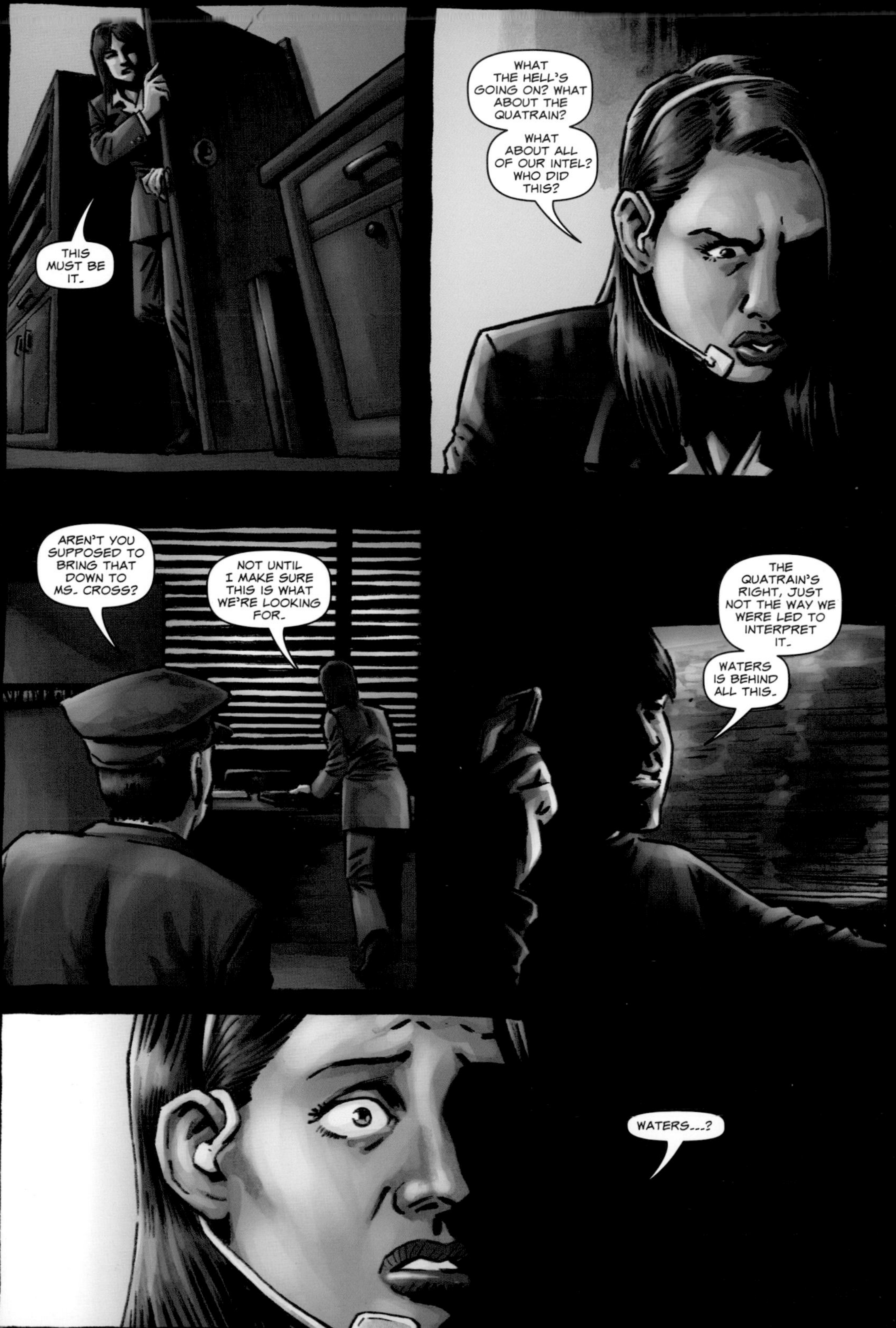
THIS MUST BE IT.
WHAT THE HELL'S GOING ON? WHAT ABOUT THE QUATRAIN?
WHAT ABOUT ALL OF OUR INTEL? WHO DID THIS?
AREN'T YOU SUPPOSED TO BRING THAT DOWN TO MS. CROSS?
NOT UNTIL I MAKE SURE THIS IS WHAT WE'RE LOOKING FOR.
THE QUATRAIN'S RIGHT, JUST NOT THE WAY WE WERE LED TO INTERPRET IT.
WATERS IS BEHIND ALL THIS.
WATERS...?

OH, GOD... STEVE, I'VE GOT TO PUT YOU ON HOLD A SECOND.

GET MARIE ON THE LINE NOW!

SHE'S IN WATERS' OFFICE!

I'M ON IT.

CLICK

DEE·DEE·DEET

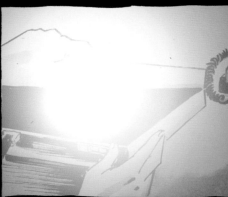

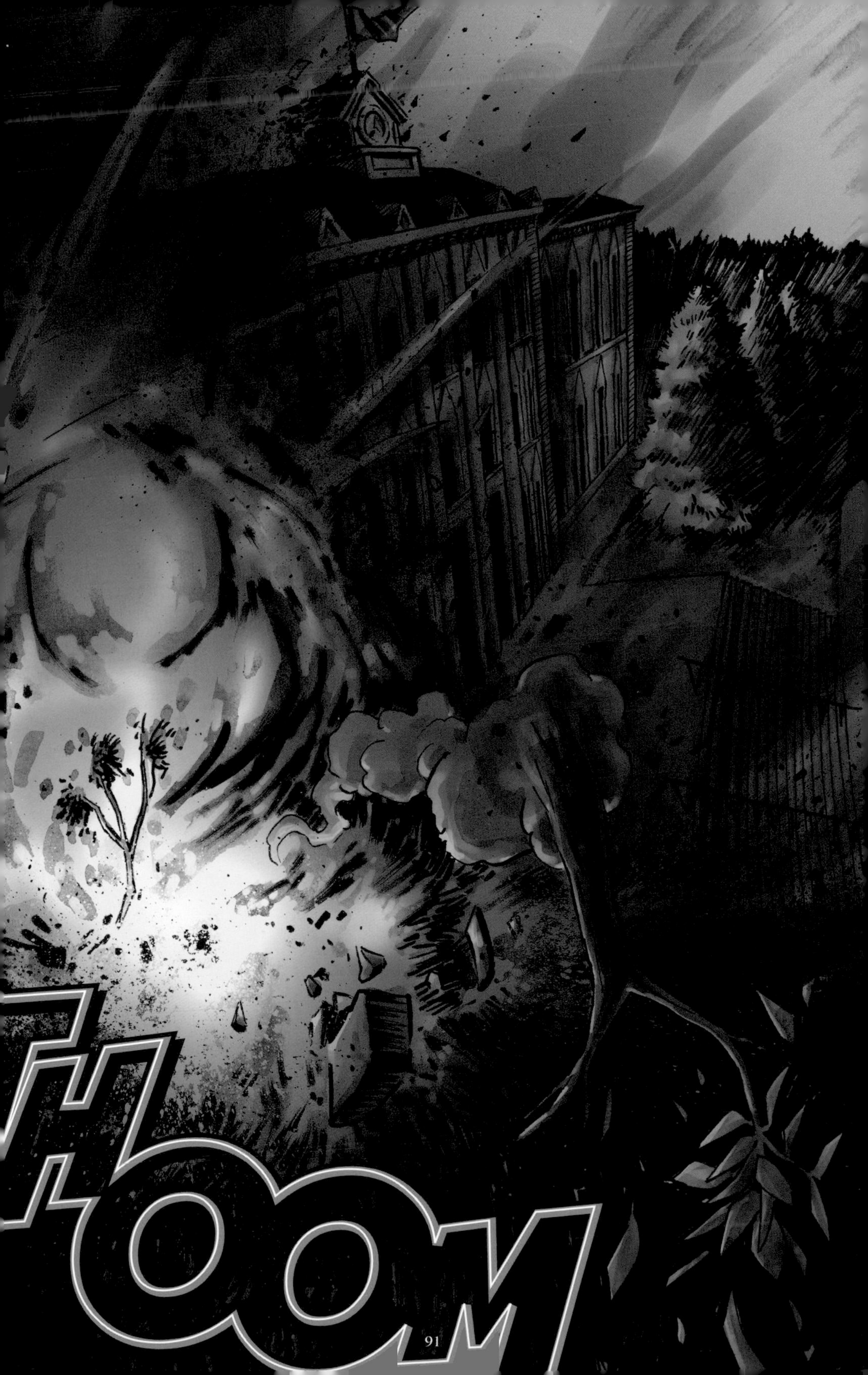
THOOM

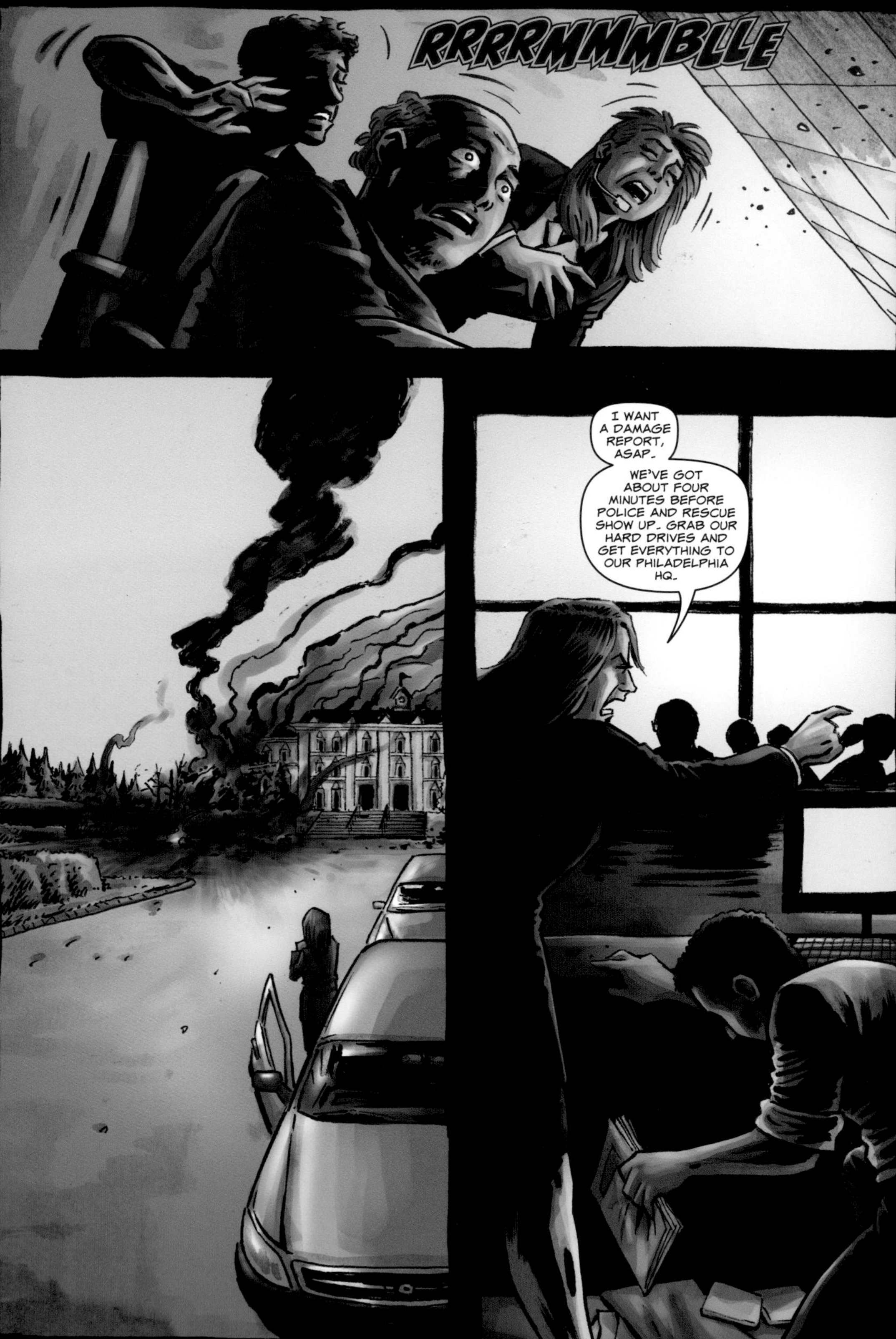
RRRRMMMMBLLE
I WANT A DAMAGE REPORT, ASAP.
WE'VE GOT ABOUT FOUR MINUTES BEFORE POLICE AND RESCUE SHOW UP. GRAB OUR HARD DRIVES AND GET EVERYTHING TO OUR PHILADELPHIA HQ.

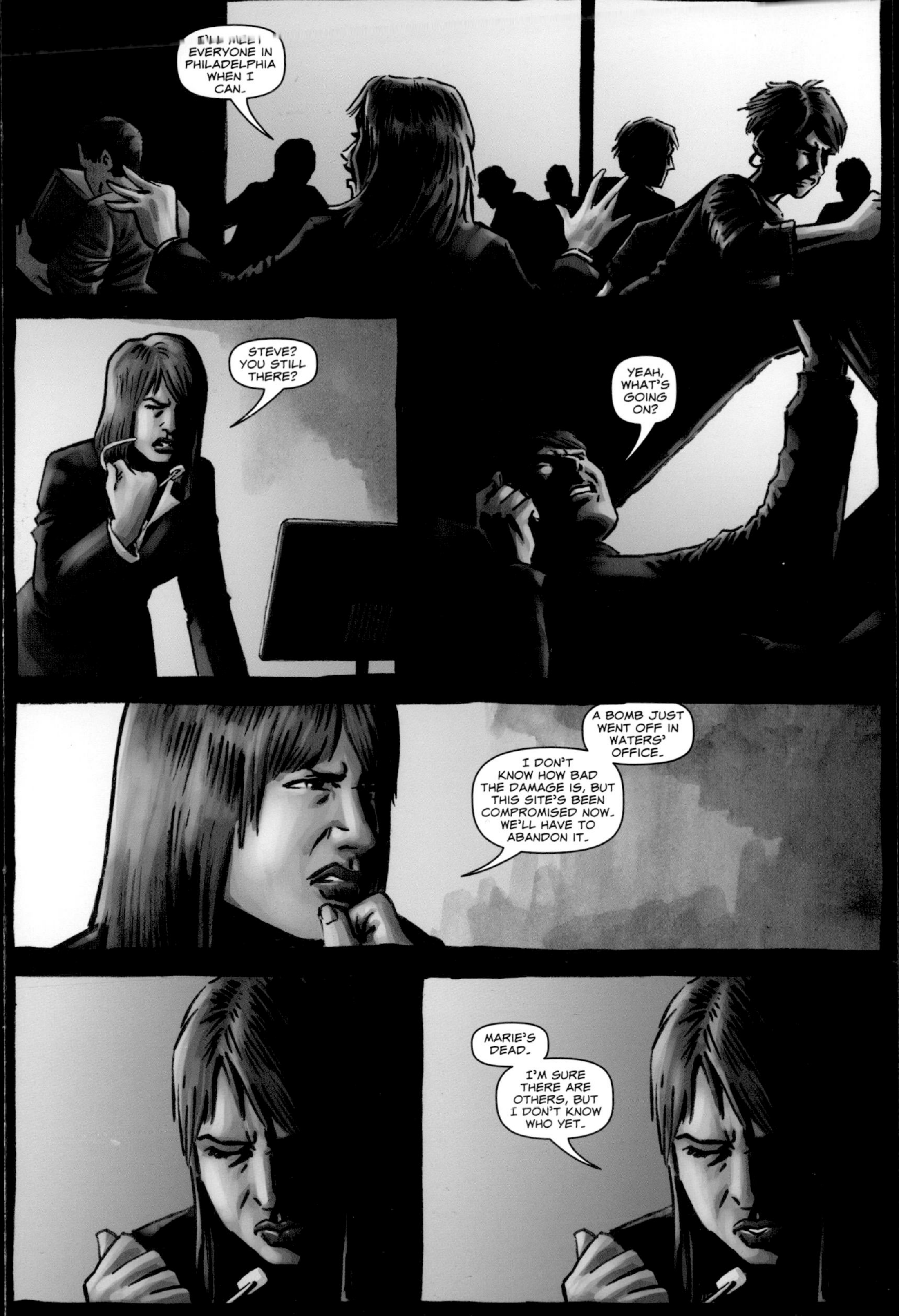
I'LL MEET EVERYONE IN PHILADELPHIA WHEN I CAN.
STEVE? YOU STILL THERE?
YEAH, WHAT'S GOING ON?
A BOMB JUST WENT OFF IN WATERS' OFFICE.
I DON'T KNOW HOW BAD THE DAMAGE IS, BUT THIS SITE'S BEEN COMPROMISED NOW. WE'LL HAVE TO ABANDON IT.
MARIE'S DEAD.
I'M SURE THERE ARE OTHERS, BUT I DON'T KNOW WHO YET.

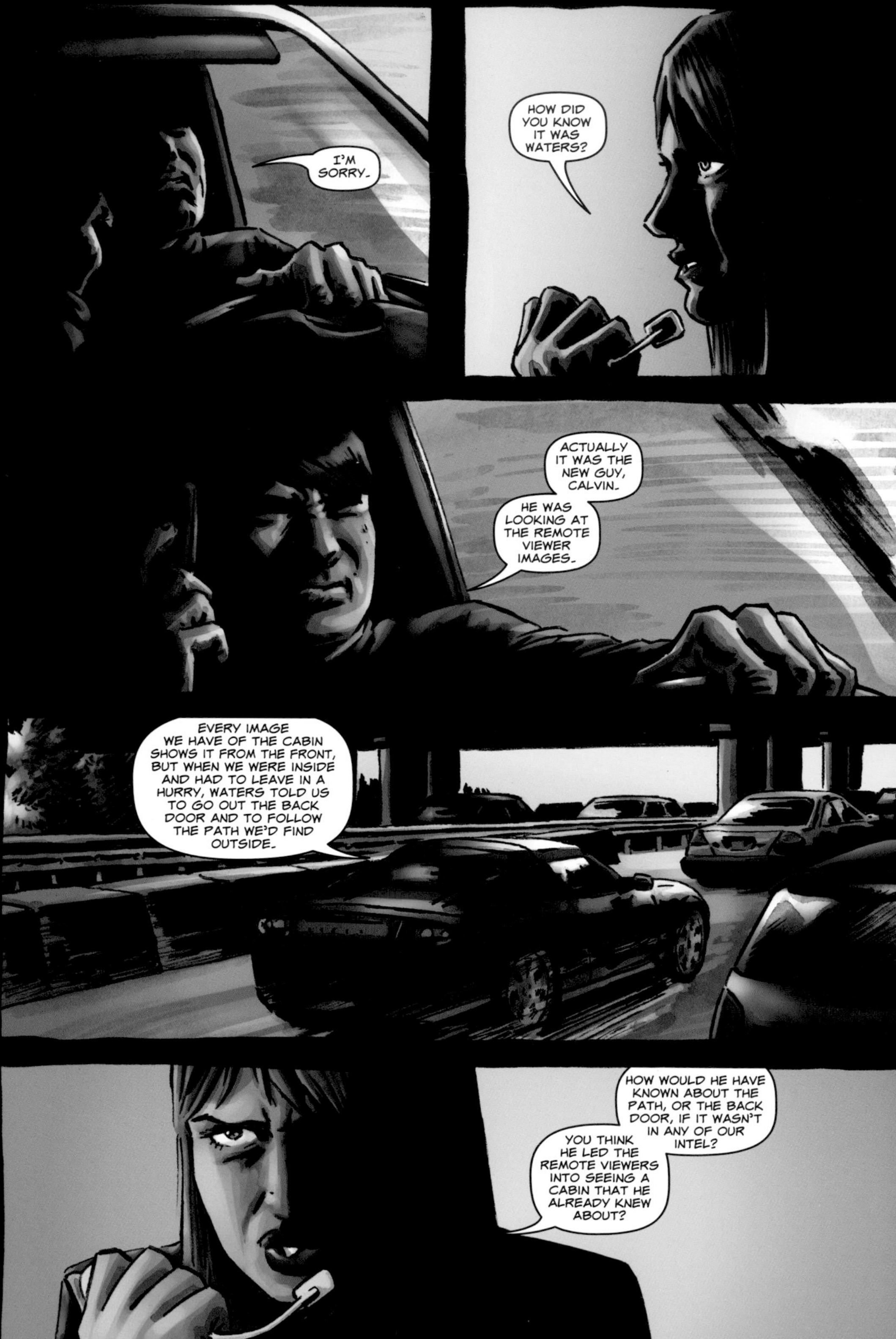
I'M SORRY.
HOW DID YOU KNOW IT WAS WATERS?
ACTUALLY IT WAS THE NEW GUY, CALVIN.
HE WAS LOOKING AT THE REMOTE VIEWER IMAGES.
EVERY IMAGE WE HAVE OF THE CABIN SHOWS IT FROM THE FRONT, BUT WHEN WE WERE INSIDE AND HAD TO LEAVE IN A HURRY, WATERS TOLD US TO GO OUT THE BACK DOOR AND TO FOLLOW THE PATH WE'D FIND OUTSIDE.
HOW WOULD HE HAVE KNOWN ABOUT THE PATH, OR THE BACK DOOR, IF IT WASN'T IN ANY OF OUR INTEL?
YOU THINK HE LED THE REMOTE VIEWERS INTO SEEING A CABIN THAT HE ALREADY KNEW ABOUT?

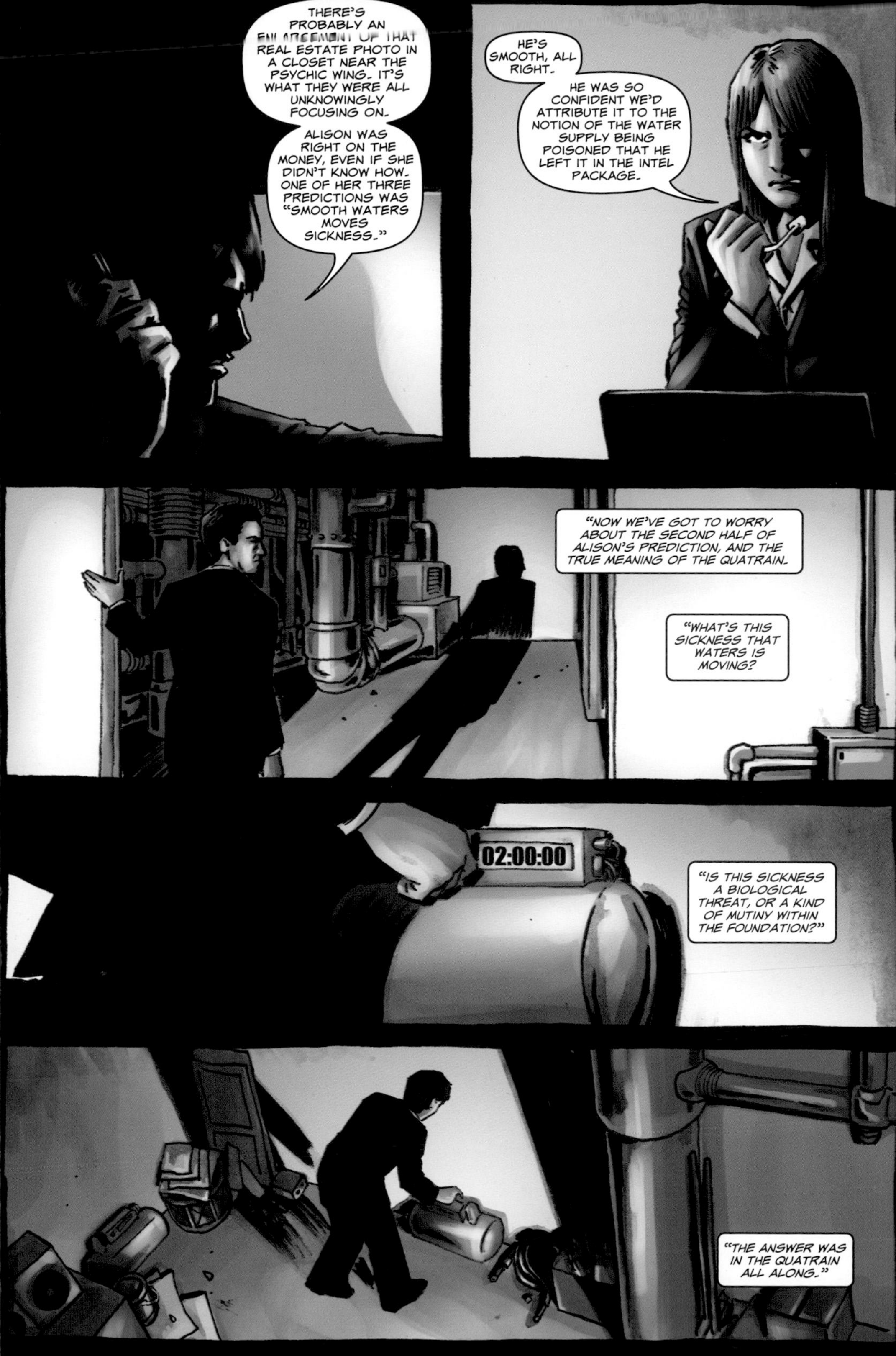
THERE'S PROBABLY AN ENLARGEMENT OF THAT REAL ESTATE PHOTO IN A CLOSET NEAR THE PSYCHIC WING. IT'S WHAT THEY WERE ALL UNKNOWINGLY FOCUSING ON.
ALISON WAS RIGHT ON THE MONEY, EVEN IF SHE DIDN'T KNOW HOW. ONE OF HER THREE PREDICTIONS WAS "SMOOTH WATERS MOVES SICKNESS."
HE'S SMOOTH, ALL RIGHT.
HE WAS SO CONFIDENT WE'D ATTRIBUTE IT TO THE NOTION OF THE WATER SUPPLY BEING POISONED THAT HE LEFT IT IN THE INTEL PACKAGE.
"NOW WE'VE GOT TO WORRY ABOUT THE SECOND HALF OF ALISON'S PREDICTION, AND THE TRUE MEANING OF THE QUATRAIN.
"WHAT'S THIS SICKNESS THAT WATERS IS MOVING?
02:00:00
"IS THIS SICKNESS A BIOLOGICAL THREAT, OR A KIND OF MUTINY WITHIN THE FOUNDATION?"
"THE ANSWER WAS IN THE QUATRAIN ALL ALONG."

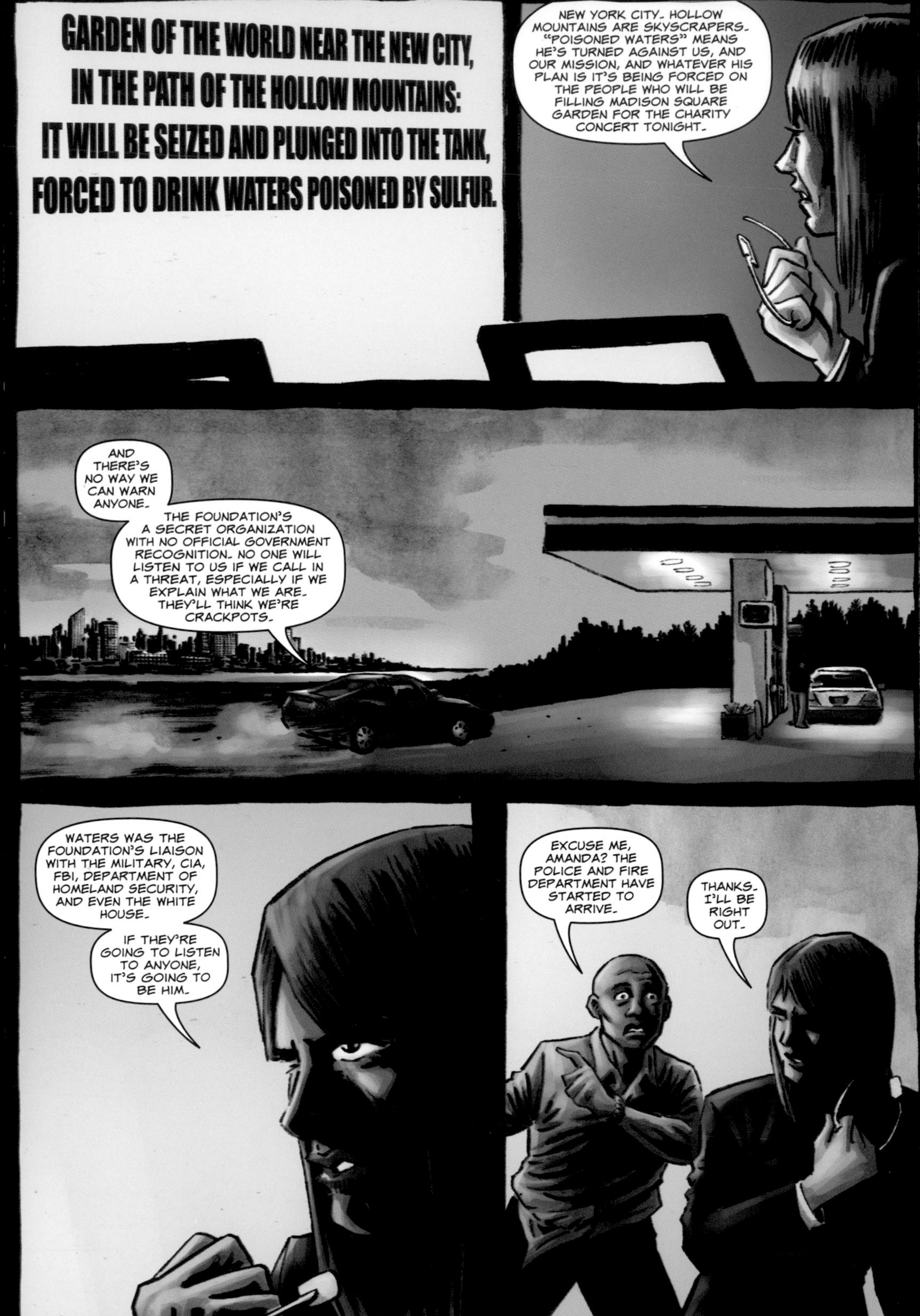
GARDEN OF THE WORLD NEAR THE NEW CITY, IN THE PATH OF THE HOLLOW MOUNTAINS: IT WILL BE SEIZED AND PLUNGED INTO THE TANK, FORCED TO DRINK WATERS POISONED BY SULFUR.
NEW YORK CITY. HOLLOW MOUNTAINS ARE SKYSCRAPERS. "POISONED WATERS" MEANS HE'S TURNED AGAINST US, AND OUR MISSION, AND WHATEVER HIS PLAN IS IT'S BEING FORCED ON THE PEOPLE WHO WILL BE FILLING MADISON SQUARE GARDEN FOR THE CHARITY CONCERT TONIGHT.
AND THERE'S NO WAY WE CAN WARN ANYONE.
THE FOUNDATION'S A SECRET ORGANIZATION WITH NO OFFICIAL GOVERNMENT RECOGNITION. NO ONE WILL LISTEN TO US IF WE CALL IN A THREAT, ESPECIALLY IF WE EXPLAIN WHAT WE ARE. THEY'LL THINK WE'RE CRACKPOTS.
WATERS WAS THE FOUNDATION'S LIAISON WITH THE MILITARY, CIA, FBI, DEPARTMENT OF HOMELAND SECURITY, AND EVEN THE WHITE HOUSE.
IF THEY'RE GOING TO LISTEN TO ANYONE, IT'S GOING TO BE HIM.
EXCUSE ME, AMANDA? THE POLICE AND FIRE DEPARTMENT HAVE STARTED TO ARRIVE.
THANKS. I'LL BE RIGHT OUT.

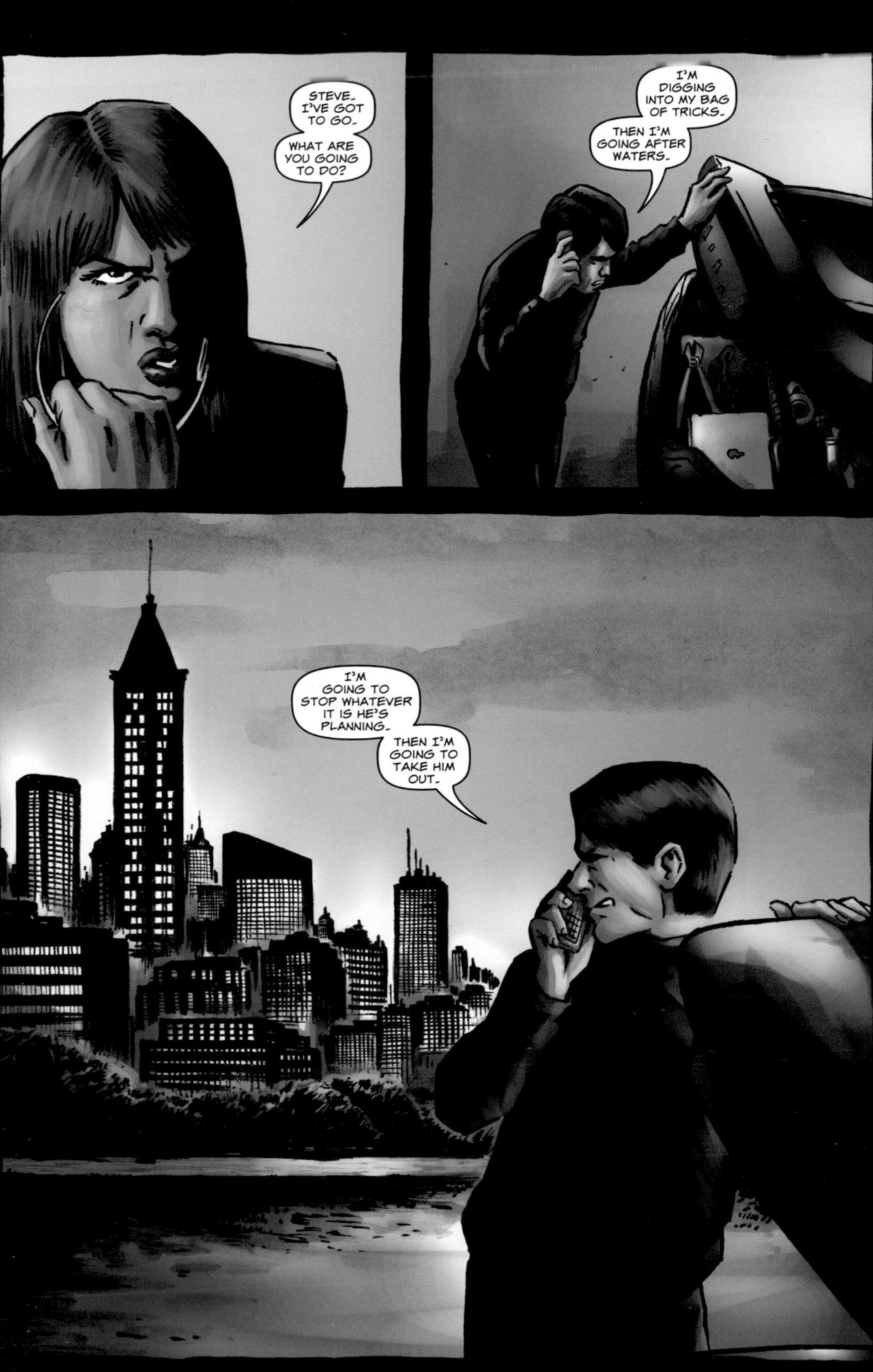
STEVE. I'VE GOT TO GO.
WHAT ARE YOU GOING TO DO?
I'M DIGGING INTO MY BAG OF TRICKS.
THEN I'M GOING AFTER WATERS.
I'M GOING TO STOP WHATEVER IT IS HE'S PLANNING.
THEN I'M GOING TO TAKE HIM OUT.

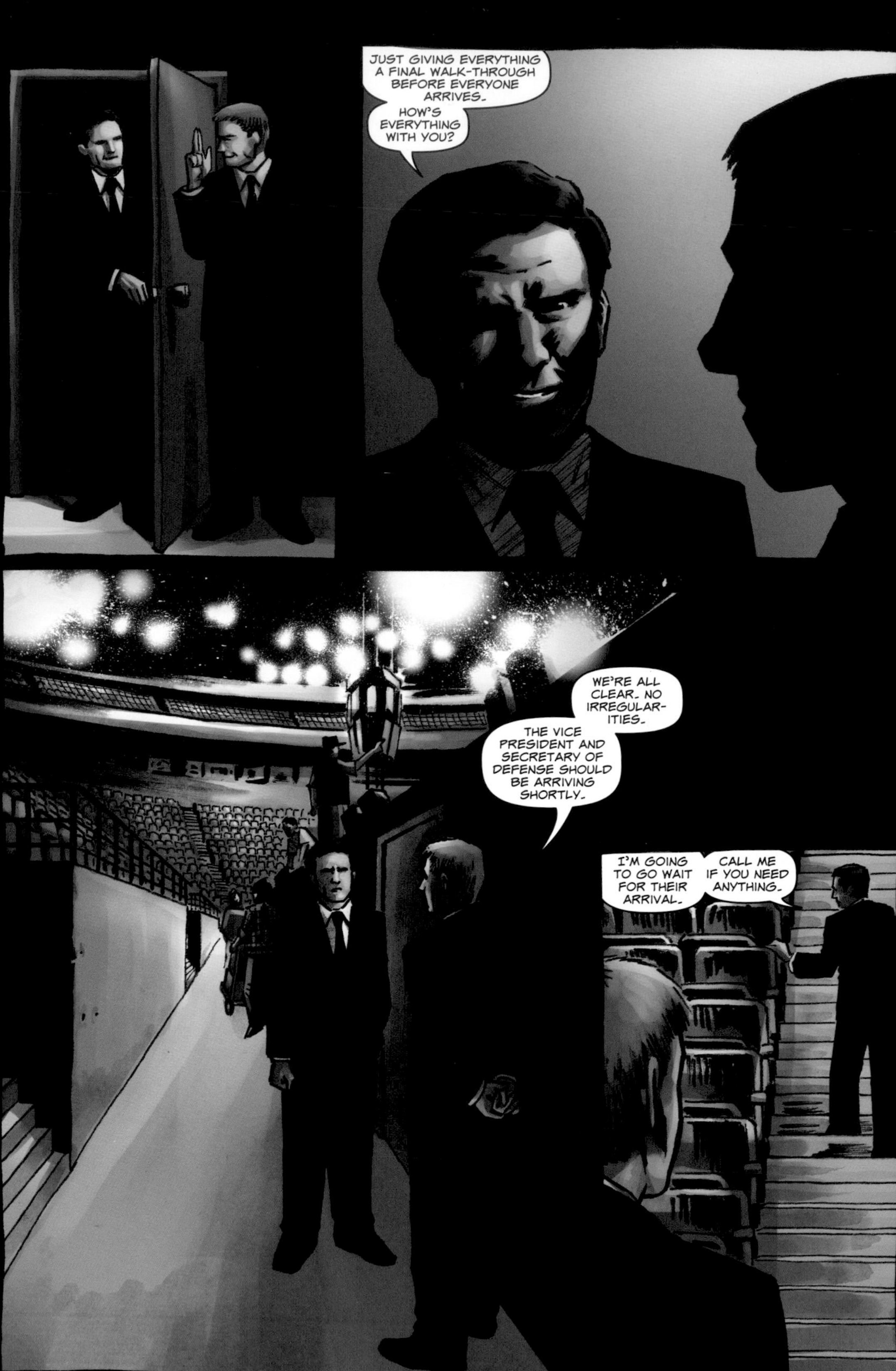
JUST GIVING EVERYTHING A FINAL WALK-THROUGH BEFORE EVERYONE ARRIVES.
HOW'S EVERYTHING WITH YOU?
WE'RE ALL CLEAR. NO IRREGULAR-ITIES.
THE VICE PRESIDENT AND SECRETARY OF DEFENSE SHOULD BE ARRIVING SHORTLY.
I'M GOING TO GO WAIT FOR THEIR ARRIVAL.
CALL ME IF YOU NEED ANYTHING.

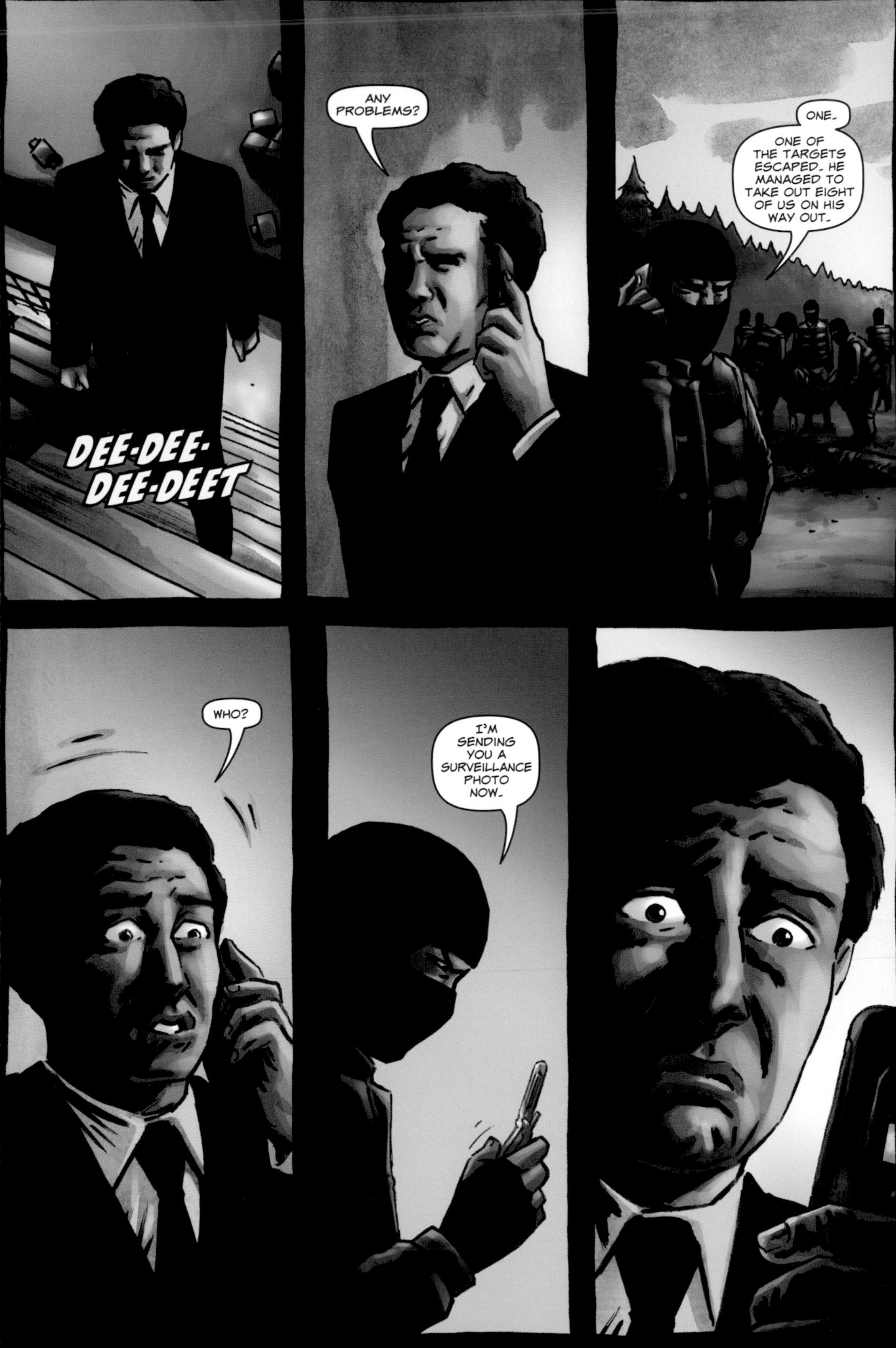

DEE-DEE-DEE-DEET
ANY PROBLEMS?
ONE.
ONE OF THE TARGETS ESCAPED. HE MANAGED TO TAKE OUT EIGHT OF US ON HIS WAY OUT.
WHO?
I'M SENDING YOU A SURVEILLANCE PHOTO NOW.

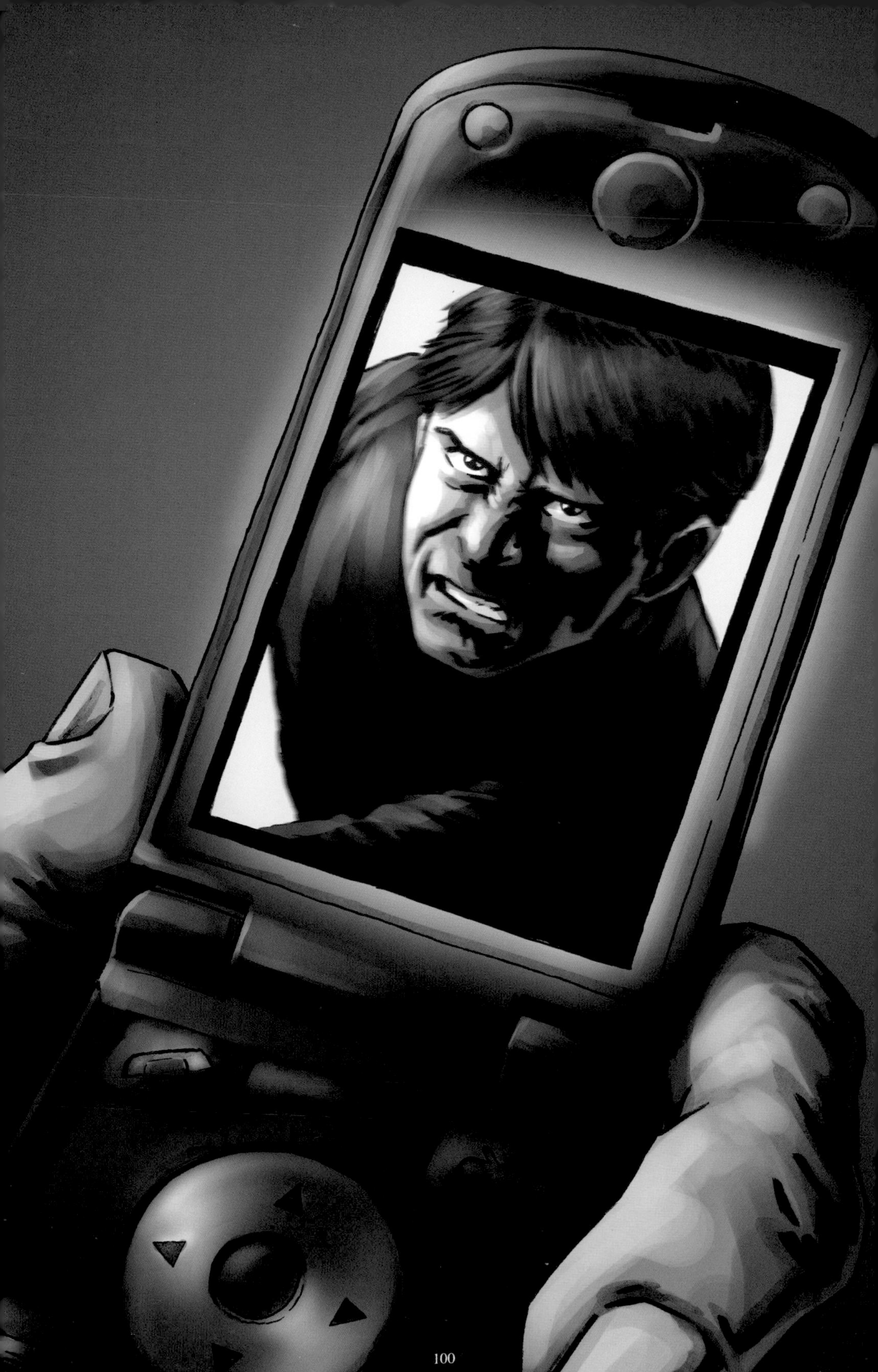

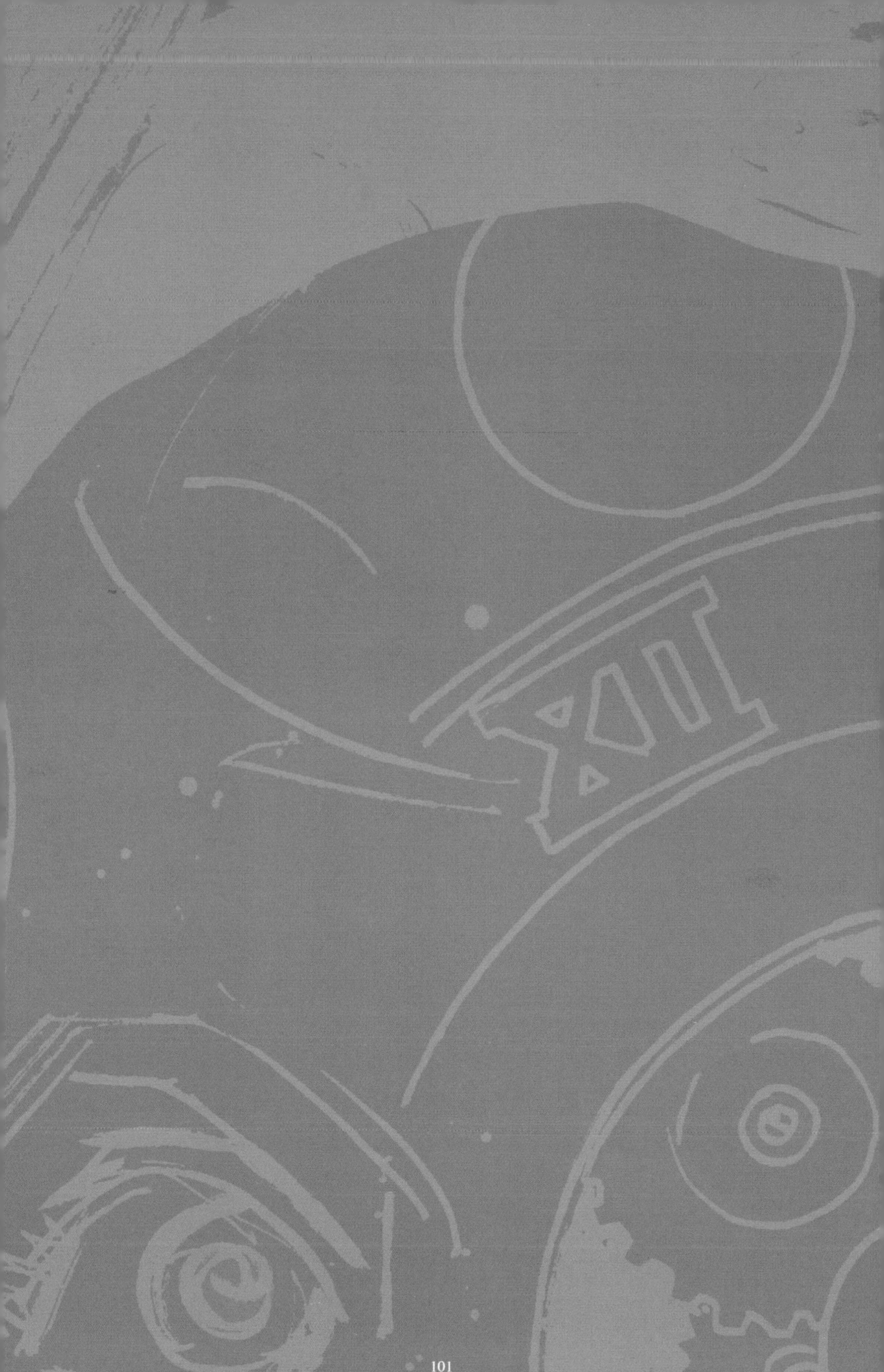
XII

Chapter Five

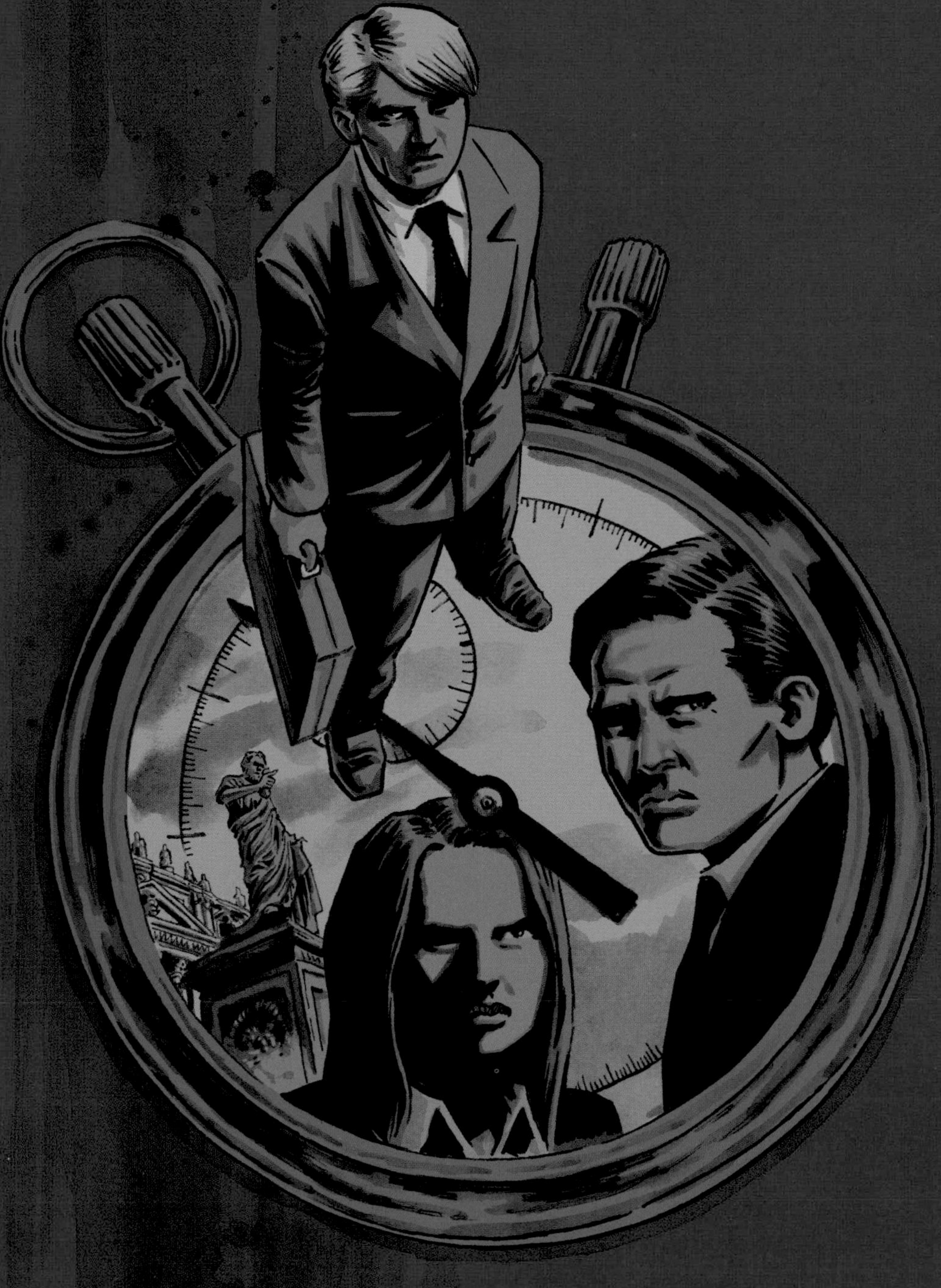

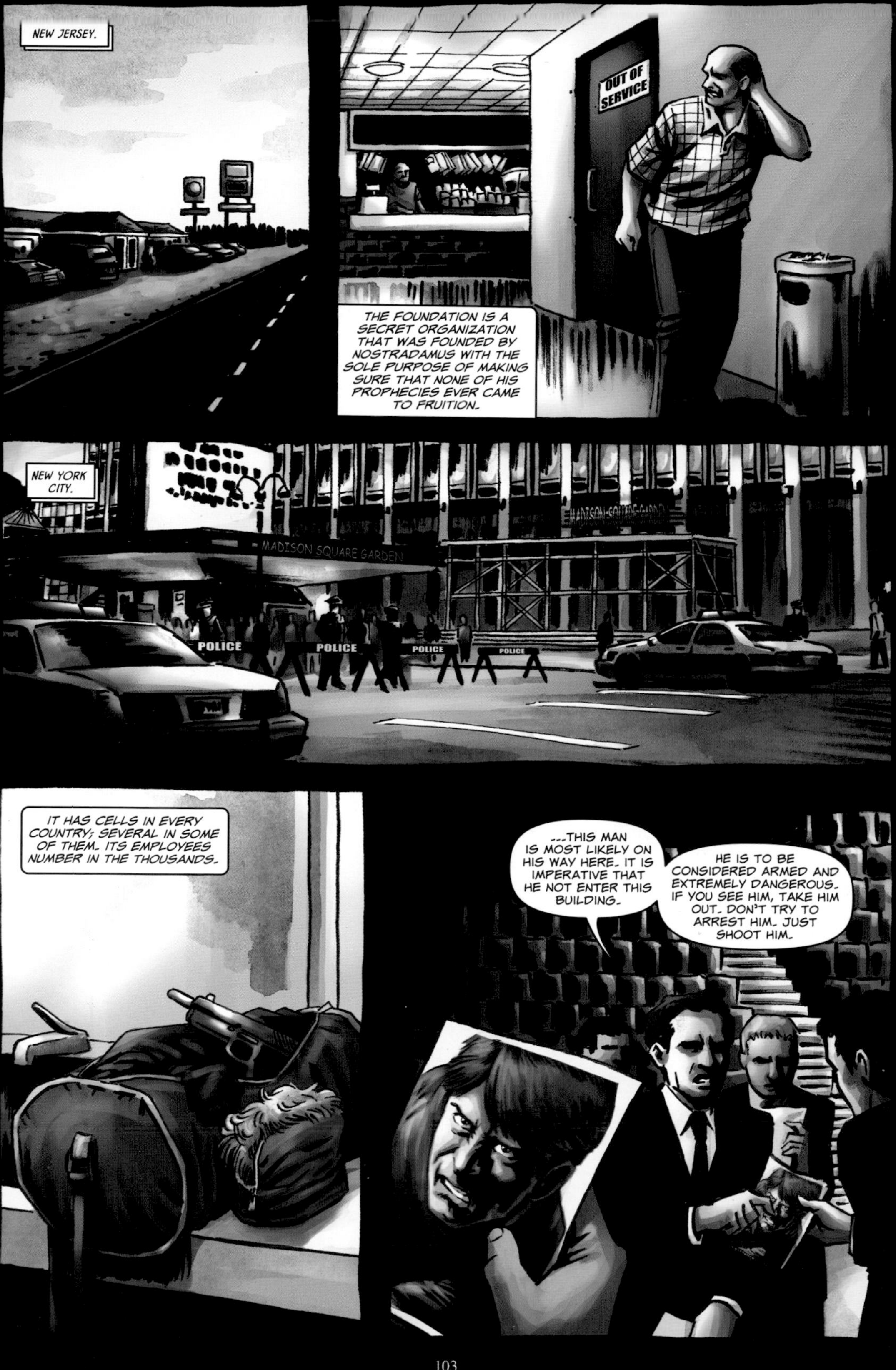
NEW JERSEY.
OUT OF SERVICE
THE FOUNDATION IS A SECRET ORGANIZATION THAT WAS FOUNDED BY NOSTRADAMUS WITH THE SOLE PURPOSE OF MAKING SURE THAT NONE OF HIS PROPHECIES EVER CAME TO FRUITION.
NEW YORK CITY.
MADISON SQUARE GARDEN
POLICE
POLICE
POLICE
POLICE
IT HAS CELLS IN EVERY COUNTRY; SEVERAL IN SOME OF THEM. ITS EMPLOYEES NUMBER IN THE THOUSANDS.
...THIS MAN IS MOST LIKELY ON HIS WAY HERE. IT IS IMPERATIVE THAT HE NOT ENTER THIS BUILDING.
HE IS TO BE CONSIDERED ARMED AND EXTREMELY DANGEROUS. IF YOU SEE HIM, TAKE HIM OUT. DON'T TRY TO ARREST HIM. JUST SHOOT HIM.

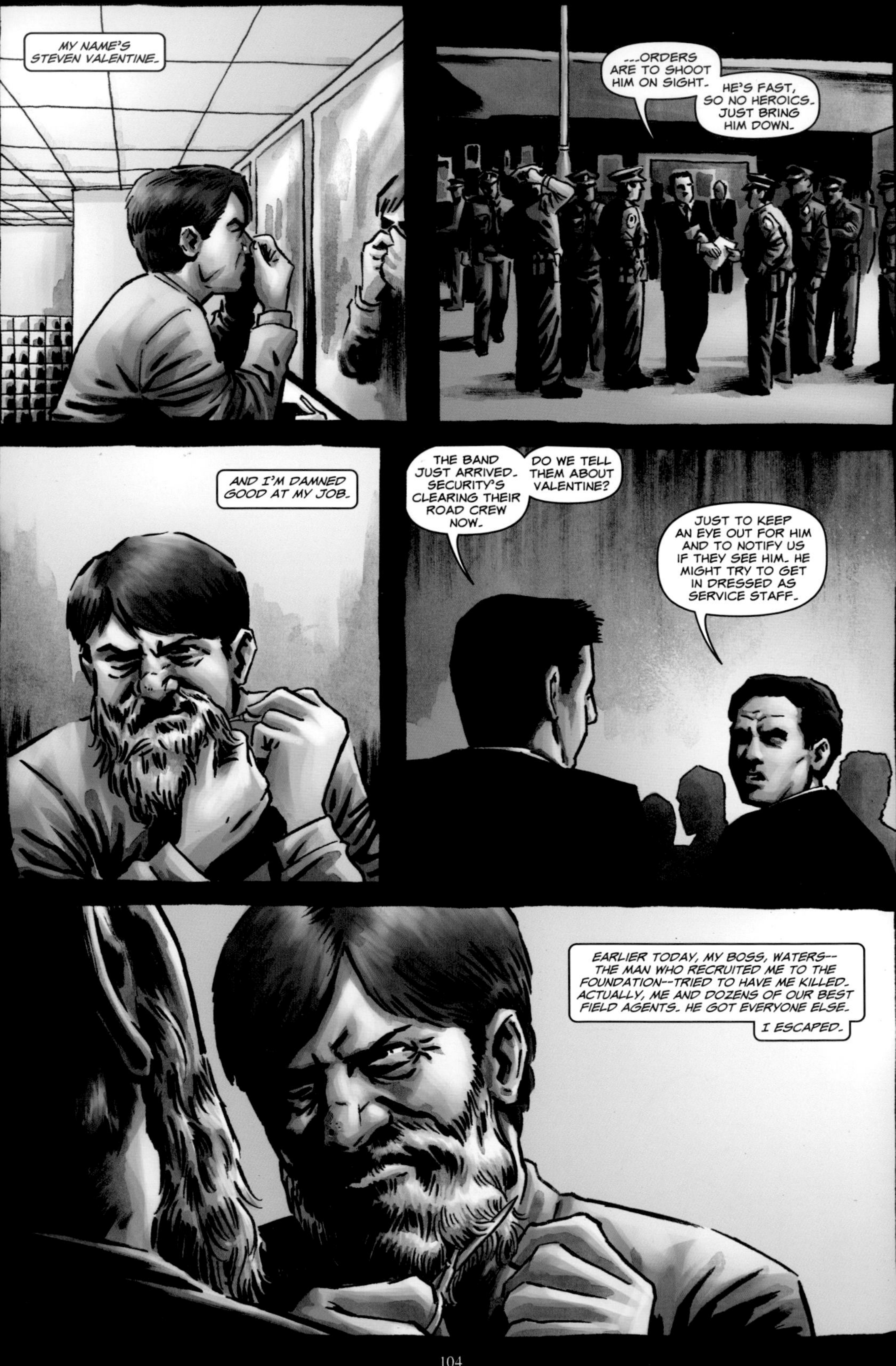
MY NAME'S STEVEN VALENTINE.
...ORDERS ARE TO SHOOT HIM ON SIGHT.
HE'S FAST, SO NO HEROICS. JUST BRING HIM DOWN.
AND I'M DAMNED GOOD AT MY JOB.
THE BAND JUST ARRIVED. SECURITY'S CLEARING THEIR ROAD CREW NOW.
DO WE TELL THEM ABOUT VALENTINE?
JUST TO KEEP AN EYE OUT FOR HIM AND TO NOTIFY US IF THEY SEE HIM. HE MIGHT TRY TO GET IN DRESSED AS SERVICE STAFF.
EARLIER TODAY, MY BOSS, WATERS-- THE MAN WHO RECRUITED ME TO THE FOUNDATION--TRIED TO HAVE ME KILLED. ACTUALLY, ME AND DOZENS OF OUR BEST FIELD AGENTS. HE GOT EVERYONE ELSE.
I ESCAPED.

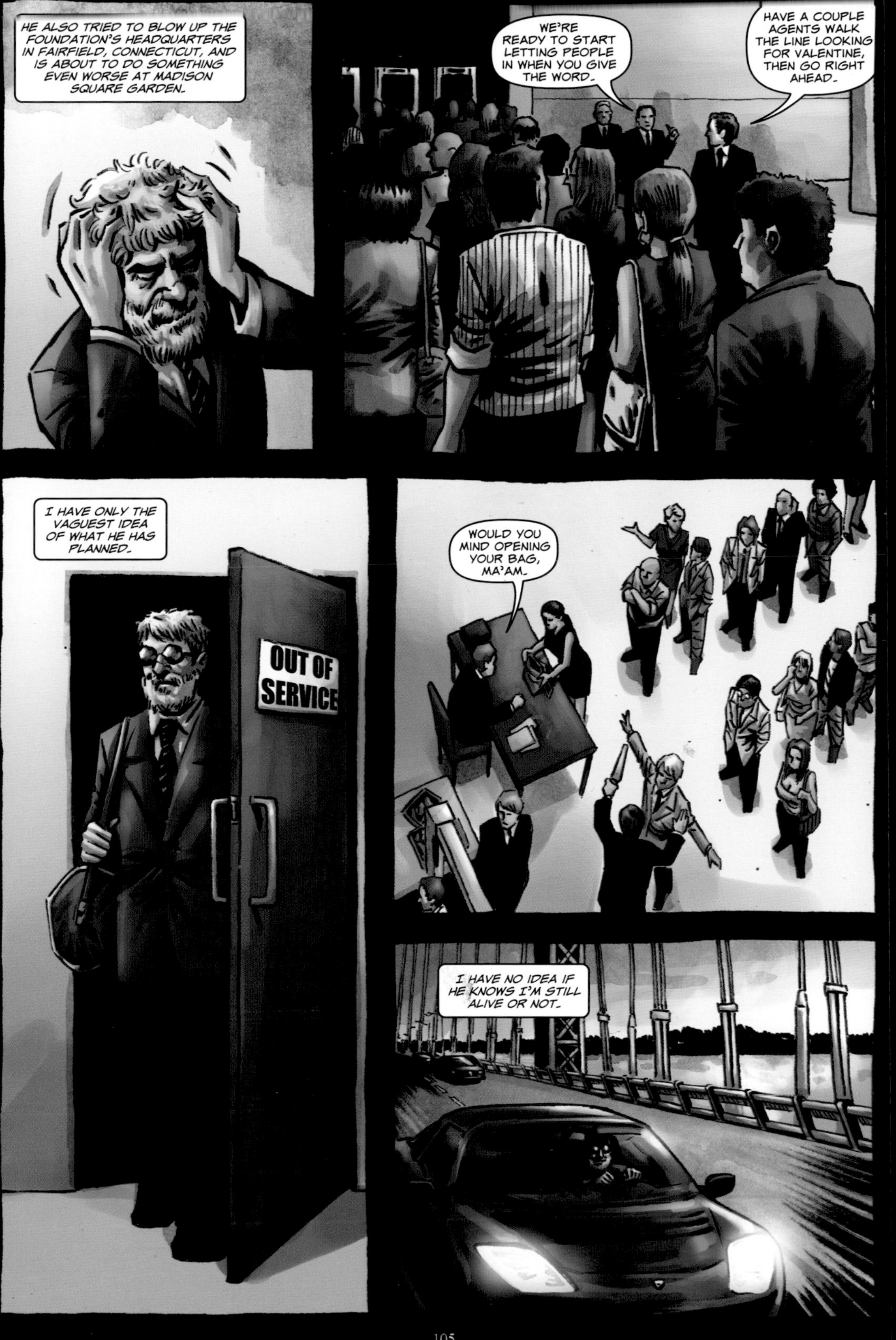
HE ALSO TRIED TO BLOW UP THE FOUNDATION'S HEADQUARTERS IN FAIRFIELD, CONNECTICUT, AND IS ABOUT TO DO SOMETHING EVEN WORSE AT MADISON SQUARE GARDEN.
WE'RE READY TO START LETTING PEOPLE IN WHEN YOU GIVE THE WORD.
HAVE A COUPLE AGENTS WALK THE LINE LOOKING FOR VALENTINE, THEN GO RIGHT AHEAD.
I HAVE ONLY THE VAGUEST IDEA OF WHAT HE HAS PLANNED.
OUT OF SERVICE
WOULD YOU MIND OPENING YOUR BAG, MA'AM.
I HAVE NO IDEA IF HE KNOWS I'M STILL ALIVE OR NOT.

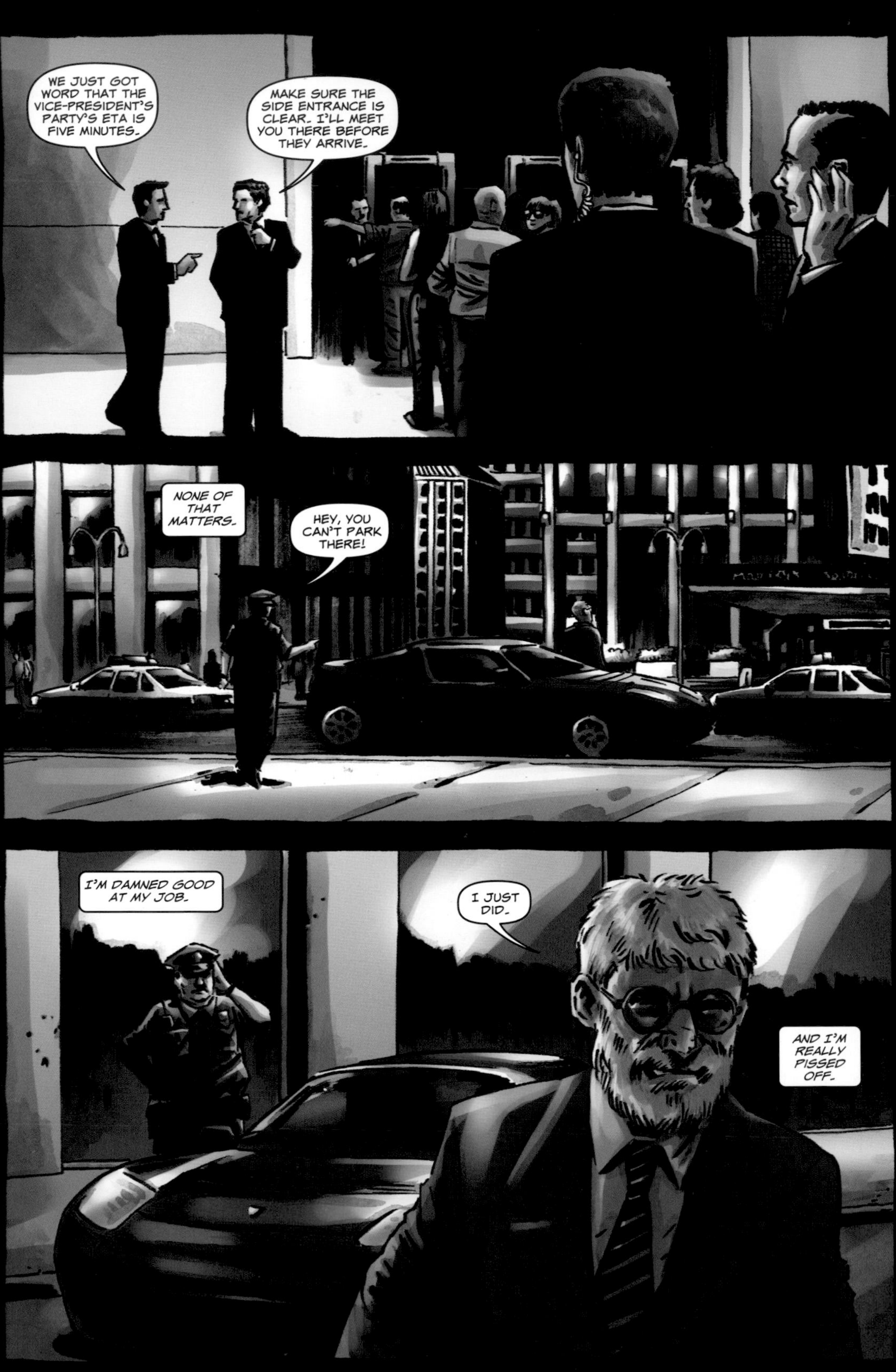
WE JUST GOT WORD THAT THE VICE-PRESIDENT'S PARTY'S ETA IS FIVE MINUTES.
MAKE SURE THE SIDE ENTRANCE IS CLEAR. I'LL MEET YOU THERE BEFORE THEY ARRIVE.
NONE OF THAT MATTERS.
HEY, YOU CAN'T PARK THERE!
I'M DAMNED GOOD AT MY JOB.
I JUST DID.
AND I'M REALLY PISSED OFF.

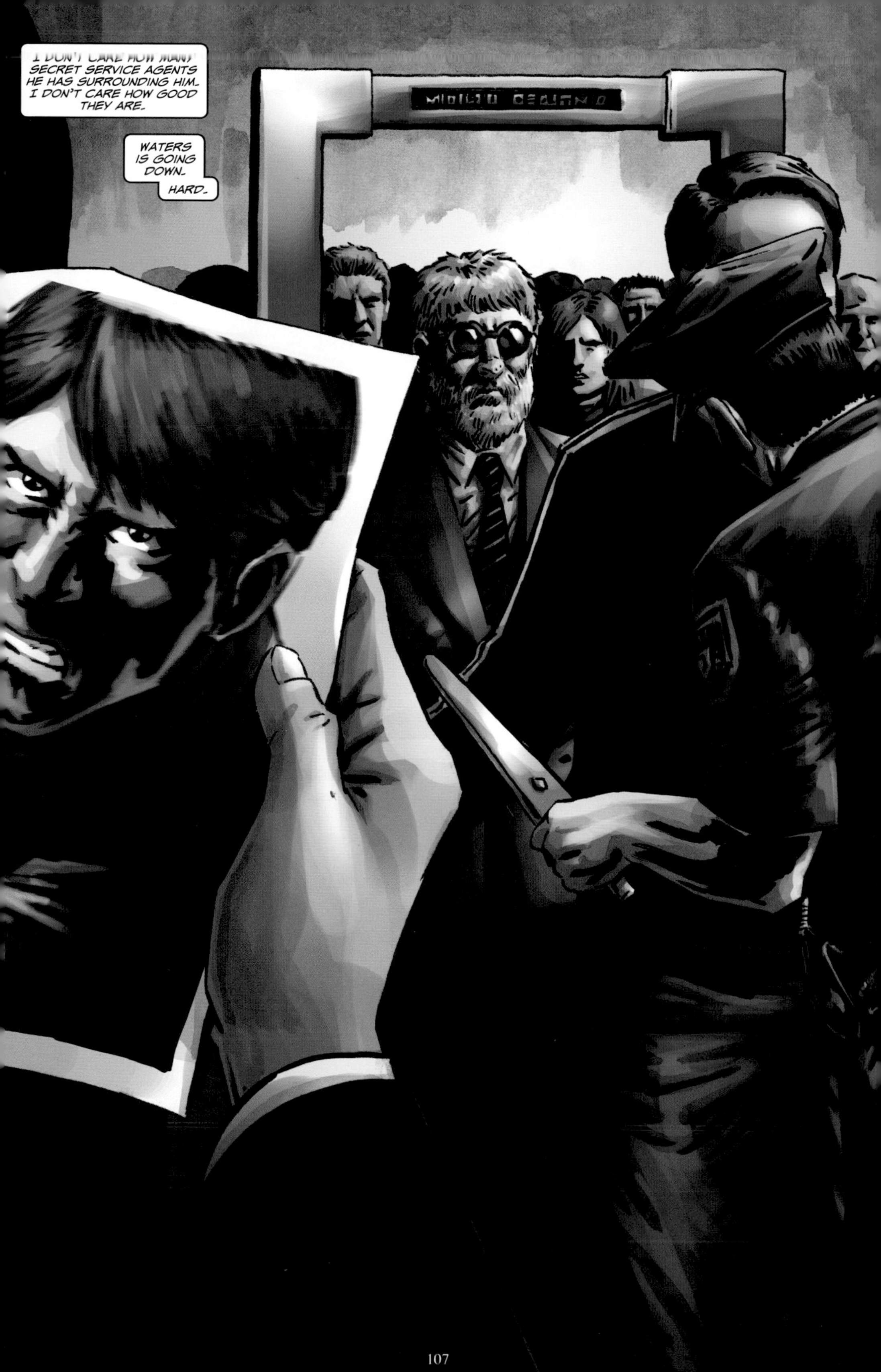
I DON'T CARE HOW MANY SECRET SERVICE AGENTS HE HAS SURROUNDING HIM. I DON'T CARE HOW GOOD THEY ARE.
WATERS IS GOING DOWN.
HARD.

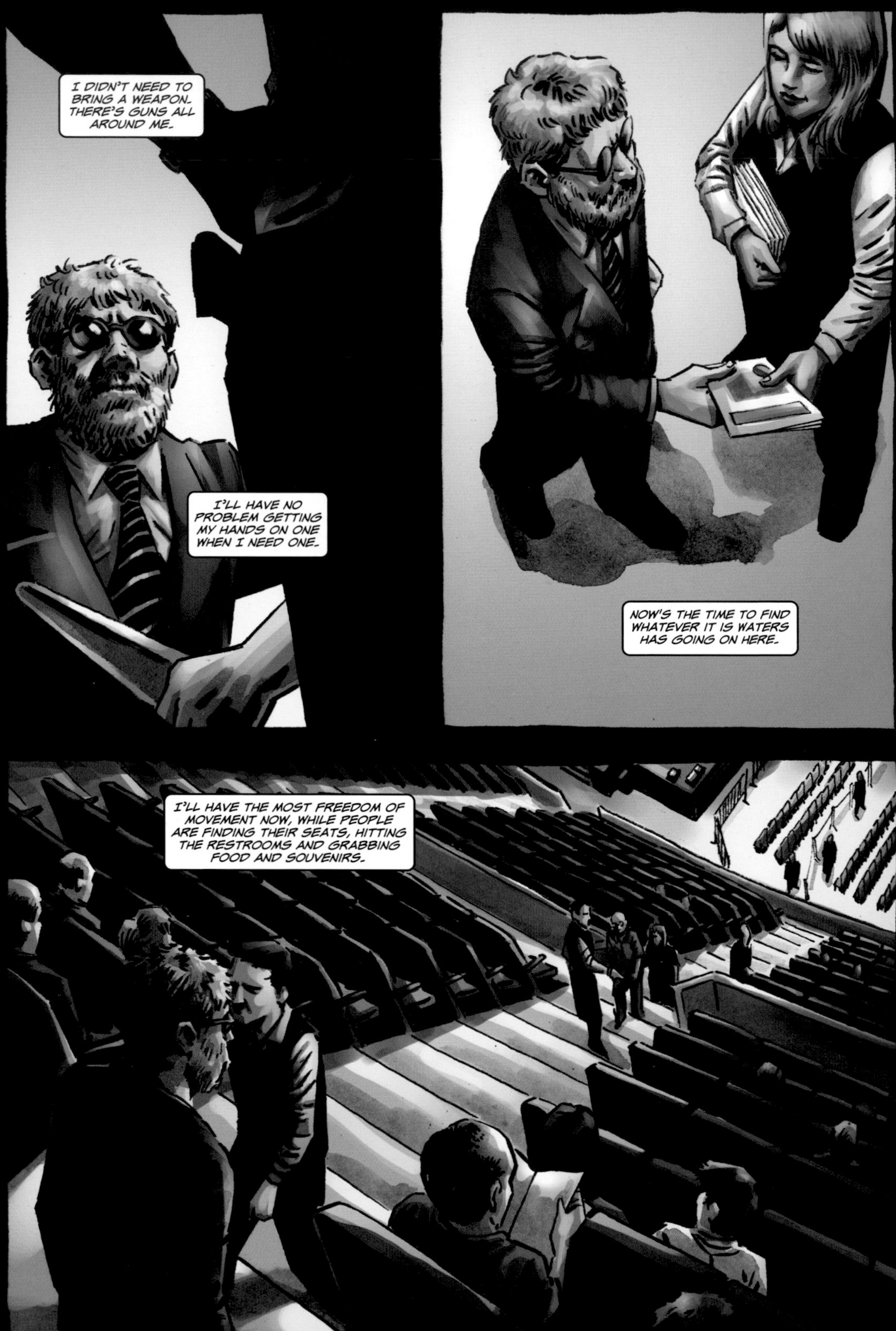

I DIDN'T NEED TO BRING A WEAPON. THERE'S GUNS ALL AROUND ME.
I'LL HAVE NO PROBLEM GETTING MY HANDS ON ONE WHEN I NEED ONE.
NOW'S THE TIME TO FIND WHATEVER IT IS WATERS HAS GOING ON HERE.
I'LL HAVE THE MOST FREEDOM OF MOVEMENT NOW, WHILE PEOPLE ARE FINDING THEIR SEATS, HITTING THE RESTROOMS AND GRABBING FOOD AND SOUVENIRS.

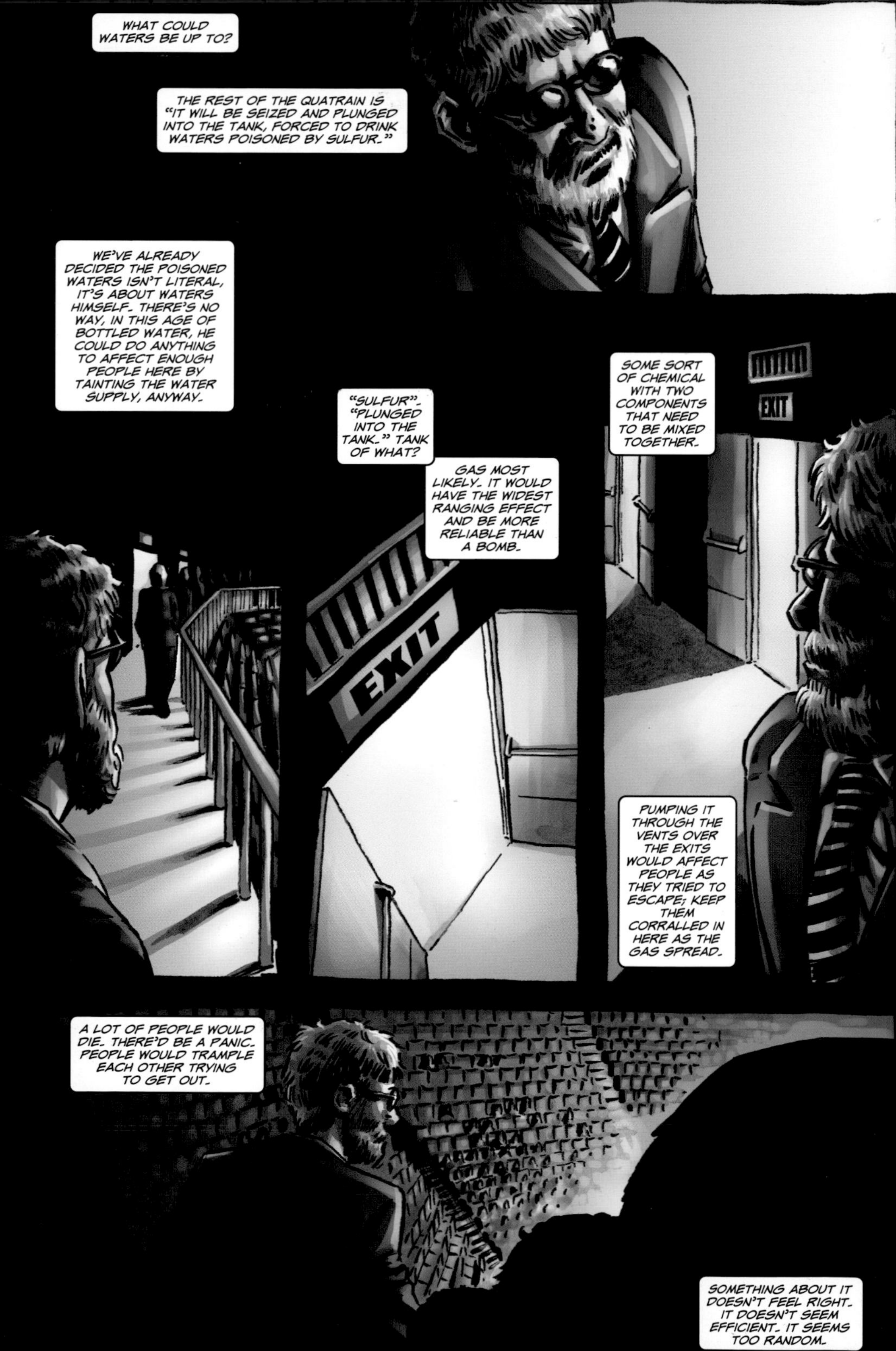
WHAT COULD WATERS BE UP TO?
THE REST OF THE QUATRAIN IS "IT WILL BE SEIZED AND PLUNGED INTO THE TANK, FORCED TO DRINK WATERS POISONED BY SULFUR."
WE'VE ALREADY DECIDED THE POISONED WATERS ISN'T LITERAL, IT'S ABOUT WATERS HIMSELF. THERE'S NO WAY, IN THIS AGE OF BOTTLED WATER, HE COULD DO ANYTHING TO AFFECT ENOUGH PEOPLE HERE BY TAINTING THE WATER SUPPLY, ANYWAY.
"SULFUR". "PLUNGED INTO THE TANK." TANK OF WHAT?
GAS MOST LIKELY. IT WOULD HAVE THE WIDEST RANGING EFFECT AND BE MORE RELIABLE THAN A BOMB.
EXIT
SOME SORT OF CHEMICAL WITH TWO COMPONENTS THAT NEED TO BE MIXED TOGETHER.
EXIT
PUMPING IT THROUGH THE VENTS OVER THE EXITS WOULD AFFECT PEOPLE AS THEY TRIED TO ESCAPE; KEEP THEM CORRALLED IN HERE AS THE GAS SPREAD.
A LOT OF PEOPLE WOULD DIE. THERE'D BE A PANIC. PEOPLE WOULD TRAMPLE EACH OTHER TRYING TO GET OUT.
SOMETHING ABOUT IT DOESN'T FEEL RIGHT. IT DOESN'T SEEM EFFICIENT. IT SEEMS TOO RANDOM.

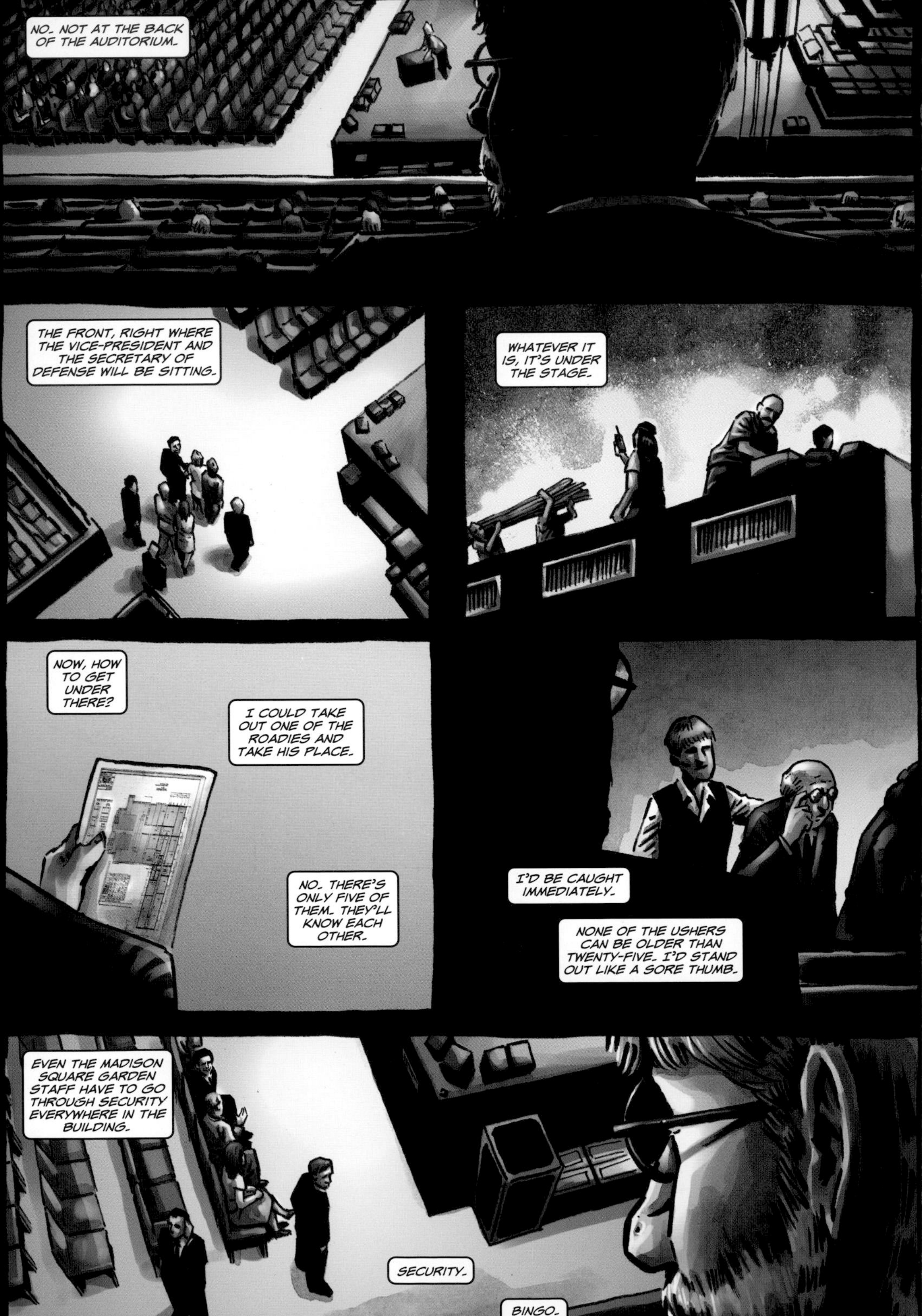
NO. NOT AT THE BACK OF THE AUDITORIUM.
THE FRONT, RIGHT WHERE THE VICE-PRESIDENT AND THE SECRETARY OF DEFENSE WILL BE SITTING.
WHATEVER IT IS, IT'S UNDER THE STAGE.
NOW, HOW TO GET UNDER THERE?
I COULD TAKE OUT ONE OF THE ROADIES AND TAKE HIS PLACE.
NO. THERE'S ONLY FIVE OF THEM. THEY'LL KNOW EACH OTHER.
I'D BE CAUGHT IMMEDIATELY.
NONE OF THE USHERS CAN BE OLDER THAN TWENTY-FIVE. I'D STAND OUT LIKE A SORE THUMB.
EVEN THE MADISON SQUARE GARDEN STAFF HAVE TO GO THROUGH SECURITY EVERYWHERE IN THE BUILDING.
SECURITY.
BINGO.

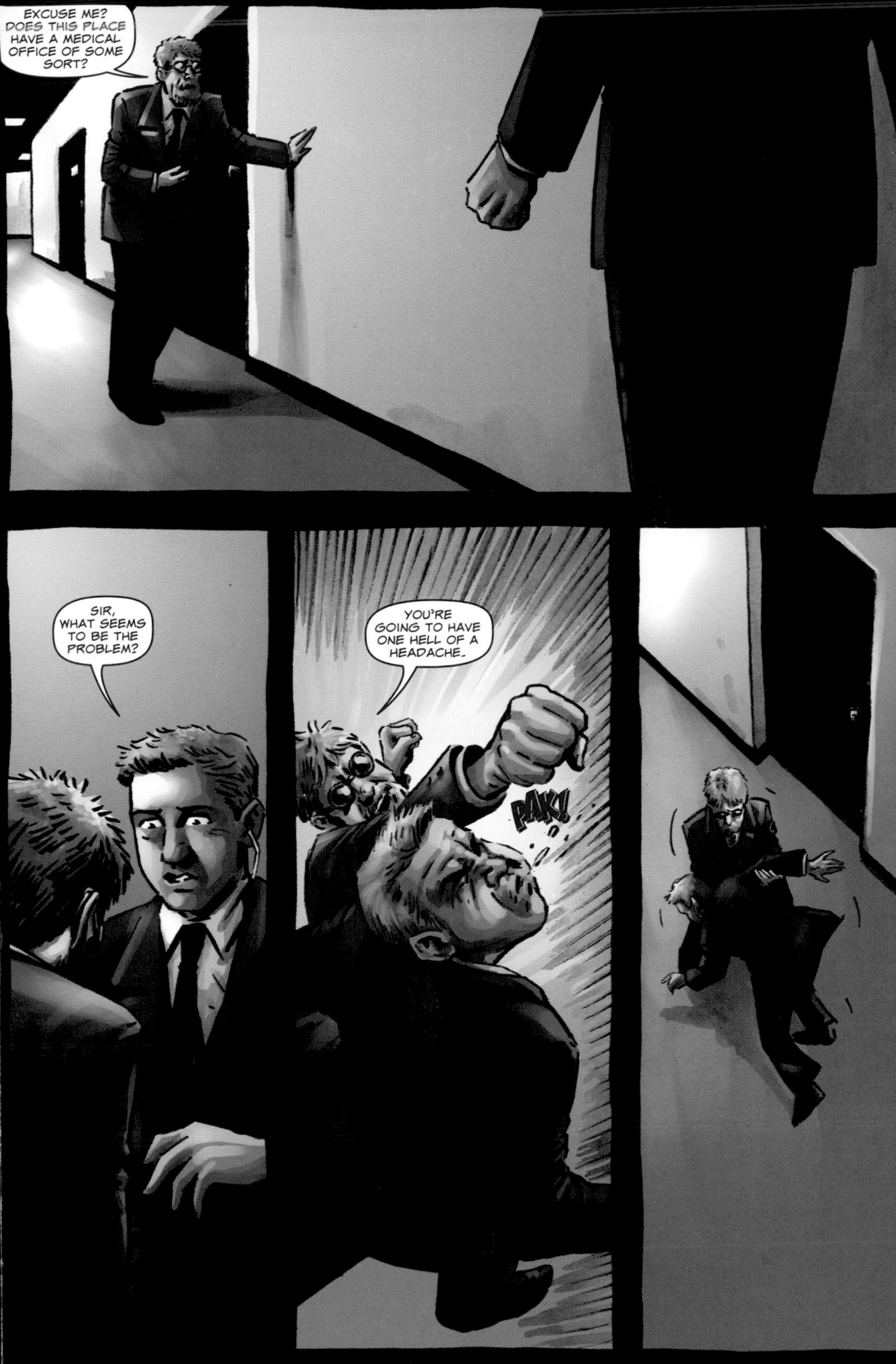
EXCUSE ME? DOES THIS PLACE HAVE A MEDICAL OFFICE OF SOME SORT?
SIR, WHAT SEEMS TO BE THE PROBLEM?
YOU'RE GOING TO HAVE ONE HELL OF A HEADACHE.
PAK!

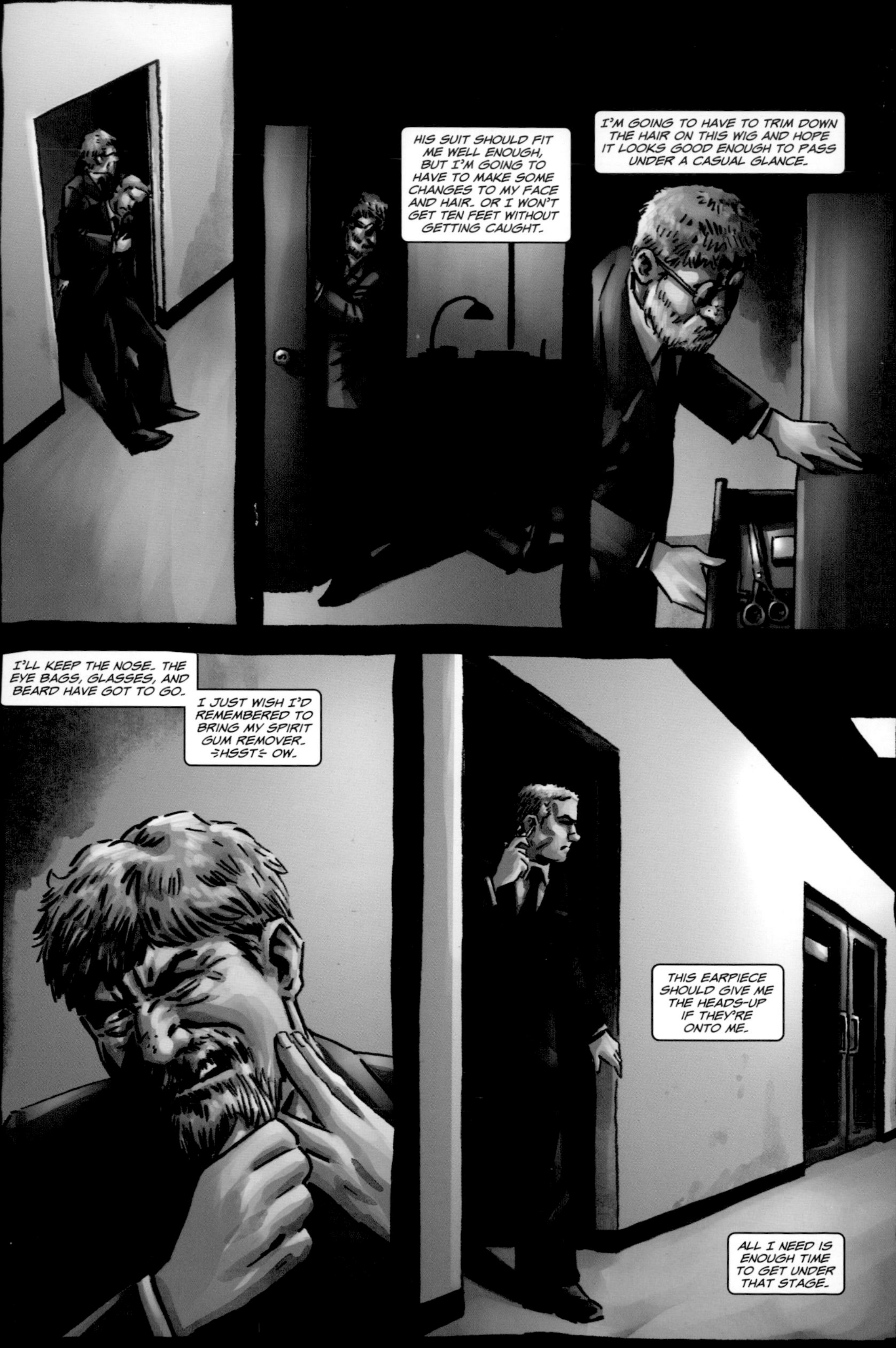
HIS SUIT SHOULD FIT ME WELL ENOUGH, BUT I'M GOING TO HAVE TO MAKE SOME CHANGES TO MY FACE AND HAIR. OR I WON'T GET TEN FEET WITHOUT GETTING CAUGHT.
I'M GOING TO HAVE TO TRIM DOWN THE HAIR ON THIS WIG AND HOPE IT LOOKS GOOD ENOUGH TO PASS UNDER A CASUAL GLANCE.
I'LL KEEP THE NOSE. THE EYE BAGS, GLASSES, AND BEARD HAVE GOT TO GO.
I JUST WISH I'D REMEMBERED TO BRING MY SPIRIT GUM REMOVER. =HSST= OW.
THIS EARPIECE SHOULD GIVE ME THE HEADS-UP IF THEY'RE ONTO ME.
ALL I NEED IS ENOUGH TIME TO GET UNDER THAT STAGE.

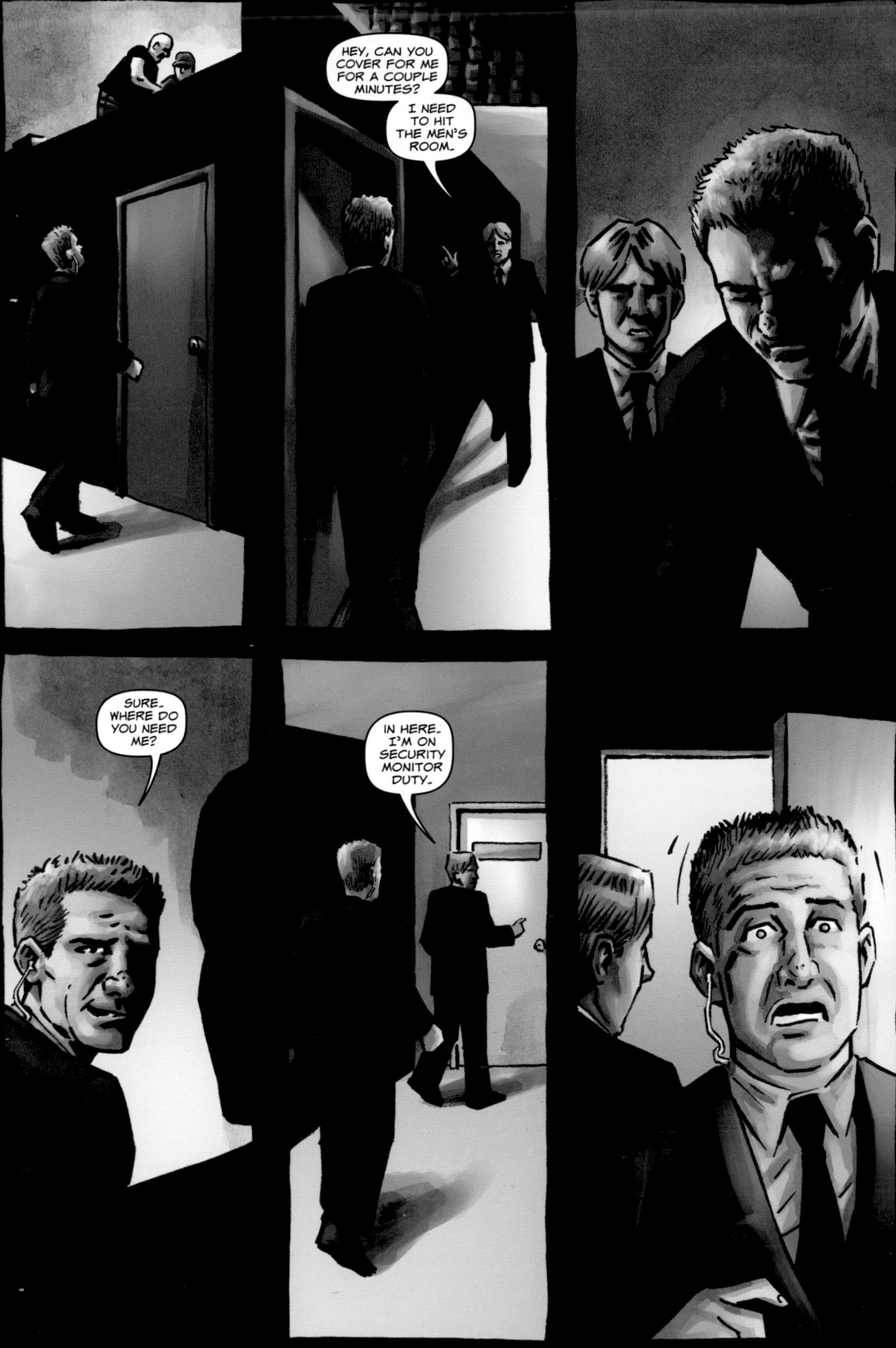
HEY, CAN YOU COVER FOR ME FOR A COUPLE MINUTES?
I NEED TO HIT THE MEN'S ROOM.
SURE. WHERE DO YOU NEED ME?
IN HERE. I'M ON SECURITY MONITOR DUTY.

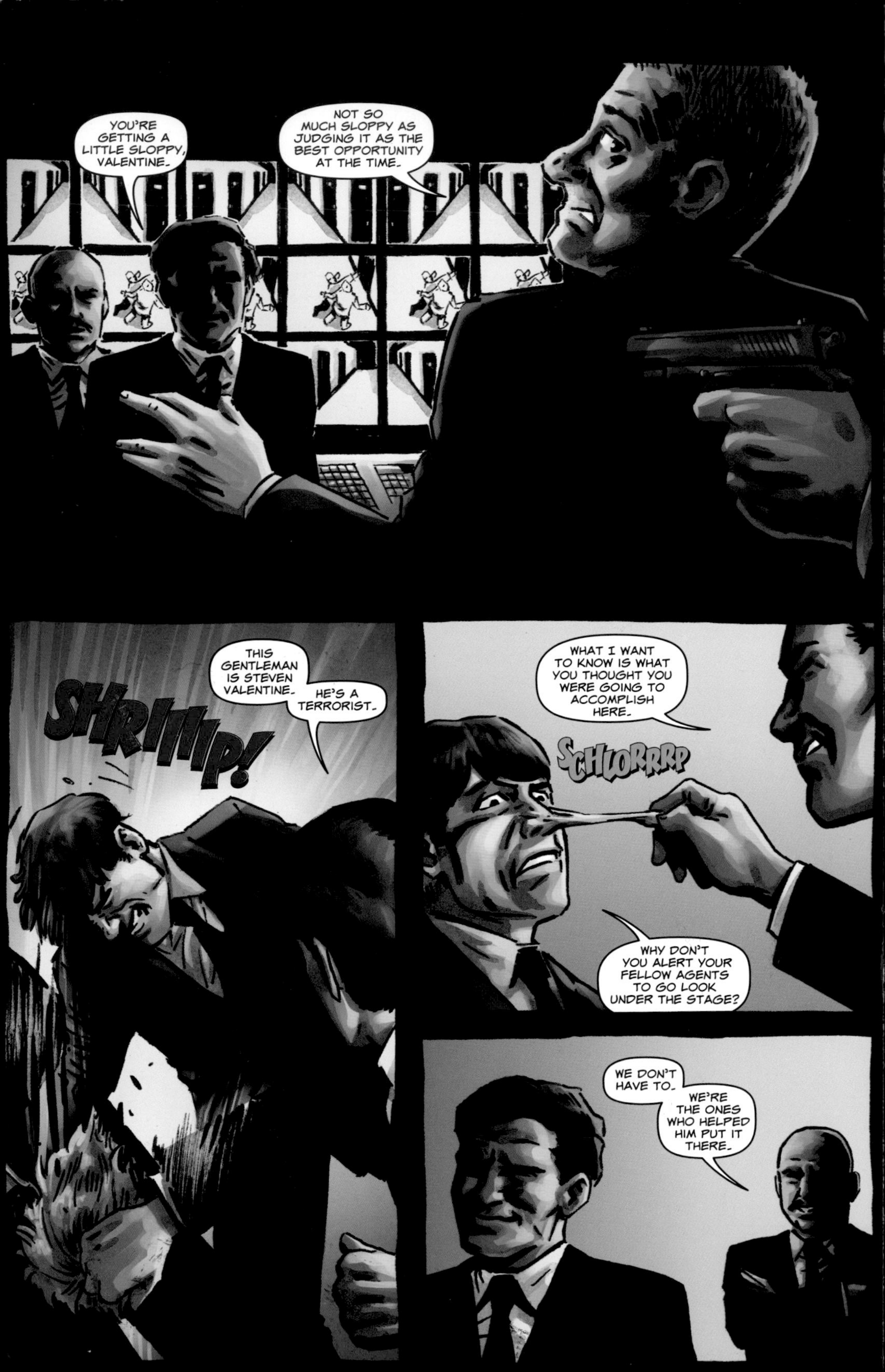

YOU'RE GETTING A LITTLE SLOPPY, VALENTINE.
NOT SO MUCH SLOPPY AS JUDGING IT AS THE BEST OPPORTUNITY AT THE TIME.
THIS GENTLEMAN IS STEVEN VALENTINE.
HE'S A TERRORIST.
SHRIIIP!
WHAT I WANT TO KNOW IS WHAT YOU THOUGHT YOU WERE GOING TO ACCOMPLISH HERE.
SCHLORRRP
WHY DON'T YOU ALERT YOUR FELLOW AGENTS TO GO LOOK UNDER THE STAGE?
WE DON'T HAVE TO.
WE'RE THE ONES WHO HELPED HIM PUT IT THERE.

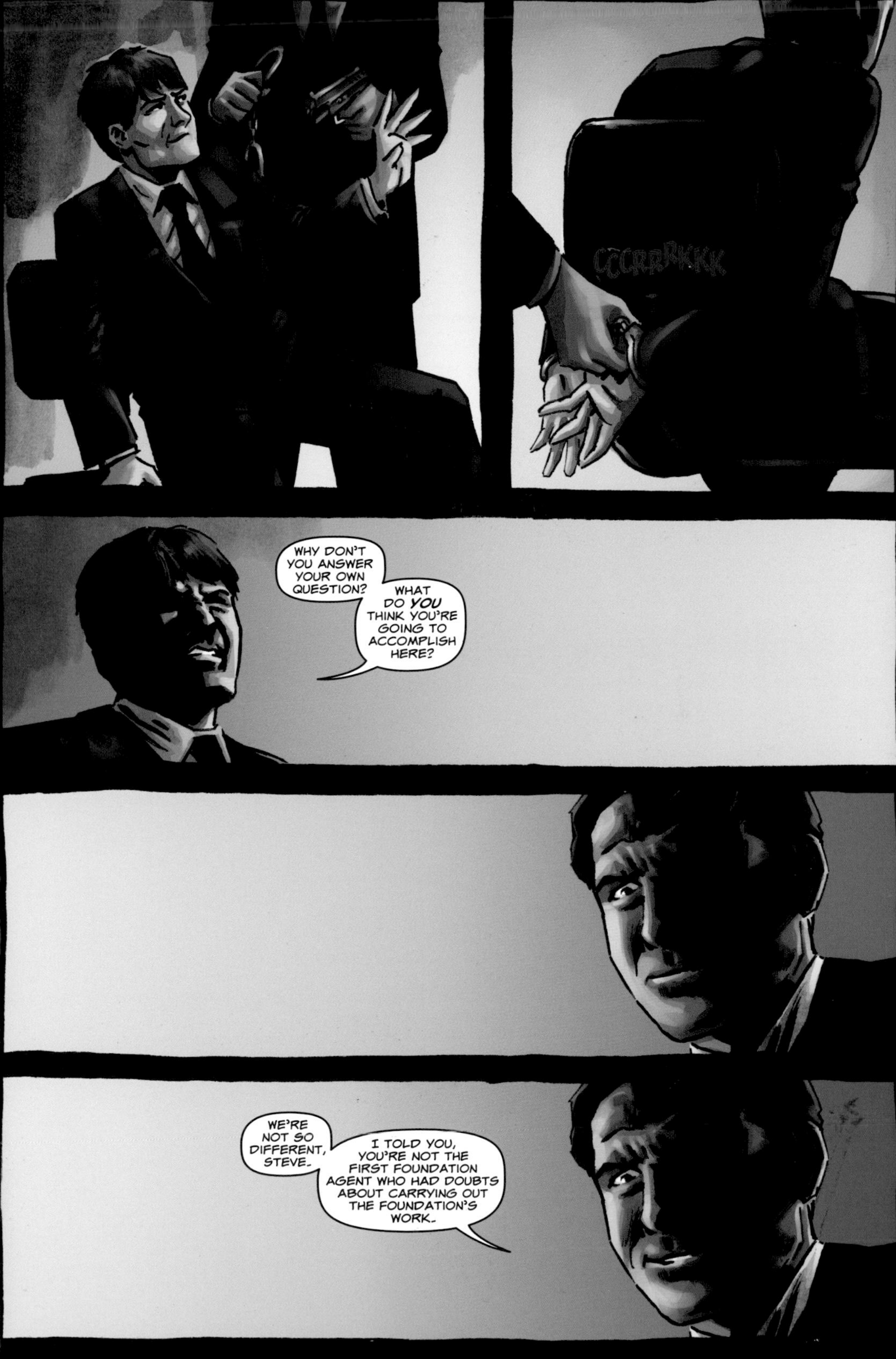
CCCRRRKKK
WHY DON'T YOU ANSWER YOUR OWN QUESTION?
WHAT DO *YOU* THINK YOU'RE GOING TO ACCOMPLISH HERE?
WE'RE NOT SO DIFFERENT, STEVE.
I TOLD YOU, YOU'RE NOT THE FIRST FOUNDATION AGENT WHO HAD DOUBTS ABOUT CARRYING OUT THE FOUNDATION'S WORK.

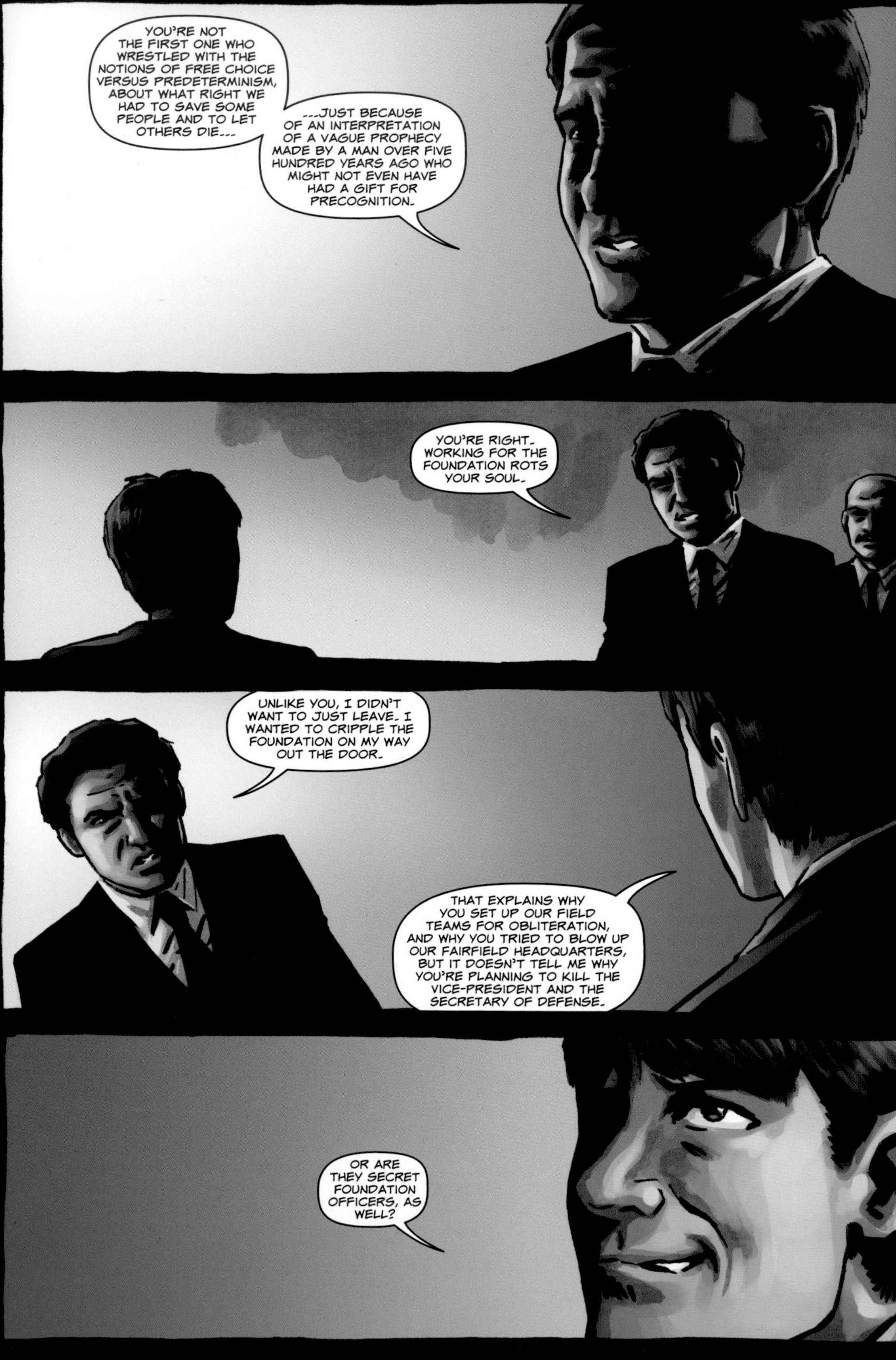
YOU'RE NOT THE FIRST ONE WHO WRESTLED WITH THE NOTIONS OF FREE CHOICE VERSUS PREDETERMINISM, ABOUT WHAT RIGHT WE HAD TO SAVE SOME PEOPLE AND TO LET OTHERS DIE...
...JUST BECAUSE OF AN INTERPRETATION OF A VAGUE PROPHECY MADE BY A MAN OVER FIVE HUNDRED YEARS AGO WHO MIGHT NOT EVEN HAVE HAD A GIFT FOR PRECOGNITION.
YOU'RE RIGHT. WORKING FOR THE FOUNDATION ROTS YOUR SOUL.
UNLIKE YOU, I DIDN'T WANT TO JUST LEAVE. I WANTED TO CRIPPLE THE FOUNDATION ON MY WAY OUT THE DOOR.
THAT EXPLAINS WHY YOU SET UP OUR FIELD TEAMS FOR OBLITERATION, AND WHY YOU TRIED TO BLOW UP OUR FAIRFIELD HEADQUARTERS, BUT IT DOESN'T TELL ME WHY YOU'RE PLANNING TO KILL THE VICE-PRESIDENT AND THE SECRETARY OF DEFENSE.
OR ARE THEY SECRET FOUNDATION OFFICERS, AS WELL?

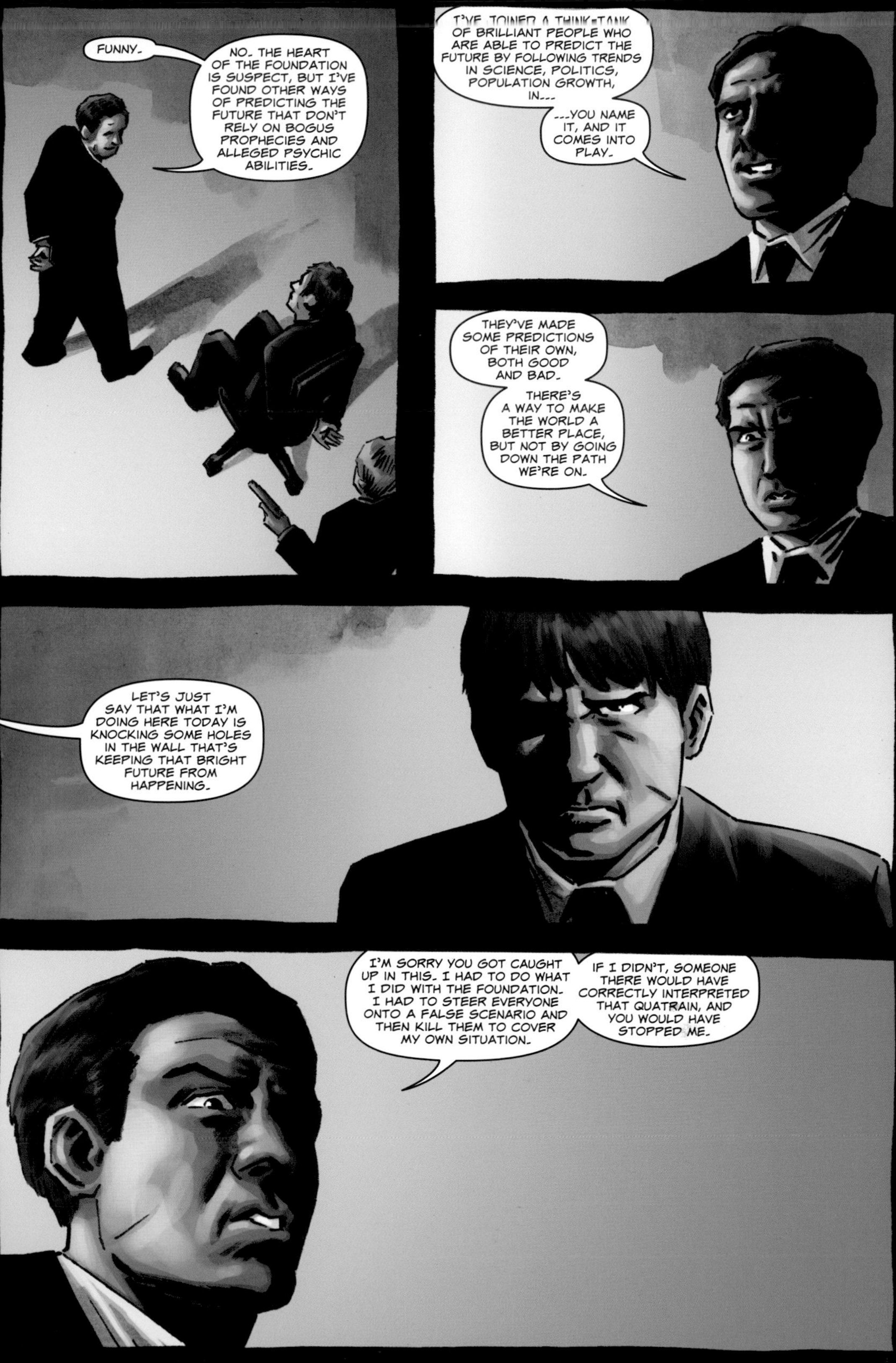
FUNNY.
NO. THE HEART OF THE FOUNDATION IS SUSPECT, BUT I'VE FOUND OTHER WAYS OF PREDICTING THE FUTURE THAT DON'T RELY ON BOGUS PROPHECIES AND ALLEGED PSYCHIC ABILITIES.
I'VE JOINED A THINK-TANK OF BRILLIANT PEOPLE WHO ARE ABLE TO PREDICT THE FUTURE BY FOLLOWING TRENDS IN SCIENCE, POLITICS, POPULATION GROWTH, IN...
...YOU NAME IT, AND IT COMES INTO PLAY.
THEY'VE MADE SOME PREDICTIONS OF THEIR OWN, BOTH GOOD AND BAD.
THERE'S A WAY TO MAKE THE WORLD A BETTER PLACE, BUT NOT BY GOING DOWN THE PATH WE'RE ON.
LET'S JUST SAY THAT WHAT I'M DOING HERE TODAY IS KNOCKING SOME HOLES IN THE WALL THAT'S KEEPING THAT BRIGHT FUTURE FROM HAPPENING.
I'M SORRY YOU GOT CAUGHT UP IN THIS. I HAD TO DO WHAT I DID WITH THE FOUNDATION. I HAD TO STEER EVERYONE ONTO A FALSE SCENARIO AND THEN KILL THEM TO COVER MY OWN SITUATION.
IF I DIDN'T, SOMEONE THERE WOULD HAVE CORRECTLY INTERPRETED THAT QUATRAIN, AND YOU WOULD HAVE STOPPED ME.

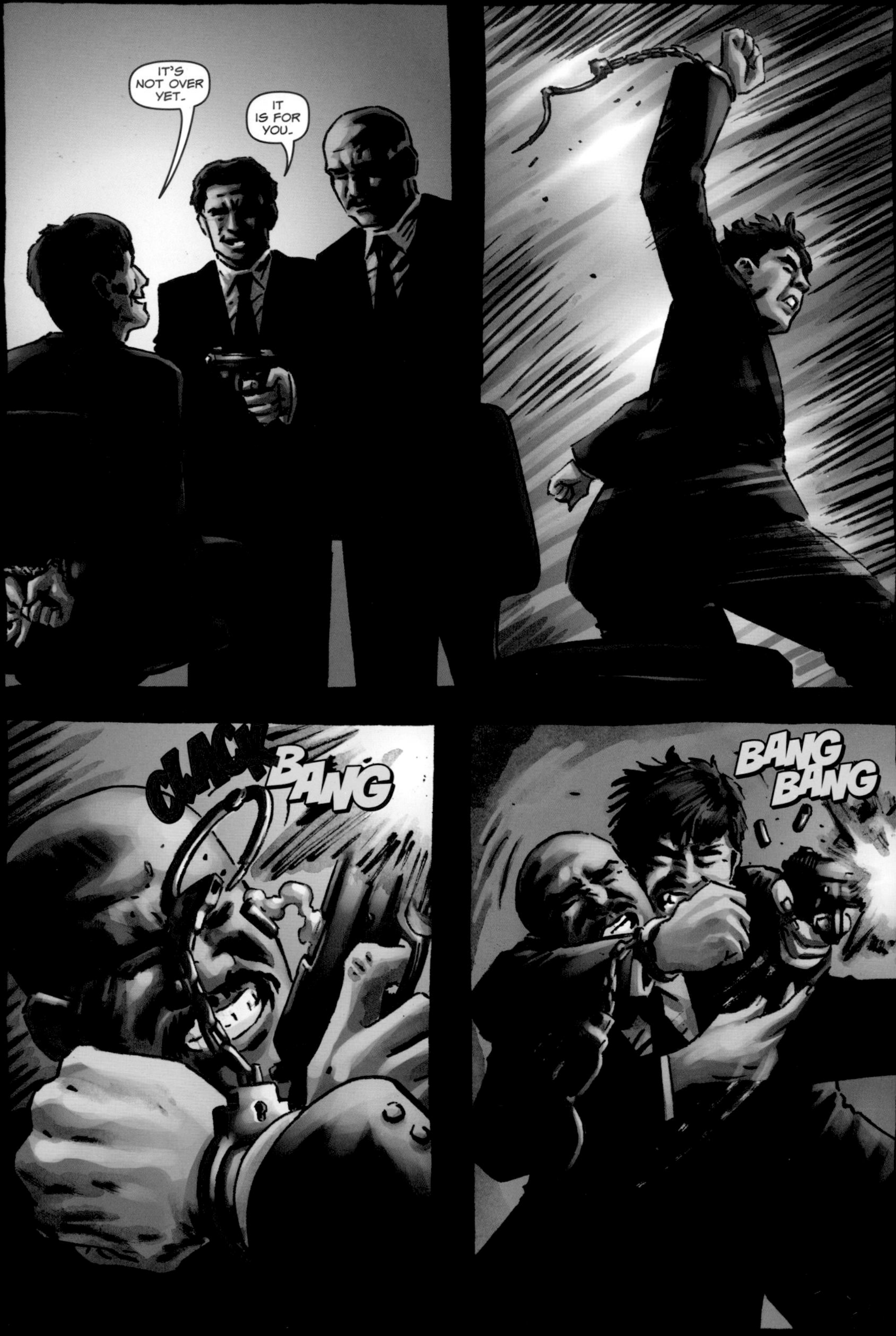
IT'S NOT OVER YET.
IT IS FOR YOU.
CLACK
BANG
BANG
BANG

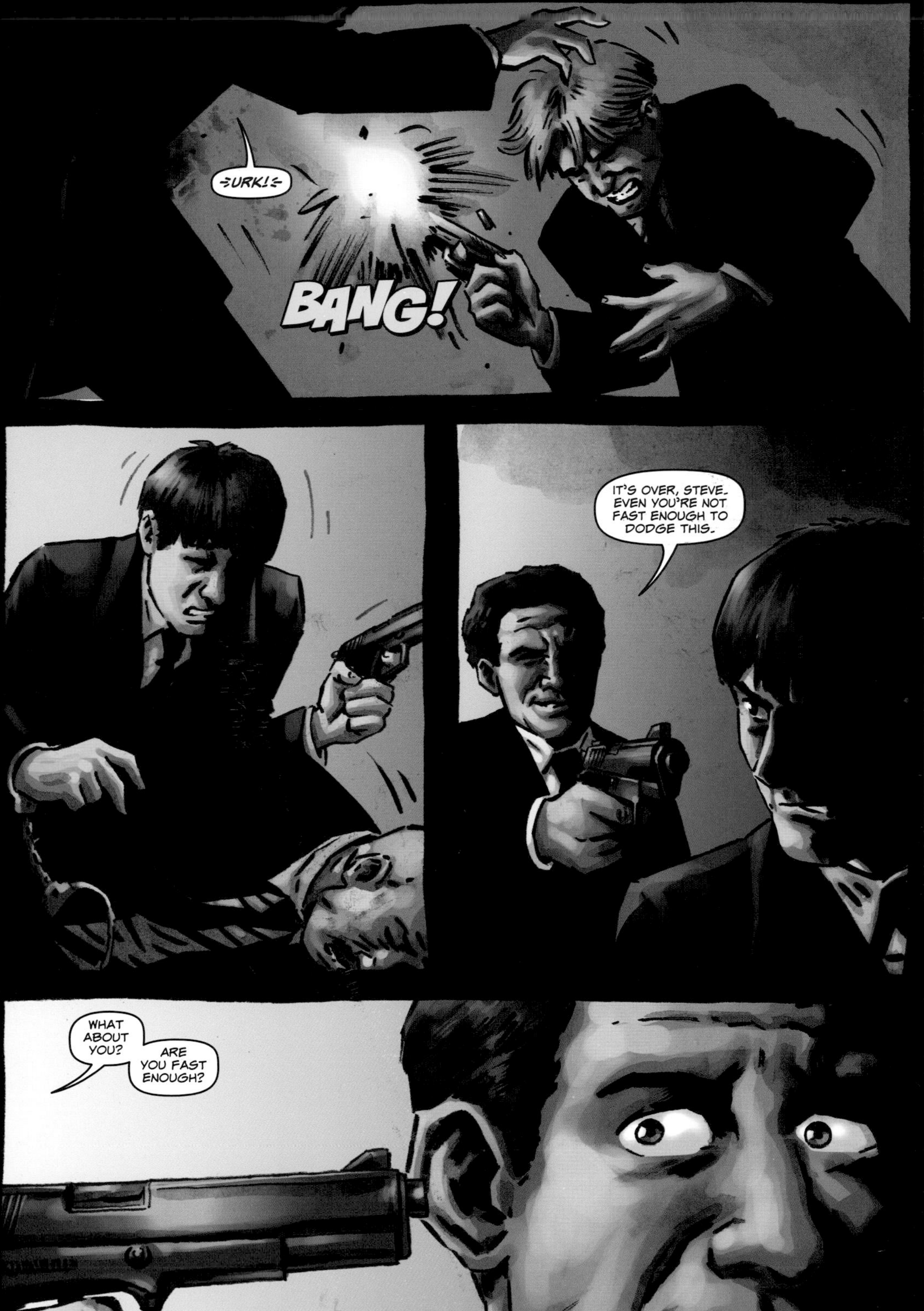
URK!
BANG!
IT'S OVER, STEVE. EVEN YOU'RE NOT FAST ENOUGH TO DODGE THIS.
WHAT ABOUT YOU?
ARE YOU FAST ENOUGH?

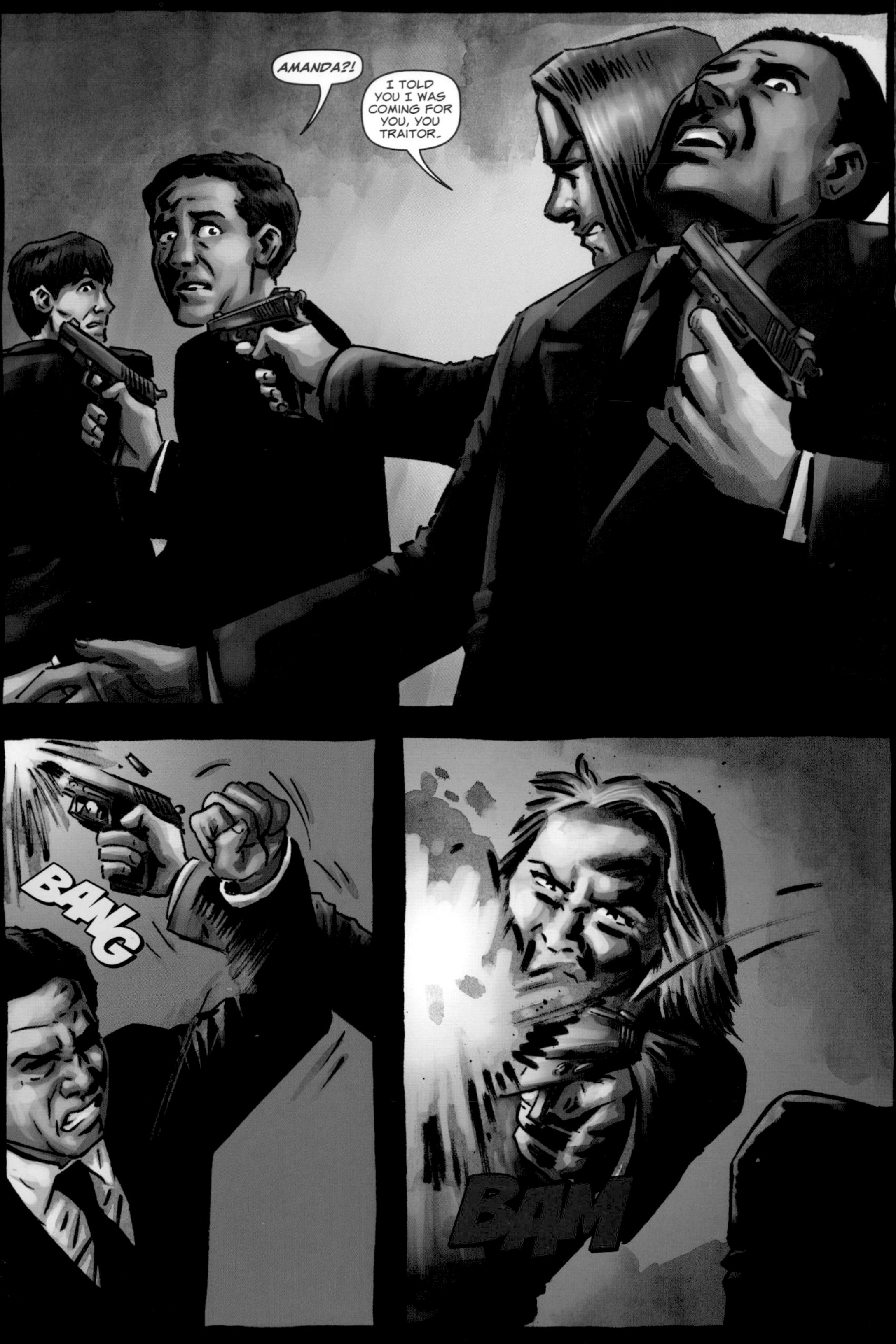
AMANDA?!
I TOLD YOU I WAS COMING FOR YOU, YOU TRAITOR.
BANG
BAM

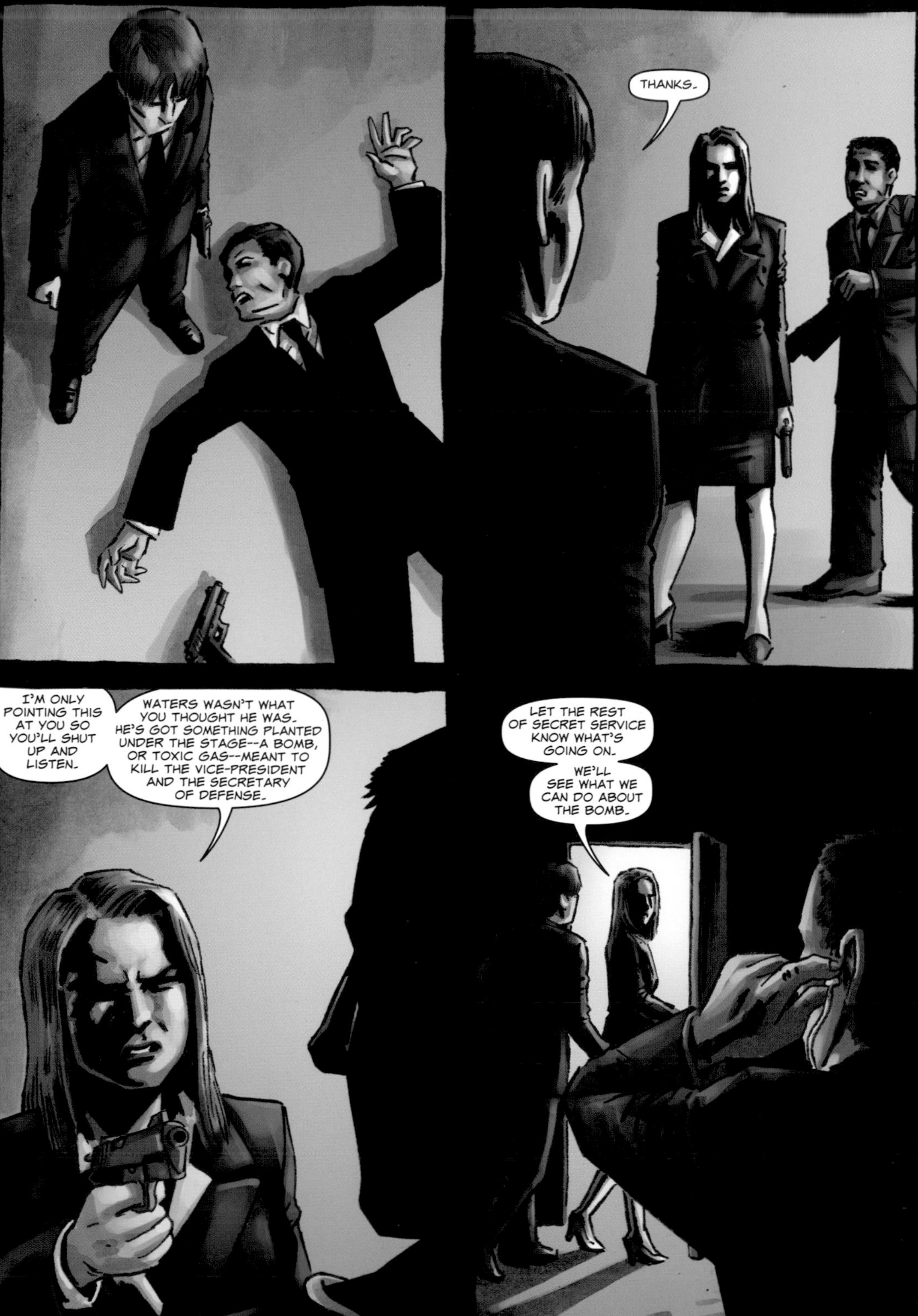
THANKS.
I'M ONLY POINTING THIS AT YOU SO YOU'LL SHUT UP AND LISTEN.
WATERS WASN'T WHAT YOU THOUGHT HE WAS. HE'S GOT SOMETHING PLANTED UNDER THE STAGE--A BOMB, OR TOXIC GAS--MEANT TO KILL THE VICE-PRESIDENT AND THE SECRETARY OF DEFENSE.
LET THE REST OF SECRET SERVICE KNOW WHAT'S GOING ON.
WE'LL SEE WHAT WE CAN DO ABOUT THE BOMB.

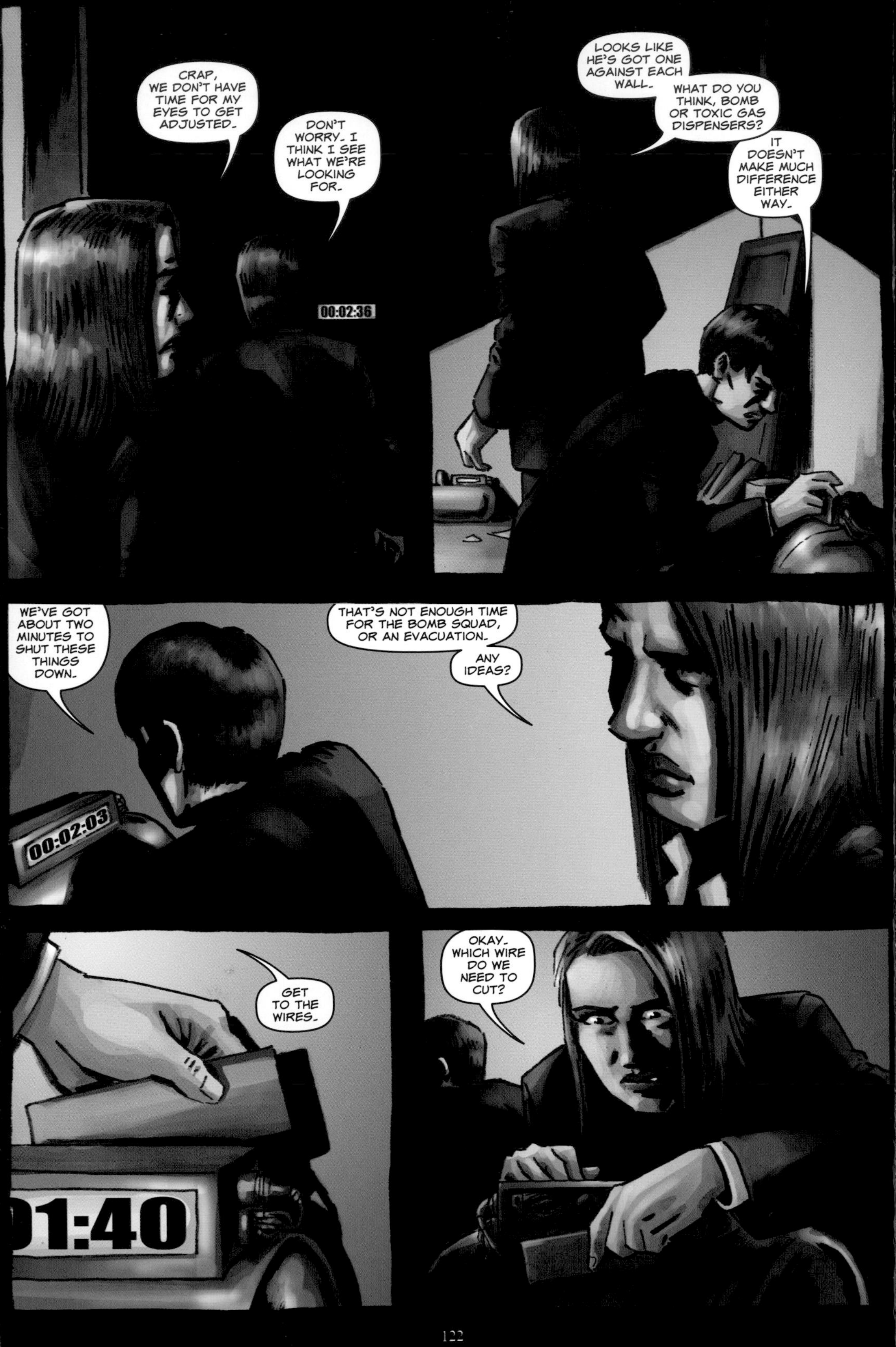
CRAP, WE DON'T HAVE TIME FOR MY EYES TO GET ADJUSTED.
DON'T WORRY. I THINK I SEE WHAT WE'RE LOOKING FOR.
00:02:36
LOOKS LIKE HE'S GOT ONE AGAINST EACH WALL.
WHAT DO YOU THINK, BOMB OR TOXIC GAS DISPENSERS?
IT DOESN'T MAKE MUCH DIFFERENCE EITHER WAY.
WE'VE GOT ABOUT TWO MINUTES TO SHUT THESE THINGS DOWN.
00:02:03
THAT'S NOT ENOUGH TIME FOR THE BOMB SQUAD, OR AN EVACUATION.
ANY IDEAS?
GET TO THE WIRES.
01:40
OKAY. WHICH WIRE DO WE NEED TO CUT?

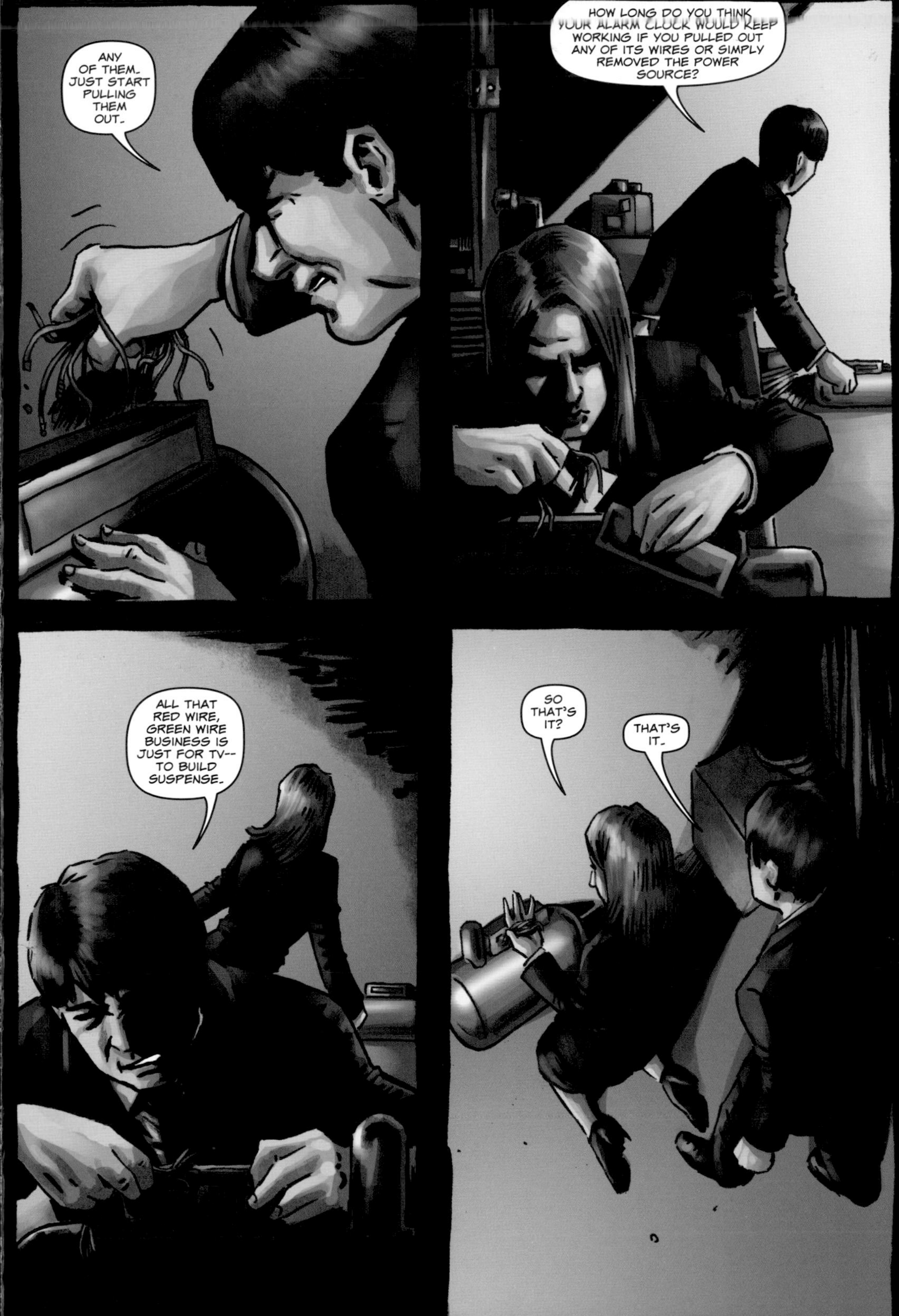
ANY OF THEM. JUST START PULLING THEM OUT.
HOW LONG DO YOU THINK YOUR ALARM CLOCK WOULD KEEP WORKING IF YOU PULLED OUT ANY OF ITS WIRES OR SIMPLY REMOVED THE POWER SOURCE?
ALL THAT RED WIRE, GREEN WIRE BUSINESS IS JUST FOR TV-- TO BUILD SUSPENSE.
SO THAT'S IT?
THAT'S IT.

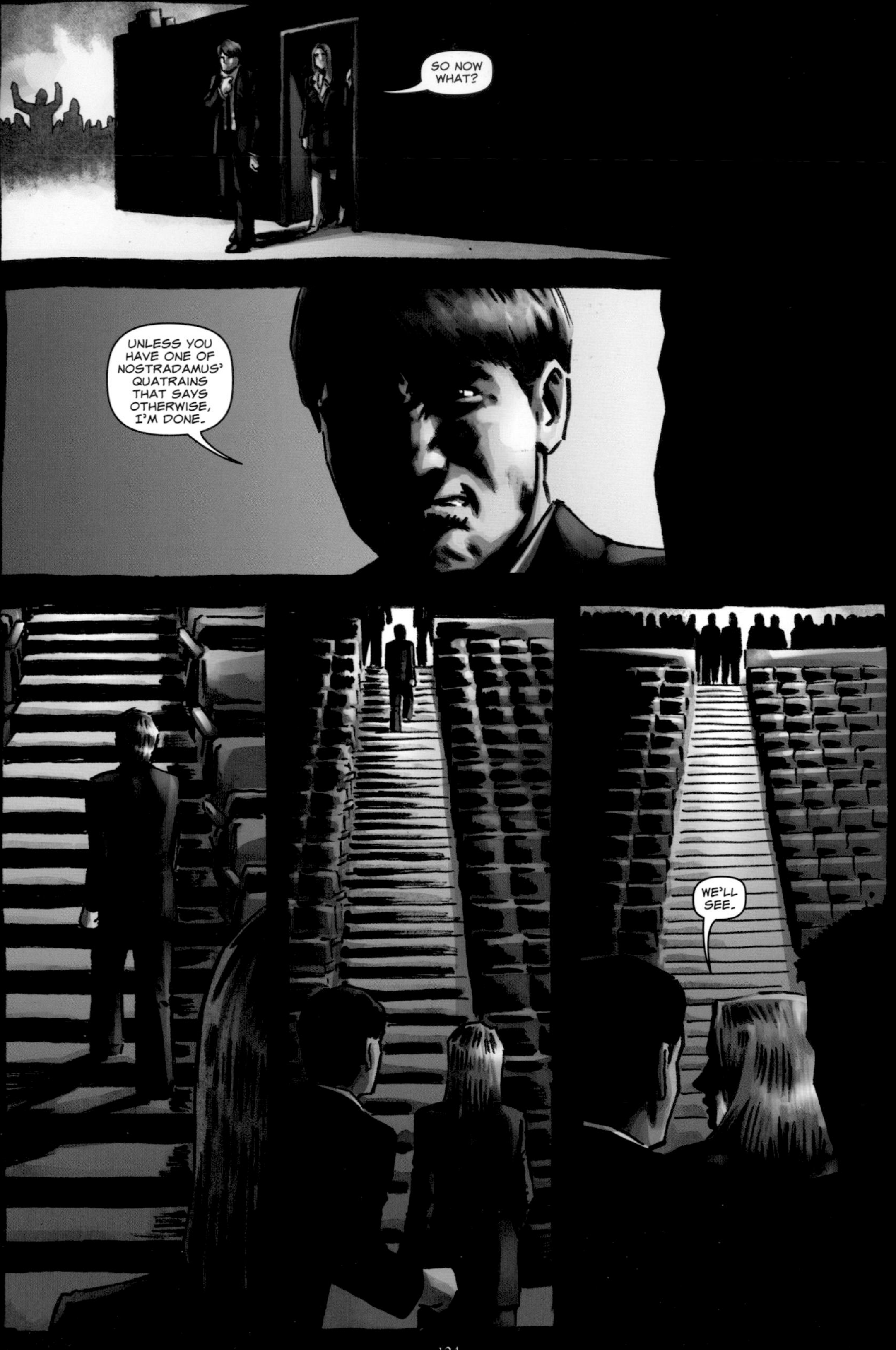
SO NOW WHAT?
UNLESS YOU HAVE ONE OF NOSTRADAMUS' QUATRAINS THAT SAYS OTHERWISE, I'M DONE.
WE'LL SEE.

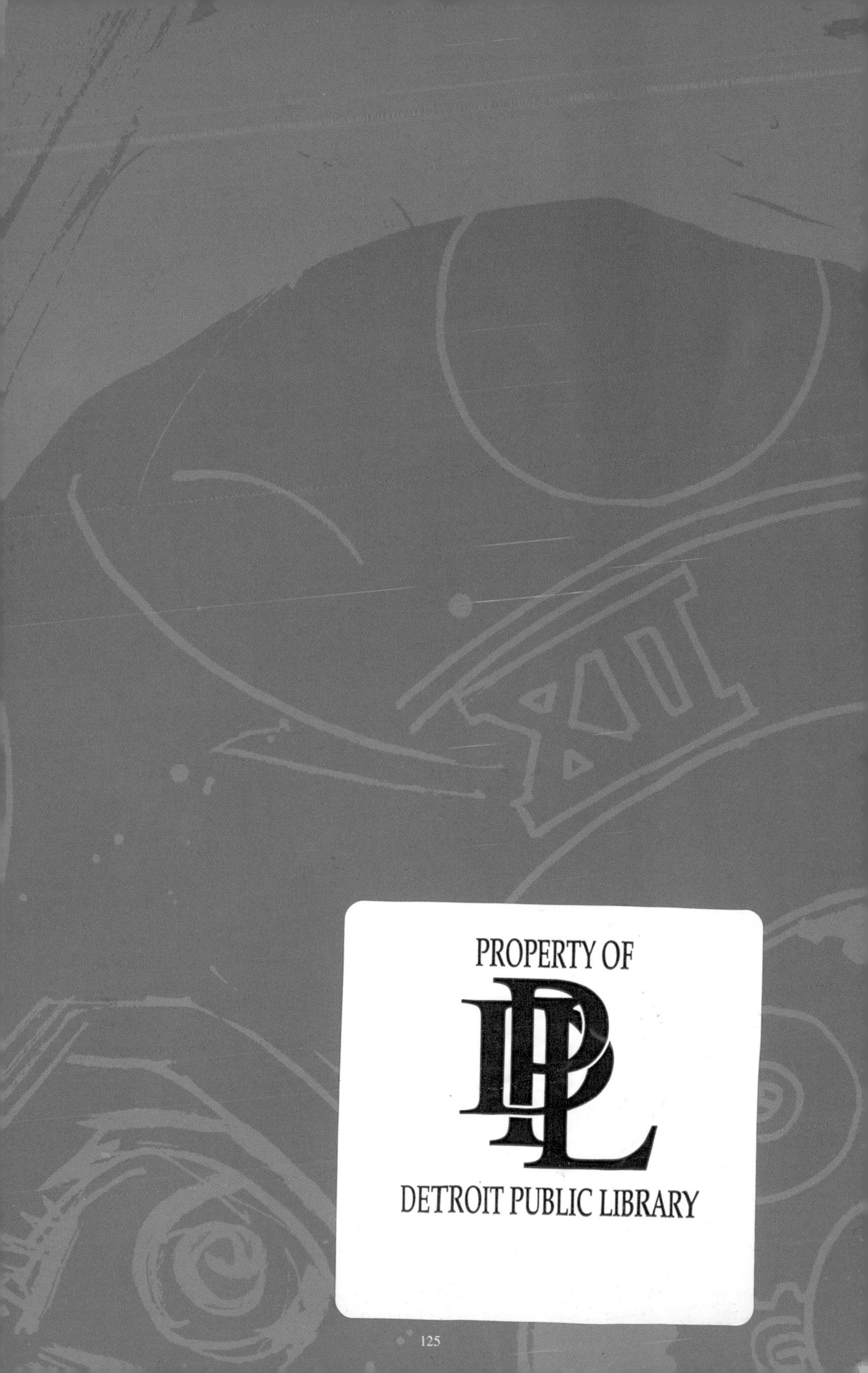

BOOM! STUDIOS **TRADE PAPERBACKS**

WHAT'S THE BIG IDEA?
www.BOOM-STUDIOS.com

ANDREW COSBY · JOHANNA STOKES · RHOALD MARCELLUS
DEATH VALLEY
Travis Klein
Ryan Zimmerman
Samantha Lyons
Death Valley High Yearbook - photography by Kaare Andrews

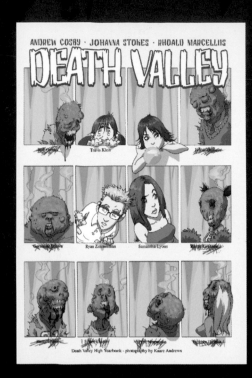

DEATH VALLEY

written by Johanna Stokes
and Andrew Cosby
drawn by Rhoald Marcellus
cover by Kaare Andrews
$14.99, full color, 128 pages

ISBN13: 978-1-934506-08-0

Samantha's graduating from high school in the Valley - getting together with her pals to throw an End of the World party to celebrate, everyone ends up accidentally locked in a bomb shelter. When Samantha and her pals emerge, they find that the entire world has changed, and the dead now walk the Earth... It's Dawn of the Dead by way of The O.C.! From EUREKA TV show writers writers Andrew Cosby and Johanna Stokes (Mr. Stuffins and The Savage Brothers)!

Giffen and DeMatteis'
PLANETARY
BRIGADE

PLANETARY BRIGADE

written by Keith Giffen
and J.M. DeMatteis
drawn by various
$14.99, full color, 128 pages

ISBN13: 978-1-934506-10-3

More Giffen and DeMatteis Bwaha-ha-ha hilarity! From the hit-writers of Justice League International comes their own, quirky, turn on a league of super-heroes! The Planetary Brigade is a group of heroes fronted by Hero Squared's Captain Valor and Grim Knight. Meet Mr. Brilliant - Earth has never met a smarter, or more smug, hero. Earth Goddess - by day, she's a sweet, unassuming wallflower, but when the Earth needs her, she turns into a gargantuan guardian of the planet. Purring Pussycat -sweet, sexy... what's she hiding? The Third Eye - spiritual mystic. The Mauve Visitor - strange visitor from another world, or cute little Smurf-like dude? Together, they're in a league all their own.

GIFFEN · DEMATTEIS · ABRAHAM
HERO 2
SQUARED

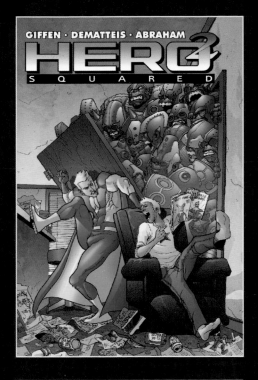

HERO SQUARED VOLUME 1

Written by Keith Giffen
and J.M. DeMatteis
Drawn by Joe Abraham
$14.99, full color, 136 pages

ISBN13: 978-1-934506-00-4

Collecting the sold-out X-Tra Sized Special one-shot - which was such a success that it lead to a three issue miniseries - this book is packed with extras. In print for the first time will be the popular web comic promotion that Keith Giffen plotted and penciled, and which DeMatteis scripted along with Giffen's original character designs and Joe Abraham's concept sketches. Also in print for the first time is a Keith Giffen plot, which can now be compared side-by-side with DeMatteis' final script!

ZOMBIE TALES

ZOMBIE TALES

written and drawn by various
$14.99, full color, 144 pages

ISBN13: 978-1-934506-02-8

The best-selling zombie anthology finally gets collected, featuring work from the best of the best: material written by Mark Waid, Keith Giffen, Eureka creator Andrew Cosby, Transformers The Movie writer John Rogers, Eureka TV show writer Johanna Stokes, Fall of Cthulhu writer Michael Alan Nelson, and more! Artists featured are a non-stop constellation of names: Keith Giffen, Fallen Angel's J.K. Woodward, Painkiller Jane's Lee Moder, 100 Bullets' Dave Johnson, Mark Badger, and many many more! This edition collects Zombie Tales #1, Zombie Tales: Oblivion, and Zombie Tales: The Dead. Don't wait 28 days later for the new dawn of the walking dead!

TALENT
written by Christopher Golden
and Tom Sniegoski
drawn by Paul Azaceta
$14.99, full color, 128 pages

ISBN13: 978-1-934506-05-9

The sold-out sensation is finally collected! Optioned in a five way studio bidding war by Universal Pictures, Talent tracks Nicholas Dane, miraculous sole survior of a plane crash. As mysterious men arrive to kill Dane, he discovers he can channel the talents of the victims of the crash! Discover why Ain't It Cool News said "Since the company's inception, Boom! has been creating quite a rumble in the comics world, but with Talent, they're definitely living up to their name. Highly recommended."

JEREMIAH HARM
written by Keith Giffen
and Alan Grant
drawn by Rael Lyra
and Rafael Albuquerque
$14.99, full color, 128 pages

ISBN13: 978-1-934506-12-7

From Keith Giffen (52, Annihilation) and Alan Grant (Batman, Lobo) comes this hard-hitting sci-fi series with a gritty tone and a brutal anti-hero as the lead! When three of the galaxy's most fearsome criminals escape confinement on a prison planet and wind up on Earth, the authorities have no choice but to free the most wanted man in the universe - Jeremiah Harm - to track these fugitives down and stop them. He doesn't love you, he doesn't want to be your friend, he isn't your super-hero - and God help you if you find yourself in Harm's way! Featuring art from Rael Lyra (Dragonlance: Legend of Huma) and Rafael Albuquerque (Blue Beetle).